Wide-Eyed Wisdom

WIDE-EYED
Wisdom

Keith A. Miller

with

Teresa Miller-Weston

COVENANT DEVELOPMENT GROUP, INC.

Copyright © 2020 Keith A. Miller.

All rights reserved. No part of this publication may be reproduced, distributed, or transmitted in any form or by any means, including photocopying, recording, or other electronic or mechanical methods, without the prior written permission of the author, except in the case of brief quotations embodied in critical reviews and certain other noncommercial uses permitted by copyright law.

ISBN: 978-1-7348865-0-4

Library of Congress Control Number: 2020912762

Printed by Gorham Printing, Inc. – Centralia, Washington.

First printing edition 2020.

Published by Covenant Development Group Inc.
Oregon City, OR 97045

Cover Art: Dmitriy L. Shumskiy
Cover Design: Teresa Miller-Weston

www.wide-eyedwisdom.com

DEDICATION

To our grandchildren – the greatest blessings we could have ever hoped for.
Jocelyn, "The Astute"
James, "The Curious"
Jonathan, "The Iron Man"

FROM THE AUTHOR

As I worked on this book, I read an article regarding the impending retirement crisis[1]. The article recapped a study pointing out that more than half of working people have virtually nothing saved for retirement. Zero. Zip. Nada. Wait, what? Half of working adults are wholly unprepared for their "golden years" – that beautiful period we all aspire to – where the only boss you answer to is yourself, and your meeting attendees include, "Me, Myself and I". What were they thinking?

Can you imagine working 40-some years, without at least some preparation for your future? I have lost count of the number of folks I have talked with, who have reached that magical retirement milestone only to see their income stream shrink to a trickle. The smallest overspend or unexpected expense creates a dilemma of whether to eat or fill a prescription. Many retiree bank accounts have nothing left at the end of the month – most certainly no money for hobbies, entertainment, or even modest travel.

What a wakeup call! More of us have got to figure out how to align our pre-retirement life, with the pressures, demands, and needs of today, so we can support the realities of what is needed for our future. *Houston, we have a problem!*

You are probably thinking, "oh great another book about finances, and how to prepare for retirement". This book is about so much more than finances. But, given the importance of money, finances cannot be avoided. The retirement-savings study pointed out a symptom of a bigger problem – many of us lack the **knowledge**, **understanding**, and **self-discipline** to prepare for a fulfilling future.

WIDE-EYED WISDOM

Finances aside there are other issues that we must focus on, as early in life as possible, to chart our path and live the life that we desire.

This book is <u>not</u> specifically about preparing for retirement. This book is a collection of valuable wisdom that I have learned throughout my life, that you can employ in your own journey - the sooner the better! Retirement just happens to be near the culmination of your journey. Use the wisdom you learn in this book, then enjoy the journey as you prepare for today, tomorrow, and your future.

I know that much of what I have learned over the years could have been used much earlier in my life. Fortunately for me, as a teenager I decided to commit to a life plan filled with experiences and opportunities. Later, with my young wife, we developed a plan for our marriage and future family. Our shared mission motivated me to develop personally and professionally, so I could provide for our family.

> "Youth is wasted on the young."[2]
>
> George Bernard Shaw

The primary reason I wrote this book was to document valuable life lessons for our grandchildren – Jocelyn, James, and Jonathan. These three have given Cindy and I renewed purpose and meaning. We look at our three grandchildren and say to one another that we did a good job, and that these little ones are here because of us. Well others might have had a bit to do with them arriving here too. Jokes aside, I want to give our grandchildren the gift of my hard-earned knowledge, understanding and wisdom, that for years to come will make a positive difference for them, and perhaps future generations. For others that may read this book you too can set a new course for yourself and your family.

The second reason I wrote this book is that I love to mentor and coach. This book is one way to continue my personal quest to help others.

The life lessons in the following pages will help people of any age. If you are a teenager or twenty something, pay attention now and don't wait to take action! You have an opportunity to chart an exciting and fulfilling life, with the people, lifestyle and means to support your passions. Of course, many reading this book may be far removed from the teen years, take heart – the next best time to make a positive difference in your life is today.

Once you learn a bit about my background, perhaps you will see why I am so passionate. Even though I do not know all of you, I believe in you and suspect you have untapped potential.

FROM THE AUTHOR

Born the seventh of eight children I can tell you quite a bit about what it was like to grow up in a large lower middle-class family. Eight children were born over a span of twenty-plus years.

We lived in a small farming community in the San Joaquin Valley of California. When I was born the population of the town was about 8,000. Summers were hot. People used to say, "it is a dry heat". As a child I imagined it was probably as hot as the Sahara Desert.

School was an important center of community activity. Parents wanted a better life for their kids and placed a premium on learning. High school sporting events and other school related activities were (and still are) a big deal. Farming was a huge part of the community. The valley is still a world class producer of grapes, peaches, nectarines, plums, oranges, lemons, and a variety of other crops. Our San Joaquin Valley focused on feeding the U.S. (From the hard-working people of the Valley to you, you're welcome.)

Unfortunately for the young people that grew up in our small town, if you didn't own a business or a farm, there wasn't a wide selection of careers. The best paying jobs were teachers, business owners, farmers, and builders. All noble professions that are necessary in every community, but also evidence of few professional opportunities. Most, (and I was one of them) left the community soon after high school was finished.

Growing up in a large family, we did not have many material possessions. Although, I can tell you that we never felt poor. My mom made clothes for my three sisters. Hand me down clothes were the rule for the five boys. Mom displayed elementary school class pictures of three brothers wearing a red polo shirt – the *same* red polo shirt. New clothes were purchased sparingly, and almost always at "back to school" time.

My brother in-law Tom, God rest his soul, was like a father, brother, and best friend to me. He grew up in Kansas and would tell stories about his modest childhood. He used to say that he wore hand me down pants that had "knee patches in the ankles", (that was true because Tom's older brother was about a foot taller).

All the kids in our family were taught a great work ethic. This value has served me well throughout my career.

There wasn't much money available for the wants of so many children. As a pre-teen or teen, if my siblings or I wanted to buy something we had to work to earn the money to pay for it. We all worked, performing a variety of odd jobs from the time we were in grade school through high school and college.

All eight of us kids were taught self-discipline, honesty, integrity, and a value system that put others first. These values came from both mom and dad. They were both "caregivers" during their lifetime, giving all they had to take care of a large family and many times friends of ours.

Our house was a comfortable place where the kids in the neighborhood were always welcome. Growing up, most of us neighborhood kids spent those hot summer days and nights using our boundless energy along with a strong feeling of invincibility to create our own fun – I learned first-hand why there were rules. There were no video games and no internet. The boys in the neighborhood formed strong bonds – we were brothers from different mothers. We went to school together, played together, ate together, fished, and hunted together, had fun together (sometimes pushing the line between what was acceptable and not), protected one another, and at times grieved together.

As teens we experienced the immaturity that accompanies youth. None of us quite knew how to move ahead in the world or how to chart our direction. We also did not understand our individual capabilities.

Back then, after you left home you either made it on your own or you might have starved. There was no "boomerang effect" (moving back in with mom and dad so they could take care of you). Not that our parents wouldn't have helped us…it just wasn't in our DNA to fail to support ourselves.

Those were great times. I miss the neighborhood guys I grew up with – we have all gone in different directions, and live hundreds of miles apart. We raised families, and several of us are now grandparents. We have all matured and developed in different ways. Fortunately, we were given a firm foundation with similar core beliefs. Each of us chose a different path, or the path chose us.

One common denominator growing up was that our parents did the best they knew how, with the resources and education they possessed. Now, many years later I have realized that we were all capable of becoming _more_ confident, _more_ powerful, and _more_ influential. We didn't know what we didn't know, nor did we know where to find the counsel we each needed to realize our potential.

We each learned major life lessons early in our lives. Life experiences seem to be one of the best teachers, although at times painfully so. At the age of 13, I unexpectedly grew up and shouldered a man's burden, literally overnight. Our

FROM THE AUTHOR

whole family was dealt a serious life curve. Dad left mom one evening and I experienced my first taste of "real life". I don't have any idea how tough it was on my mom or how she felt when dad left. Although I did witness some things that would have challenged the coping skills of the most mature adults.

The months and years following my parents' split were rough. First the feeling of being different, embarrassed, and ashamed. I felt like an outcast. But the more I thought about our family situation the more I realized that I was just like everyone else. No one is immune to serious problems and setbacks. The family situations for many of my schoolmates were just as serious. Years earlier in elementary school, two friends lost their moms, one to heart disease and the other to cancer. Several other friends were being raised by a single parent.

I tell that story to exhibit how quickly (and unexpectedly) major life problems will impact you at some future point. The negative experiences seem so unfair. And there is no way of stopping the inevitable. You may be thinking about the times that you have experienced serious life events. You are not alone. You are rubbing elbows with countless people that have experienced serious setbacks. Make the best of the situation, grow, and move forward.

Personal tragedies aside, one thing I can say is that all of us neighborhood kids could have used additional guidance. We needed wisdom that would have helped us then, and exponentially more as we journeyed through our adult lives.

This book is my attempt to give you some of the most important life lessons that I learned and used throughout my journey. I can't tell you how to do everything step by step. And I don't want to. Take ownership of your life by investing time and research on the subjects you find most helpful. Whatever you find in these pages that speaks to you, may it be the genesis for acquiring more knowledge and understanding. Learn as much as you can now and use the new knowledge and understanding to shape your future.

Sincerely,

Keith A. Miller

CONTENTS

From the Author	i
Introduction	1
CHAPTER ONE: It's Time to Adult Now *Identify your life plan and personal values*	3
CHAPTER TWO: Getting Started *Understand your capabilities and evaluate your career options*	11
CHAPTER THREE: Let's Get Personal – Your MONEY *Create a personal budget, learn how to spend smart, save wisely, and use financial tools to your advantage*	47
CHAPTER FOUR: Moving on Up *On the job habits to employ for a successful career*	107
CHAPTER FIVE: Hurry Up and Fail *Embrace failure as a valuable teacher and motivator*	145
CHAPTER SIX: Life – *Master Class* *Skills to enhance your personal knowledge quotient, including Negotiations, DIY and Emergency Preparedness*	155
CHAPTER SEVEN: Finance – *Master Class* *Advanced financial acumen to build even greater wealth*	177
CHAPTER EIGHT: Career – *Master Class* *The leadership skills and personal career commitment to get you to the top*	207
CHAPTER NINE: Get in the Game *Open letter and challenge from the author*	227

Acknowledgements	237
Resources	239
Works Cited	251
About the Authors	255

INTRODUCTION

Have you ever heard the phrase, "I wish I knew then what I know now"? If you are like me, you would have liked to have been taught life wisdom at a much earlier age. Maybe I just wasn't ready to listen and really hear what was said. Or, like so many have said to me, "we just didn't discuss those things at home".

As young adults we all leave the nest – at least most of us do. As we go, there are life wisdom gaps we must fill with valuable knowledge and understanding. Filling these wisdom gaps will help us to think broadly, research and study for ourselves, become better life planners, and ultimately master our own direction.

> "Life would be infinitely happier if we could only be born at the age of eighty and gradually approach eighteen."[3]
>
> *Mark Twain*

Think about it – while on a trip, when you have navigation capabilities including turn by turn instructions and hazards marked along the way, aren't you more likely to get to where you want to go? Life isn't a whole lot different. When you know your intended destination, you can build a plan that will get you there. As you travel, you make many course adjustments to meet the stops, starts, hazards, and turns.

This book is about learning some life lessons, and enacting them as early as possible, to prepare for and control your own successful life journey. If you put additional work into your early learning, your life journey will be much more likely to follow the route you intend to take. Without additional work, chances are you will be dumped on a path the world chooses for you. As you make quality decisions at a young age the result will be greater confidence, stability, opportunity, rewards, and control.

My hope is that you will read some bits of wisdom and become motivated enough to seek and gain additional knowledge and understanding. Think for yourself instead of following the herd. Commit yourself to additional learning so that you understand how, when, what and why.

> "I expect to pass through life but once. If therefore, there can be any kindness I can show, or any good thing I can do to any fellow being, let me do it now, and not defer or neglect it as I shall not pass this way again."[4]
>
> *William Penn*

Just a few bits of wisdom combined with an assertive and inquisitive mind may be what you need to launch into your optimal direction.

Still interested? Are you willing to invest some of your time into your own development? If so, continue reading and prepare to be challenged to take control, learn, and think for yourself.

CHAPTER ONE
IT'S TIME TO ADULT NOW

In this chapter you will learn about your foundation. I am going to challenge you to mature in a few areas, right away. You will identify what is important to you and develop a draft of your long-term life vision. This chapter is short but no-less important than those that follow. You should exit this chapter with a good idea of your value system and vision for your future.

In 1789, Benjamin Franklin wrote, "In this world nothing can be said to be certain, except death and taxes."[5] I'd like to add you can be certain that a fair amount of living will occur in there too. There are several cycles, moving from one life stage to the next as we age. The process from birth through adulthood is to gradually gain experience, knowledge, understanding and responsibility (well, at least for some of us).

At the time, childhood and the teen years may feel like a veritable eternity. But as you can see (and may know from experience), childhood is just a blink – the bulk of our life is spent, say it with me, "adulting".

A look at our LIFE CYCLE

Infancy/Childhood	Teen	Young Adult		Adult			Retirement/Golden Years		
Birth	10's	20's	30's	40's	50's	60's	70's	80's	90's

"Adulting"

WIDE-EYED WISDOM

Today, Peter Pan syndrome is rampant. Folks fail to realize that they must grow up! Growing up means enjoying both privileges <u>and</u> responsibilities. We live in a "gimmie" society – feeling entitled to all the perks and benefits of growing up without the hard work and responsibility. Look at your personal life and those close to you, I bet you are familiar with a few of these:

- *The teen with a new cellphone in hand (paid for by mom and dad) wanting complete privacy, and no expectations regarding her behavior or performance in school.*
- *The newly minted driver who wants a car, gas money and insurance, without a job or any means to pay for it (that is what mom and dad are for, right?).*
- *The college student all too eager to "be out on his own", who blames the "bad" teacher for a poor or failing grade.*
- *The freshly minted college graduate, unable to find a job that will pay enough to support her modern lifestyle, who blames the university and education system for her failure to land a career job.*
- *The office worker who has worked years in the same job (yet has not improved his skillset or sought greater responsibility), squeals to anyone and everyone, because he has been passed over for a promotion yet again.*
- *The retiree who blames the system because she can't afford to live without outside assistance (by the way, she spent little (if any) effort in planning and preparing for the decades of living after retirement).*
- *A mistake is made but no one will take responsibility. "Some kid must have done it." If they ever catch "some kid", he or she will be in a lot of trouble.*

It is no secret! It's just reality – once you have reached adulthood no one is responsible to take care of you but you. No one. Not your mom or dad, your grandparents, the government, or any institution – you are responsible for yourself. So, you do you.

Throughout this book we are going to operate under the assumption that you accept and take ownership of this core message – **you are responsible for yourself, your life, and your future**. If you aren't ready to assume ownership, put this book down. You aren't ready to learn or commit to a plan for yourself. I hope you come back soon – the earlier in life that you thoughtfully and proactively make your plan, implement meaningful decisions, and follow through, the greater positive impact you will have on your life.

CHAPTER ONE: IT'S TIME TO ADULT NOW

It is time to adult now. Before we dig into the tools and tactics, we will dive into your vision and defining values to be used as a guide for decision making.

Understanding your Vision and Values

If you ever attend a party or gathering and conversation is lacking, ask perhaps the greatest philosophical question of all time, "So what's the meaning of life?" If you can make it past the crickets chirping in the background, you just might strike up a lively and enlightening conversation. What you will find is that this is one of those questions for which man has yearned for an answer for millennia. The responses will likely reflect unique worldviews. Despite what the media often reports, Hollywood reflects, or Facebook circulates, not all people view and interpret the world through the same lens of experience, culture, or beliefs.

I am not here to tell you which worldview you should follow – most likely you have already arrived at some framework from which to view the world. I want you to understand that as an adult, how you view the world, and your place in it, will help define your life vision. Big picture, your life vision can become your life plan. You don't need to have your whole life figured out – there's no way you could – but you do need a start, or perspective from which to view the world, and your place in it. Most importantly you must be able to describe your big goals (this action will result in your life plan).

If you set out on a road trip of the United States, it doesn't help to have a map of Uzbekistan. Your life journey is no different. You need a map that will guide you to your desired destination. You are much more likely to be satisfied when you plot a course (and make regular course corrections) in support of the vision and values that ground you. This requires some philosophizing and introspection. Please take time to be thoughtful. To get started, ask yourself a few questions:

- Do I have any core beliefs? Why do I hold them to be true, relevant, and important?
- What are my religious beliefs? How should this impact my decisions and actions in life?
- What personal characteristics do I want to own and model?
- Who do I want to interact with? (One of my mentors would say that if you hang out with dogs long enough you are bound to get fleas.)
- Are there any social missions/causes that I connect with?

WIDE-EYED WISDOM

- Is there a person or group of people to whom I am committed?
- Is there a subject/field of study with which I am enamored?
- Do you crave notoriety and fame? Or perhaps a family-oriented life?
- Where do you want to live?
- What sort of lifestyle do you envision?

Your perspective today will shift and mature as you grow and become exposed to more people and experiences. Your life mission may look something like this:
- *I want to experience new cultures and help the sick and impoverished around the world.*
- *Coming from a broken home, I want to make my future family life the highest priority while pursuing a career that allows me to financially support our needs.*
- *I just love acting and being on stage. I want to be in the entertainment industry and surround myself with creative people every day.*
- *I see myself as Mr. Big Shot – I thrive on high-pace, high-pressure, and the hustle and bustle of the big city.*

Do you have some ideas? Great! Make note of your vision so that you can thoughtfully and purposefully respond to choices, opportunities, and challenges in your life, in a way that satisfies your core beliefs.

Now that you have some understanding of the big picture vision for your life, you need to hone-in on personal values that serve as your internal sounding board. Think of values as the tools to help you decide which route to take on your life plan journey. And when you are faced with an unexpected detour, keep your values front and center as you recalibrate your route. You can hold many values to be true, but at the end of the day it is unlikely that you will be able to satisfy every one of your values with every decision you make. In that case you must make a choice. But before you do that, identify the top five values that will always be a litmus test for your decisions. Life isn't perfect, and it isn't easy. At times you must make tough choices, sometimes at the cost of something you value. Save yourself the heartache – know what is important to you and be able to spot your deal-breakers.

Values
- *Honesty*
- *Integrity*
- *Family*
- *Achievement*
- *Money*
- *Loyalty*
- *Hard Work*
- *Fame*
- *Travel*
- *Experiences*
- *Knowledge*
- *Success*

CHAPTER ONE: IT'S TIME TO ADULT NOW

Years ago, I had an incredible opportunity to purchase a small wholesale distributor raking in over $1 million net profit per year. The income stream was excellent, and I wouldn't need to uproot my family – we had already moved multiple times, back and forth from California to Oregon, and our kids were now in school. We all felt at home in the Pacific Northwest. But there was a catch, about 80-90% of the profits were generated from the sale of tobacco products. The income potential was more than appealing – it would have changed our lives, but I didn't love the idea of benefitting from a harmful addictive substance. In the end, my core value of **Integrity** made the decision for me. To knowingly support and promote the tobacco industry would have conflicted with my Integrity – I didn't want to profit from something that causes such devastating illness and disease. If my values were unclear, I would have chosen the money.

Can you see how identifying your core values will help navigate the bumpy waters of decision making? Depending on what stage of life you are in, you may find that the priority of your values may shift. A few years back, our daughter Teresa had to make a tough decision. She has always been a high-achiever – high school valedictorian and summa cum laude college graduate. Her education success led to an excellent job straight out of college. The Fortune 100 company she worked for recognized her talent and invested in her professional development. Nearly six years into her career, corporate went through significant restructuring throughout the country, part of which eliminated the position she held. While she had an opportunity to move into another position, it would have required increased hours and commitment that she just was not willing to give, since it would conflict with her value for **Family**, and require too much time away from her young child. Now a handful of years down the road, and two more children added to the brood, she is thankful that she was able to focus on her kids and spend the time that so many parents miss. She is now looking forward to getting back into her career once her youngest is in school.

Keep in mind that during the time our daughter worked through her career and family decisions, she was modeling core value examples to her immediate and extended family and friends.

WIDE-EYED WISDOM

> "Create a vision for the life you really want and then work relentlessly towards making it a reality."[6]
>
> *Roy T. Bennett*

Life will present you with many opportunities and challenges. What a blessing! Know who you are, who you want to be, and what is important to you and why. With this knowledge in your pocket, you can adjust your route to keep you on track with your life plan.

Complete the exercise below – it will help you identify what is important in your life.

Vision & Values Exercise
See Resources – Exhibit 1 p. 240, for a list of Value Words

A. Describe in a sentence or two your vision for your life (ie. Life Plan).
    _____
    _____
    _____
    _____

B. List the 5 words that best describe your values.
    1. _____
    2. _____
    3. _____
    4. _____
    5. _____

C. Rank your values words in order of importance.
    1. _____
    2. _____
    3. _____
    4. _____
    5. _____

D. How well does your value list support your life vision?
    _____
    _____

CHAPTER ONE: IT'S TIME TO ADULT NOW

E. Would you trade any of your five stated values for any other value?
   - Yes
   - No

F. If you answered yes. What new value word(s) would you add, and which original value word would you delete? List your new five value words.
   1. _____
   2. _____
   3. _____
   4. _____
   5. _____

G. Prioritize Your Values from question F.
   1. _____
   2. _____
   3. _____
   4. _____
   5. _____

I'm not a psychologist, but if you are willing to give up the values you listed at the start of the exercise (those listed in questions B. and C.) and later trade for other values, the new values may be more important to you than those you started with and have now crossed out.

You have just developed a mini rough draft of your desired life plan and supporting values. Congratulations on taking the first step – it is an important one!

This exercise just scratched the surface - there is more to consider as you build and enact a comprehensive life plan. Take the time now to visit our website at www.wide-eyedwisdom.com. You will find a detailed Life Plan exercise that will bring clarity and direction to the multi-faceted nature of your amazing life so that you spend your days proactively working toward what is important to you. Plus, you will get to meet "The Wise Guide". Don't wait or you might miss out on this critical and foundational building block to a purposeful and prosperous life.

CHAPTER TWO
GETTING STARTED

Now that the foundation has been laid, you must develop a thoughtful and proactive approach to achieve your life plan. Let's get started on your path, including the knowledge and understanding you should pursue.

So far, you have learned the following:
1. There is wisdom to gain throughout life – the earlier that it is put to work, the more beneficial it will be to you! (Hint – that is the purpose of this book.)
2. You are responsible for your future
3. You have created a rough draft of your life plan and supporting values.

Chapter Two is devoted to your preparations to launch into the world. You will come away with the following:
- Understand the importance of Life-Long Learning
- Identify Education Paths
- Guidance for Career Decision Making
- Tips to Prepare for your Career

Let's get started developing your reality. To achieve your life plan, you must acquire the knowledge, understanding, and skills, to take advantage of opportunities that arise (and those you make).

WIDE-EYED WISDOM

Invest in Yourself

I have heard it said that the deposits you put into your self-development are much like monetary deposits. Just like an investment, the more you deposit/invest in yourself each year, the more you grow. Imagine that you invest 10% annually in your development while others invest only 1% in their development. As you invest continually for 5, 10, 25-years…you will have raised your knowledge, understanding and your ceiling well beyond the people that are your competition for your preferred career. Eventually your compound knowledge and understanding, much like a monetary investment, grows to astounding levels.

Ever heard of Warren Buffet, the "Oracle of Omaha"? Here is what he thinks about self-development.

> "The best investment you can make…is an investment in yourself, the more you learn the more you'll earn."[7]
>
> *Warren Buffett*

A great example of investing in personal knowledge and understanding is our daughter. At a young age she became a voracious reader. With reading as her foundation, her interests are broad, and she finds that she is successful at anything she chooses to do.

When our daughter was a pre-teen, I asked her how she knew so much about so many subjects. She replied, "I don't know why I know, I just know". No doubt her depth of knowledge at a young age was the direct result of what she had retained, a result of regular reading.

She has since motivated our granddaughter to become an avid reader. Now ten years old, our granddaughter is an intelligent and knowledgeable girl. Her understanding of the world has grown well beyond her years. Now our daughter is working to interest her boys, ages five and three, the same way she taught her little girl (though at the moment the two boys are more partial to superheroes and destruction than reading – one step at a time, right?).

CHAPTER TWO: GETTING STARTED

Intelligence, Knowledge and Understanding

Intelligence

What is intelligence? **Intelligence** is *the capacity to learn and critically interact with the inputs around us.*[8]

Yes, it is true that some folks are more intelligent than others. It is also true that genetics, an accident, drug parents and a myriad of other factors will cause disabilities in many people, which can impair intelligence.

I'm reminded of a colleague years ago who would regularly hum, "If I Only Had a Brain" (song from *The Wizard of* Oz) while working. Despite what we may hear or observe about humanity, the overwhelming mass of people *are* intelligent enough to accomplish great things – don't buy into the excuse that you aren't smart enough! By virtue of having the skills to read this book and digest the messages, you are intelligent and can accomplish plenty.

Knowledge

If most of us are intelligent, why is there such a wide disparity in our skills and abilities? That's because *Intelligence* and *Knowledge* are not the same thing. Think of intelligence as your capacity (gas tank), and knowledge as the quantity and quality of inputs (the amount and type of fuel). The larger the tank, plus the greater quantity and quality of fuel, the faster and farther the vehicle can travel.

Our minds are incredible machines – the grey matter inside is just waiting for synapses and connections to be made. Those who invest the time and resources into stimulating this mental tool by filling their knowledge tank, are likely to surpass someone who just happens to be naturally intelligent. After all, what good is a large gas tank if you are not going to fill it with lots of quality fuel? Maybe that is why some people lack "common sense".

Knowledge is gained through many experiences. The rate of knowledge gain depends upon the experience. The more rote (repetitive) the input, the slower the gain. Eventually there is little to no additional growth. People that gain knowledge quickly do so through a commitment to lifelong education, and by taking on a variety of new challenges and experiences. These people take ownership of their intelligence capacity and fill it constantly. Eventually, they just know.

WIDE-EYED WISDOM

Knowledge Gains: Increasing knowledge is up to the individual. No other person can make you increase your knowledge. *You own your personal development. Training and education are only as valuable as the commitment and effort you put in.*

What should you study? Your life plan and values will provide the subject matter. If you don't know what to study, find mentors that will speak candidly with you. Listen to them. Then find the materials. It is in your hands. Don't make lame excuses. You are an intelligent person.

Read: Become a voracious reader. Pick a variety of topics and read about them. You will find what you are interested in through the various books you read. Have you ever watched the game show *Jeopardy*? The contestants always have at least one thing in common - they are all voracious readers.

I read books about ways to sharpen my professional skills. My commitment to be the best at what I do requires constant development. Reading helps me make rapid gains in knowledge and understanding. I don't wait for an organization sponsored class. I read.

Influence others to read regularly, especially children. Do what you can to awaken and expand a child's imagination. Children's books are designed to stretch the imagination of youngsters. Encourage kids to become active engaged readers. When they read, they will build knowledge. Their brain tanks, overflowing with high octane knowledge, will fuel their motors and take them far.

Why Gain Knowledge?

Knowledge can…

- Increase your confidence
- Drive purposeful and informed decision making
- Expand your curiosity
- Enhance independent thinking
- Increase ideas and possibilities
- Develop "Expert" power
- Improve leadership skills
- Reduce surprises and fear of the unknown
- Increase your awareness and anticipation
- Make cause and effect better understood
- Increase your professional value and raise your ceiling
- Enhance your teaching ability

CHAPTER TWO: GETTING STARTED

Classes: Take advantage of opportunities to learn from experts. Whether the class is part of your schooling, adult education, or offered by your organization, commit to the opportunity, and take away as much as you can. Those that make the most of learning opportunities will stand a much better chance of reaching their goals than those who fail to seek lifelong learning.

Teach/Lead a Class: I have been asked on numerous occasions to lead adult education classes. To be ready for the class, my advance preparation had to be awesome (after all, I did not want to look like a dufus). Each time I prepared to lead a class I learned more than I knew about the subject previously.

If you are asked to teach a subject, run to the opportunity. Yep, I said *run to the opportunity*, not run *from* the opportunity. You will be stretched to learn. Your knowledge, understanding and confidence, will grow. Increased confidence leads to personal and professional success.

On the Job: On the job learning is valuable but can be dangerous, depending upon what you do with it.

First the value. There is nothing like actual hands-on work experience. You learn and then will understand what you are doing and how to do it. I encourage you to learn "why", in addition to what and how. If you know why, you will be a proficient problem solver, and more importantly, prepared to imagine and implement better ways to do the job. Know why the work or process is structured a certain way, and you will learn to anticipate when things are about to go wrong and how to make necessary changes.

Now for the danger. Some of us rely solely on an organization to train us and keep our skills current. Organizations are not responsible for keeping your skills current. You are the proud owner of skill development. If you don't keep your personal skills current, you may find yourself with many years of experience performing outdated tasks.

Other Sources: Gain knowledge wherever you can – and engage your senses. You can learn from books, museums, travel, articles, observation, questions, friends, trivia games, a classroom setting or a TV show, or tackling a new or challenging project. The younger you are when you learn how to gain knowledge, the better. Your school and professional habits will be much more disciplined, and the result will be a greater level of success. You have the mental capacity, so pay attention, and become a diligent listener and learner.

Add "Lifelong Learner" to your resume, continue to gain knowledge, understanding, and power, right up to your exit from this world.

Understanding

Without understanding, you will not be nearly as powerful. To make intelligent decisions and exhibit the best behaviors and examples, develop understanding based on the knowledge that has filled your tank. Think back to our example of the large gas tank that represents intelligence. Filling the tank with fuel represents gaining a significant amount of knowledge. Using the same word picture, *Understanding* is the complex drive train, computer systems, electronics, and other systems required to operate your vehicle, including your operator training. These complex systems and tools can be used to get the most out of your intelligence and knowledge. Once you are armed with understanding how to operate your vehicle, you will be able make optimal decisions around all actions necessary to have a safe and successful journey. Understanding of how to operate your vehicle is critical and necessary to arrive comfortably, safely and on-time to your desired destination.

Understanding will empower you to see potential solutions and ramifications in your minds-eye. From that point, you can play out the consequences of various potential decisions. Instead of acting on impulse, you will make decisions using excellent, advanced, and intentional reasoning.

Self-Discipline

If you hope to be successful in life, self-discipline is something you must make a habit of as early as possible – get ready to hear me talk about this ability throughout the book. Without the appropriate amount of self-discipline, you will have difficulty in your relationships, with commitment, performance in school, career, and your finances – just to name a few. Self-discipline must be learned, practiced, relearned, and practiced again. Self-discipline will help you make sound decisions and actions that support your life plan. Undisciplined decisions and lack of effort will dump you on a very undesirable path. Absent

CHAPTER TWO: GETTING STARTED

self-discipline you will not reach your life plan goals unless by dumb luck, good fortune lands in your lap. If you happen to experience good luck, without self-discipline, chances are you will waste your good fortune. You will read about some lottery winners later that emphasizes this point.

Have you ever heard of Jesse Owens? He excelled in the summer Olympics of 1936, in Germany, at one of the darkest times in the history of our world. Mr. Owens won four gold medals and buried the idea of Hitler's Aryan supremacy.

> "We all have dreams, but in order to make dreams come into reality, it takes an awful lot of determination, dedication, self-discipline and effort."[9]
>
> *Jesse Owens*

Self-discipline is the foundation, a requirement, for the subject matter in this book – this important ability has no expiration date. Successful people are masters at self-discipline. Supremely talented but undisciplined people become shooting stars – they burn bright but lack staying power and fizzle out quickly.

Career Time: Choose a Path...A True Story

It was late fall in Central California. The mornings were beginning to get brisk, but we still had those warm dry afternoons. The sweet agricultural aroma was in the air, a blend of dairy cows and rotting fruit.

It was 1976 and I was a senior in high school. Our high school was typical of those in most small California valley towns. I think the school was built in the 1940's, it was difficult to tell. Buildings were added over time as the town's population grew. The classrooms on one side of the high school reminded me of elementary school buildings. Large chalk boards, tile floors, musty smells, and the pile of books on the shelves that looked like they hadn't been moved in eons.

The Vietnam War had ended in April of 1975. I'll never forget reading the daily casualty reports in the newspaper. Bombing, wounded, missing in action, loss of life in Vietnam and turmoil all over the U.S. The end of the Vietnam war was welcomed by all and turned out to be the start of a very peaceful and prosperous time in the United States.

I mention Vietnam because the military draft ended in 1973. The end of the war signaled the end of mandatory draft registration. With the military draft in the rearview mirror and to keep their numbers strong, each of the armed forces ramped up recruiting efforts.

WIDE-EYED WISDOM

I was one of about thirty students in Civics class (a senior year graduation requirement). If you took Civics class first semester, there was a good chance you could graduate high school at Christmas break.

The local Army recruiter was looking for the next group of soldiers and had arranged an assessment test for all seniors in the Civics classes. I suspect the arrangement with the school administration was that each student would receive personalized information about strengths, interests, and career recommendations in exchange for taking the assessment. There must have been a profile of how a person scored that would identify potential military recruits. It was the potential soldier group the recruiter really wanted to identify. The test also gave the Army recruiter the chance to speak, albeit briefly, with every graduating senior.

I had never taken an assessment test. With college entrance or finding a job smack dab in front of me, the assessment sounded like a great idea. Maybe the results would help me figure out what to do next. I thought I should go to college but wasn't totally sure.

The Army assessment test took less than an hour to complete. I don't remember exactly what was covered, though it did touch on a wide variety of subjects. There was no right or wrong answer to many of the questions.

I was really looking forward to the Army assessment results and personalized discussion. Our teacher told us the Army recruiter would be back in a week or two with our test scores. We would meet one-on-one with the recruiter to get an idea of what the Army thought would be a good career path. Other than my school grades, this would be the first time I would ever receive feedback on my potential and possible career options. I was excited to get the chance to discuss my overall strengths, interests, and potential.

Fast forward two weeks and the recruiter arrived back in Civics class. We lined up, single file, to learn our results. The recruiter sat at a small table at the front of the classroom. As each person stepped up to the table, the recruiter asked for last name and then first.

As he talked with my classmates, I could hear the recruiter say, "You scored well in math," and then he would offer something like, "You might want to investigate a career in accounting". Some of my peers received another comment or two about other careers that aligned with their strengths and interests. And on it went. Various strengths and interests for each classmate and a prognostication of what might be a good college and/or career fit for each person. Each student seemed satisfied as they exited the line and started to ponder their next step. Or, maybe to forget about the whole thing.

Finally, at the front of the line, I gave the recruiter my last name and then first. He scanned his list. His next words… "Son, do anything you want to do. Next." Wait.

CHAPTER TWO: GETTING STARTED

What just happened? I got the bums rush. What did he mean? I wanted some direction. I wanted a do over or at least ask him to be more specific. Specific direction was what we always got in school. I wanted details. Now, I was back at square one. Or had I ever left square one? It really was up to me to figure out a direction on my own, but I wasn't ready for that decision yet (I had only turned 17 a few weeks earlier).

After giving the matter a great deal of thought, I figured the recruiter's message was that I scored at a high level across the board and could probably do whatever I chose to do. But as immature as I was, how could I possibly make such a decision? Just barely 17, I still didn't have any direction and within a few months I had to make a big life decision.

*****

In your late teens did you really know what you wanted to do as a career? Were you or are you mature enough to make such a weighty life decision?

I chose a career path that I was familiar with. I had family members that worked in the same industry. I cast aside my interests and decided based on familiarity, comfort, and a shortage of self-confidence. Don't get me wrong, my career has been financially successful and provided well for my family. I've met a lot of great people. But overall, the work itself hasn't been much fun. Nor has it been that interesting.

My preferred career was sports broadcasting, until I read some words written by the late Howard Cosell of Monday Night Football fame. Based on his behavior during the Monday Night Football broadcast he was stuck on himself. I remember well when he wrote, and I am paraphrasing…that if you aren't an ex-jock then forget about sports broadcasting.[10] Boy did that sink my ship. (By the way, Cosell didn't look anything like an ex-athlete. I was too young and immature to recognize that Howard Cosell could not have been an athlete prior to his sports broadcasting career. Although, Muhammed Ali loved the man. That counts for something.)

If I had to do it all over again, I would have contacted counselors at my high school and the local university to ask for guidance, additional testing or assessments that could guide me. And, talk with someone that was working in my career of choice. At least I would have better understood my options.

I have seen many children choose to follow in their parent's career footsteps. Throughout my career in food wholesale distribution, working with independent supermarket business owners, I witnessed countless children follow their parents into the family business. Most of the kids were not interested in operating a food store. Second and third generation food store owners rarely possessed the passion and commitment necessary to take the helm of the family business. Most wanted to reap rewards without the necessary commitment to lead a successful business.

Following family members is not necessarily a bad thing – if a family business opportunity is an option for you, it should be a serious consideration. But first, gauge your passion and interest in the family business, then review your life plan before you make your decision.

As you consider your career options, think about the following:
- Seek great career counsel. Find the best professional advice. (Stay clear of people that want to give you opinions instead of facts. Opinionated people can be passionate and convincing. Be careful with free unsolicited advice, confusion may be the result. I like to say that free advice plus $1.89 may just buy you a soft drink at your local Taco Bell.)
- If you can mold your career around your passions and interests, make it happen. You will never regret doing something you love every day.
- Be willing to stretch. You are up to the challenge.
- You are not required to follow in the footsteps of family members.
- Your career path shouldn't necessarily be familiar and/or comfortable.
- For best results, your career should support your life plan.

The Fork in the Road

"If you come to a fork in the road, take it."[11]

Yogi Berra

Hall of Fame catcher and World Series Champion, New York Yankees

---

If only it were so easy.

After high school...*Do I go straight to work? Do I pursue higher education? Open a business? Hitchhike all over Europe? What do I do?*

CHAPTER TWO: GETTING STARTED

Unless you are independently wealthy you will be faced with finding a job, going to college, business ownership, joining the military, or attending trade school. Let's discuss each of these "forks" in the road.

Career preparation should be filled with research and expert counsel. First, have you identified your life plan and supporting values? If you have those nailed down, your path is probably a bit more defined. Be methodical and do your homework and consult with the right counseling experts.

What do I mean by experts? You need objective facts. Don't ask for college and career advice from people that have little more to offer than an opinion.

In my case, friends and family members were not the best source for college and career counsel. I was the seventh of eight children. I was also the first to graduate with a bachelor's degree. Some of those close to me would offer advice even though they had never earned a college degree. They meant well but career counsel was not among their strengths or expertise. Beware advice freely given about a topic/subject/experience that has no basis in personal or professional knowledge.

Instead of opinions, find the people that counsel professionally (in college and career). **Seeking this counsel is one of the most important moves you can make.** When you meet with the counselor, share your life plan and values. Or, at a minimum share your strengths and interests. Then, work from there.

Have you already decided what you want to do for a career? If so, there is most likely a clear path for you. Your fork in the road will be defined, (and by the way, you are one of the fortunate few, and I would wager that you probably have a strong passion in life that is guiding you forward, well done).

The "ideal" pathway in our world is to engage in education, at least through high school. After high school graduation, you can dive into the working world (remember, it is time to Adult now), start your own business, go to college, join the armed forces, or enroll in trade school. If you opt for college, ideally a career path has been identified that will make your "Higher Education" worth it, after all what is the use of studying Psychology if you don't want to be a Counselor or Psychologist? Unfortunately, expecting eighteen or nineteen-year-olds to be ready to commit to career decisions just might not be realistic for some. For me it certainly wasn't.

WIDE-EYED WISDOM

Let's look at several common forks in the road.

Fork 1: Higher Education (College)

It is well-known that on average, those who earn a bachelor's degree earn significantly more money than those with just a high school diploma. Certain majors are more satisfying and pay better. Consider your life plan to make sure you choose wisely. By the way, a bachelor's degree by itself is not enough (much more on that later, so stay with me on this point).

What is your higher education goal? I will wager that most would answer that their goal is to get a diploma. Guess what, that piece of paper isn't enough!

The Beer Pong Diploma – Why You Should Put in the Work Instead

** WARNING** I hear about this topic nearly every day – "The college debt crisis!" There is no doubt that college is expensive. At the time of this publishing there is nearly $1.6 TRILLION in student loan debt[12], and many students are leaving college unprepared or unable to secure a career job with enough income to repay student loans, and pay for living expenses, not to mention save for a house, other large purchases or investments.

Students are demanding, and some politicians are clamoring to "forgive" all or part of student loan debt. "The system is broken!" is the rallying cry.

Hold on – the problem here is not necessarily "the system" (by the way there are always improvements to be made in any system or organization). **Higher education is a choice**. A myriad of education options are available. Local community college followed by a university, local university, out-of-state university, private university, law school, medical school, and on... Remember,

CHAPTER TWO: GETTING STARTED

<u>you</u> are responsible for yourself, your life, your future. Don't rely on another person or entity to provide for you or make your decisions.

Your university will eventually award a diploma based on performing *just enough* sub-standard class work. You too may choose to scrape by on the minimum necessary to graduate. If you do, **you will be no more qualified** to get a job in your chosen career field than you were when you started college.

> "Opportunity is missed by most people because it is dressed in overalls and looks like work."[13]
>
> *Thomas Edison*

If you decide to pursue a college degree, take full advantage of your world class education opportunity! Be aware of your options, understand the cost, and know what career doors your preferred degree will open. Check to make sure you know what, if any, additional credentials are required to qualify for your desired career. If your career picture does not support your life plan, you may be considering the wrong path.

Stepping into college translates to "adulting". Act like it. Maybe that degree in Underwater Basket-Weaving is not such a good idea. There are quite a few majors that will not payoff for you. Know in advance what your job prospects are for your chosen field of study. Do not be one of the many that finds out after graduation that their costly diploma is nearly worthless.

The opportunities in our country are tremendous. We are so spoiled we don't realize how fortunate we have it. Maybe the real problem is that we are not committed enough to truly value the importance of a quality education. We also may not be committed to do our best when opportunity knocks.

Answer for yourself, are you serious enough about your career to do what it takes to get there? Saying yes isn't enough. You have to say yes and mean it.

Let's try this again. *What is your education goal?* Here is my take:

Your goal is to master every subject you study. Mastery is marketable in any career and in any economy. Your knowledge, understanding and professional skills will always be in demand.

Master every subject, then use that success to compete for jobs more effectively. If you commit to mastering every school subject, and practice awesome self-discipline, you will earn your degree, and find a great job in your field of study. You will secure an upwardly mobile career with a growing salary, pay back student loans, and pay taxes like many of us. Your future will be very bright, and you will avoid bemoaning the fact that you can't find a job in your field of interest.

I'm not saying that you shouldn't enjoy your college years. Your college years will go by in a blink. What I am saying is to make the most of the education opportunity. Don't spend your time majoring in lounge and after school parties at the expense of your education. There will be time for fun at school, and after you graduate. Education is the reason for going to college and should be your number one priority – leave the title of Beer Pong Champ to someone else.

College and Career Preparations Exercise

List your top three passions in life.
1. _____
2. _____
3. _____

Which of these three would be a blast to do every day and get paid?
1. _____
2. _____

We will assume that one or more of your preferred careers requires a college education. You need to do your homework before you jump into a school. Face it, college is a big commitment, with a sizeable price tag.

Your research might look like this (find a top-notch career counselor, preferably one that specializes in your preferred careers, to guide the process):
- What are the future job prospects in your career of interest?
- Does your aptitude fit your field of interest?
- Do you need to take a career assessment test?
    - What do the results of career assessment tests reveal?
- Do you need a degree or certifications beyond a bachelor's degree?
- What schools provide the necessary degree program?

CHAPTER TWO: GETTING STARTED

- - Which of those schools specialize in your career of choice?
    - How do their programs rate locally and nationally?
    - What programs are rated higher, and why?
- Is community college an option?
- Who are potential employers?
  - What are their favored schools from which to recruit?
- Which school or schools are the best fit for your academic success?
- Which schools should you visit?
  - Based on the visit, where are you most comfortable?
  - What grants, scholarships, and loans are available?
    - How do you apply?
  - What are the prospects for a part-time job?
  - What internships are available?
- Based on your college visit, which place will be enjoyable, comfortable and allow you the best opportunity to master your subjects?
- Will your high school grades qualify for entrance into your preferred university? What are the other application requirements?
- What is the estimated cost of tuition, fees, and books?
- What is the cost of housing, including food and utilities?
- How will you pay for your education (include plan for loan payments)?
- Will your degree qualify you for other careers? What are they?
  - What are the future job prospects in these careers?
  - Will you be happy working in one of those fields?
- What companies would you prefer to work for?
  - Are you willing to relocate? If so, to where?
  - What grades must you achieve to land the job with your desired organization?
  - Besides grades what are your target companies looking for in a new graduate?
- What is your earning potential?
  - Salary, bonus, stock, 401(k), benefits...
- Visit with people that work in your field of interest.
  - Ask them about: necessary education, preferred schools, job search, employers, pay and benefits, culture, changes in the field, long-term job prospects, likes and dislikes about the job.

- Will your preferred career job support your life plan?
- What haven't you asked?

Do your best to get answers as early as possible. The questions could be limitless, but this list should get you started thinking about your research. Leave no stone unturned. You have never been faced with a decision this important.

Keep in mind that the college option comes with a price tag – a big one. Don't let that scare you off but be sure that wherever your education is taking you, is worth the investment.

Fork 2: Straight to Work

You might consider going straight to work after high school. Please, do not fool yourself and say, "I'll work for a few years and go back to college". That idea rarely works. You go to work and earn more money and spend more money than you have ever seen. Your cost to live is far more than you imagined, and it takes all you earn to survive. You fall into a cycle of earning and spending. A relationship or financial commitment or both, comes along. Now, with more than enough responsibilities, college is long gone.

If there is a career that requires a high school diploma, makes you happy, and will support your life plan, then go for it. You may not be mature enough to make the decision by yourself, so get some professional counsel. I don't mean opinions. No disrespect intended to families and friends, but to solve problems a carpenter uses a hammer and a nail, an acupuncturist uses needles, a doctor writes a prescription, a demolition expert uses dynamite…you get the idea. A family member or friend approach to problem solving will be aligned with their skillset or expertise. In many cases, advice will be little more than a subjective opinion. Family and friends think they are protecting you (the truth of the matter is that they are scared to death and could never bring themselves to launch in the direction you are considering). Don't let another person's fears or limitations place limits on you. Find a career expert that will give unbiased objective counsel.

If you choose the job after high school route don't jump into work that will be obsolete in the next few years. If your industry is eventually automated

CHAPTER TWO: GETTING STARTED

or the work is moved out of the area you will be like many others in the herd, out of work, and without the skills to find another job.

There are great careers out there. Find a career that has staying power and will support your life plan. As in any career, be the best at what you do. Even when there are dips in the economy you will always be in demand.

Fork 3: Start A Business

Many people dream of owning a business. Starting/owning a business is a big task. Years ago, a group of Harvard dropouts started a company you may have heard of – Microsoft. That team knew what they wanted to do, had vision, understood how their products would change the world, and the rest is history.

Unlike Microsoft, most businesses fail in the first few years. Why? Well, excitement, emotions and lack of preparation can cloud the all-important question – *should* this business concept move forward? Emotions take hold and most people never research what is required to build a successful business.

How to Prepare

Talk to people that have owned businesses. Interview business owners, preferably in the field that you are considering. Include people that have failed, and those that have succeeded. Schedule appointments. Prepare questions and send your list of questions in advance.

Ask about:
- Initial capital investment
- Impact on family/life
- Hours
- How did they prepare?
- Would they do it again? (Why or why not?)
- What was their biggest surprise?
- What keeps them up at night?
- What do they enjoy most?
- What do they detest or dislike?
- What are the licenses and regulatory requirements?
- Risks?
- Human Resources, availability?

- What kind of financial return to expect?
- At the end of the day, are you just buying yourself a job?

Entrepreneurial Considerations
Starting your own business requires more than desire. Ask yourself…
- Do I have the personal makeup to lead my own business?
- How much risk am I willing to accept?
- Will I be able to sleep at night?
- How will I give up control to my employees?
- What am I willing to give up, to run a successful business?
- Will the business support my life plan?

Owning a business is not for everyone. Business ownership requires investment capital, knowledge, willingness, self-discipline, desire, servant leadership and commitment. Even if you have the money, plan, and people you still might fail. There are businesses where Superman or Superwoman could never be successful.

The rewards from owning a business can be great. Although initially you probably won't be taking loads of money to the bank. Realize the heartache will be there regardless of success or failure. Are you willing to take on the issues, risk, and stress? How do those sound to you?

Just like the group of Harvard dropouts, the spoils are there for the risk takers that do the necessary homework and execute with excellence. Take heart. You live in a country filled with opportunity. Why else would so many people from around the globe leave their homeland, some even risk their life, to chase dreams in the United States of America?

There is a path to success in business ownership. If others can do it then so can you – if you have what it takes.

So, you still want to own a business? Read on…If you want to start or buy a business, build with the three P's: Plan, People and Purse.

The 3 P's: PLAN
The first P is your business plan. Your business plan must be simple. Simple

CHAPTER TWO: GETTING STARTED

enough so that everyone in the organization knows what success looks like, how you are going to get there, and how their role is important.

There are plenty of excellent business planning tools available. Make sure you choose one that makes sense to you, and everyone that will be a part of executing your plan. Keep in mind the business plan is only as good as the inputs. If you cut corners, perform shoddy research, and leave out key success ingredients, you will have a bad plan.

Among the many important parts of a business plan...

- *Vision Statement:* What does the finish line or success look like?
- *Value System*: What are the words that describe your values? Those values will drive how you make decisions and the actions you will take.
- *Competitive Differentials:* What makes your business competitive in the market? Why would someone choose you over the competition? How will you raise the bar each year so that your competition is constantly reacting and chasing your leadership position?

Other important elements of your plan are realistic financial projections. You and your team must know how to judge success. How would you and your team know if you have achieved your business vision? Without regular feedback, how would you and your team know what decisions to make and tactics to use?

Complete the first P, keeping it so simple that everyone in the organization understands the goal, can easily monitor success, and knows how and why their role is necessary and important.

The 3 P's: PEOPLE

I've heard billionaire Sir Richard Branson say the people that operate his businesses are the most important ingredient of a successful organization – even above customers. Branson believes, that for employees to really want to take great care of customers, the employee must first be well taken care of. For those of you unfamiliar with Sir Richard Branson, he founded the "Virgin Group" – which controls about 400 companies.[14] If you get the chance, search for *The Rebel Billionaire* online, it was a single season reality show documenting Mr. Branson's quest to add top talent to his team – and paired incredible and daring feats (care for tea atop a hot air balloon?) with business acumen. It will give you a great appreciation for the zest for life plus intelligence and wisdom embodied in Sir Richard.

Never underestimate the importance of a great team surrounding you in your new business. As good as you might be as an owner, you can't be at your business every minute. You cannot do everything yourself, nor should you want to. To your customers and suppliers, your team is an extension of you and your business. Without a motivated, happy, and committed team you will go nowhere. In fact, unhappy employees will grumble to customers, which will send your business in the wrong direction, fast.

Spend the time to learn what it takes to build a high-quality team, and how to lead them. Commit yourself to lifelong leadership study and learning. These two subjects are complex and everchanging. This country has too few authentic leaders. We don't need another phony, so do your homework and practice high quality leadership.

Make sure you read my Essential Eleven leadership characteristics coming up in Chapter 8.

The 3 P's: PURSE

There is a cost to enter business. You must answer the question, how much money you need, and where will it come from? If you do not have enough money to get started, then you must borrow.

If you borrow, your business plan and financial projections will become critically important in securing a loan. Lenders will review your business plan and financial projections and will still require personal guarantees or collateral. When you borrow, your personal assets will be at risk.

Why Businesses Borrow Money:
- They don't have the cash to start-up
- Cash flow timing, collections lag behind payments
- Spread risk
- Expansion
- Seasonal and other business fluctuations
- Ability to make more money
- Higher return on personal cash invested

CHAPTER TWO: GETTING STARTED

Investors and lenders will use your Business Plan and Financial Projections in combination with an assessment of you and your team. Make sure all three: Plan, People, and Purse are the best.

WARNING: Potentially Catastrophic Business Entry Mistakes
The "Start A Business" section would not be complete without understanding some of the common reasons why so many businesses fail. Here are a few fun facts for you: according to the Small Business Association (SBA), 30% of small business fail within the first two years, 50% fail within the first five years, and 66% fail within the first ten years.[15]

I've listed some factors that can spell failure if you have not prepared properly. Pay close attention to each of these. If you make mistakes, even superhuman effort may not be enough to survive.

- Your Business:
  o You paid too much to buy it or start-up costs are too high.
  o The Business idea/model is outdated.
  o The Market is too small to support additional competitors.
  o Marketing efforts are unsuccessful.
  o Financial projections are too optimistic.
  o The financial return does not support the capital investment.
- For You:
  o You make emotional decisions.
  o You don't have the depth and breadth of skills to lead the business (strategy, finance, operations, leadership, etc…).
  o The business is not consistent with your Values.
  o You are unable to work independently.
  o You are unable to build a high-performance team.

Enter business with eyes-wide open, balance your optimism with the understanding that many businesses don't turn a profit the first few years.

Is it possible that you could make more money from a less risky investment? (The less risky investment may not require your personal time, effort, risk, or stress.) Refer to Chapter 8 for a quick calculation method to estimate your personal financial return. Use the calculation to compare with other potential options as you research where to place your investment dollars.

There are not enough pages to prepare you for owning a business. Faced with the decision about what fork in the road to take, make sure you have done your homework before you take this path.

Now that I have dumped a healthy amount of cold water on you…if you have the desire, commitment, resources, skills, knowledge and understanding, business ownership can be very rewarding. If you are getting into business at an early age, you can afford failure and still have a great career. Good luck and God speed.

Fork 4: Armed Forces

Serving in the armed forces is an admirable and noble calling. The personality, skills, and aptitude required are intense. You will learn skills (including self-discipline and leadership) and have experiences the rest of us only dream about.

Besides serving your country and the pride of being part of the most powerful military on earth, the armed forces may also fund your secondary education.

I don't have personal experience in the armed forces so my comments are limited, but our country would be in bad shape without the women and men that have made the sacrifices to protect us. Thank you to all who have served, and those that plan to serve – the foundational freedoms and opportunities that we have in the United States would not be possible without you.

Fork 5: Trade School

You may have a passion for working with your hands or are mechanically or technically inclined. Trade school is a good option. Some trade school careers can turn into six figure incomes. Career training is hands-on without the general education required for a bachelor's degree.

The time required, and cost for that matter, is much less than a four (or more) year secondary education. Here is just a sampling of trade school careers:[16]

CHAPTER TWO: GETTING STARTED

Trade School Careers[16]

Information Technology	Mechanical	Medical
Network Specialist	Auto Technician	Dental Hygienist
Web Developer	Aircraft Technician	Medical Tech
Construction	**Safety Services**	**And Many More…**
HVAC	Firefighter	
Plumber	Law Enforcement	
Carpenter		
Electrician		

Identify your preferred career. Research whether the position will be in demand in the future, and whether your long-term prospects, compensation, conditions, and culture, support your life plan.

Prior to enrolling, check to see which companies use trade schools as their recruiting source. Consult with a top-notch career counselor and someone that works in your field of interest, consult page 25 for research questions.

Fork in the Road – A Final Word
Remember that **you are responsible for yourself, your life, your future**. Regardless of which path you choose, make sure the available opportunities support your life plan. For those moments when you ask yourself, "How am I going to compete and reach my goals?" Just look around you. The people you are competing with are just like the peers from your grade school, middle school, high school, and college classrooms. The faces may be different, but the people are the same. If you competed well in the classroom, chances are you will repeat that success in your career. If you did not compete well in school, now is the time to get in the game and do your best.

Remember, experience in your job is not enough. Experience will get you a paycheck. You must raise your professional ceiling for career success. Investment in yourself and your career, will take you far.

WIDE-EYED WISDOM

Your First Job

Earlier you read about the importance of a strong work ethic in my family. I can't overstate the importance of a strong work ethic for career success.

My paying jobs started when I was about ten years old. In the fall, a couple of us boys would make the rounds in the neighborhood raking leaves for 50 cents or so. If the pay was a dollar, that was a big deal. Neighbors had fruitless mulberry trees that dropped leaves in waves over several weeks. This leaf drop cycle provided the opportunity for multiple paydays each fall. If you found a job at one house, you might get a repeat a week or two later. We raked the lawns and put the leaves in a nice tidy row in the street near the curb for weekly pickup (vacuum up) by the city. The work was not difficult, but we worked hard to earn our pay.

Work Ethic...

is a belief that hard work and diligence have a moral benefit and an inherent ability, virtue, or value to strengthen character and individual abilities.[17]

At the age of 11, I started delivering newspapers to about 40 to 45 households around town. Each day after school let out, my task was to fold newspapers (yes, our news back then was printed on paper – no internet or social media) and deliver them to the porches of my customers. I delivered newspapers six days a week. The second bike I ever owned was bought with my earnings, so that I could make deliveries. The three most important things I learned on my paper route were to consistently deliver on-time to the doorstep, make sure papers were dry, and manage cash flow. I never received a customer complaint. Once per month I had to collect money for the monthly subscription. I would save the monthly collections, pay wholesale price for the newspapers (I had to pay the whole bill regardless of whether I made my monthly collections), and any money left over was mine. In a good month I would clear about $45 to $50. I learned important lessons about operating a business. I had to anticipate my obligations, budget, and take care of my customers. (At the time I was an impulse buyer of baseball cards. With money in my pocket, I stopped at a local store and bought what I could afford that day. I was lucky, my mom didn't throw out my baseball cards – I still have

CHAPTER TWO: GETTING STARTED

them. By chance, my impulsive buying turned into a valuable collection. My children or grandchildren will benefit someday.)

When I turned 13, I figured I needed to find other jobs. I went to work for our retired neighbors, and by now the jobs were more complex with better pay. Now, more capable, the jobs varied from mowing and edging lawns, to painting. Elder neighbors loved to have certain ones of us do work for them. They knew each of us kids and our families and our compensation expectations fit a retired person's budget. By now we were earning folding money – bills with crooked numbers on them.

When I was 15, my brother in-law Tom bought a grocery store in Seattle, WA. He asked me to come work in Seattle for the summer. Tom could easily find enough folks to fill the available full and part-time jobs, but fortunately for me, he wanted to help me. He taught me about career, work ethic, follow-thru, customer service, social skills, and hustle. The pay was slightly more than minimum wage. The work was primarily inside stocking shelves, and frequent customer grocery carry-outs.

Later that summer, I flew back to central California. (I can still remember my flight from Seattle to Fresno, CA. It was 69 degrees and raining in Seattle when I left, and when I got off the jet at 8:30 p.m., the California heat of 95 degrees felt like a sauna.) Back home, it was easy to get my next job now that I had some work experience. The next job started in late October, and by now I was a freshly minted 16-year old. That job was also in a grocery store. My older brother worked at the same store. (*Note: I followed the comfortable path of familiarity.*) Wages were low but the employment was steady. The work was inside, which was a blessing especially during the hot summer months.

I worked six days a week. I went to work at 4 p.m. and got off at 9 p.m. four days per week. On Saturday I went to work at 9 a.m. and got off at 9 p.m., Sunday was 9 a.m. to 8 p.m. My one day off per week was either Monday or Tuesday. Doing the math, you will see that I worked more than 40-hours per week from the age of 16. My income paid for a car, clothes, dates, and funded college.

I worked too many hours during my high school years. My work schedule really put a crimp in my extracurricular activities and social life. If I had to do it over again, I would have cut back my work hours so that I could have played high school sports and enjoyed a better social life. The other impact was on my health. Sophomore year, before I had the job, my school attendance was perfect. Junior year, with a full-time job and a full-time class schedule, I missed quite a bit of school due to sickness and exhaustion. Luckily, my mom was supportive and made sure that I was rested as much as possible.

After a couple of years of working in the grocery store, I changed jobs. Another brother worked in the agriculture industry as a contractor. He operated a machine that placed glue, and then a label on the end of boxes to be used to pack grapes bound for grocery stores throughout the U.S. My brother took another job and his former employer wanted me to take his place. The opportunity was great for a school kid with limited skills. The job paid more than triple what I made at the supermarket, and I could control my hours. I could work early in the morning or late at night, it was my choice. My priority was to label enough stock, so the packing companies had enough raw material to make boxes for their fruit packing schedules. That job allowed me to cut back my work hours and enjoy more of a social life.

Summer fruit season finished, in the fall I enrolled in college and went back to work in a grocery store. My schedule included 25 to 40 hours per week at work, a full-time college class load and during the spring semester I played competitive golf. My golf schedule required two days of travel per week. One thing the college golf experience taught me was that I had to decide between working full-time at a game or devoting myself to my education. I reasoned that there are plenty of "good" but only a few "great" golfers. Only the great golfers earn a living playing professionally (and since this book is not about golf, you can guess which group I belong to). I understood my limitations. I liked golf but I didn't love it. I decided that it was imperative that I commit to my studies and excel. By now I had extra incentive, a serious girlfriend.

In my fourth and final year of college, I worked for my favorite business professor. My responsibilities included grading homework, exams, and term papers. My focus was twofold – first, to make sure that I really knew the material, and second, to be as fair as possible to each student. Knowing you have another student's grade point in your hands is a huge responsibility.

Cindy and I married the summer before I started my senior year, we were both 20-years old. Twenty is an early age to make such a big decision. These days the normal marriage age is between 28 and 31.[18] You must be thinking,

CHAPTER TWO: GETTING STARTED

"But are you still married?" The answer is, yes, we just celebrated our 40th wedding anniversary. I have no idea where I would be without Cindy's encouragement, support and from time to time her prodding to stretch and grow my self-confidence. As I approached my final year in college, it was time to take career job hunting seriously.

My college years were during President Jimmy Carter's term of office. One of the things I remember was that the economy was bad, and jobs for college students scarce. In 1979 just after overthrowing the government of the Shah of Iran (Mohammad Reza Pahlavi), Iranian "students" took control of the American embassy in Tehran (the students would be branded "terrorists" today). The terrorists took 52 American embassy workers hostage and held them for 444-days. Coincidentally, the university I attended had the second largest population of Iranian students of any campus in the United States. American sentiment toward Iran was on the ragged edge. The national guard was stationed on campus from time to time, and the local police were monitoring relations among the Iranian students and the community. Fortunately, other than a few minor skirmishes, the peace was kept.

During my senior year, it was off to the university career center. Most universities have great career centers and quite a few organizations find their new employees right on campus.

The first time I got a glimpse of "grades matter" was when one company said that if you do not have a cumulative GPA of 3.75 or better, don't bother applying. If you decide to get a college education, make the commitment, do it right the first time, and do it well. Those four or more years pay off handsomely if you have the self-discipline to put in the hard work required to master your areas of study. So, invest in yourself, not your beer belly. (It was a little unnerving during my last visit to a major university. We toured the dorms. The dorm recycling area had three kinds of cardboard – pizza boxes, soft drink boxes, and lots of beer boxes. So much for a balanced diet.)

Downside of Working While Going to School

There is no such thing as a perfect balance between work and school. Some of you will have the great gift of financial support from family. Many or perhaps most will need to work and take on debt. There will be tradeoffs among work, school, activities, and personal life. Remember, you are adulting now. This is a precursor to the choices you will make as you move into later phases of your adult life.

I was a great student but missed countless school activities due to my full-time work schedule. One positive tradeoff was that I had no college debt (between my work and my wife working full-time, we paid as I studied). But I missed out on many high school and college experiences. I could have done a better job of finding the right mix of school success first, then add work and outside activities. My regret is that during high school I missed two years of Varsity basketball, and a year of Varsity golf. I will never get that back. Although, once I graduated from college, I was more than prepared, and secured a great career job before I left my university.

Employment Recruiter

I have written about the job search process from the perspective of someone preparing to graduate with a bachelor's degree in Business Administration. Whether you achieve a degree or not, I believe the following information will help guide your job search.

If you go to college for a bachelor's degree or higher, take full advantage of the career center at your university. The people there have developed invaluable relationships with hiring organizations (and usually have some terrific internship opportunities). I learned quite a bit about resumes, cover letters, interviews, and what the recruiters were looking for in a candidate.

Most university career centers conduct job fairs (this is how our daughter connected with her first employer) where you can meet recruiters from various organizations. You will be able to talk face to face with the recruiter. Engage with them. The more you visit with recruiters the better. In many cases recruiters will come to campus to conduct job interviews. Sign up for interviews through your career center.

If you need a part-time job while going to school, visit your college career center. They may be able to point you in the right direction. Some of the part-time jobs may even be right on campus.

Career counsel, coaching and mentoring can be found at most college career centers. Your university likely has all shapes and sizes of industry

CHAPTER TWO: GETTING STARTED

contacts. Organizations are happy to talk with you and using a career center will help get you in the door.

Now, for the lessons I learned through actual job interviews on the campus of California State University, Fresno.

Lesson #1: Business Writing

You must learn how to develop a cover letter, resume, and references.

My business course requirements included a course in writing. I was not the best student in English. Consequently, my grammar, punctuation and vocabulary are not the most elegant (hence the "Plain English" you read in this book. What I mean by the term is to speak simply and directly so that everyone understands what you mean). While grammar, punctuation and vocabulary are still not strengths of mine, each have improved with the help of a college course, and practice during my career.

Writing a professional letter, and developing a great resume were part of the writing course work. I learned that what you say is important. Probably more important is how you say it. I also learned to develop a crisp message that could be understood by everyone – which takes time and practice.

Regardless of where you are in your journey, be sure to take a writing course and then practice the craft.

Lesson #2: Recruiting Gems

The recruiters I met in college were all hand-picked. Each was bright, articulate, and professional. You could tell that each organization was serious about hiring the best. As I went through rounds of interviews, I was able to learn about the hiring process. Every company representative was forthcoming with information. When you are interviewed, show genuine interest, and ask great questions.

My favorite question was to ask the recruiter what type of person fit their hiring profile. Their answers yielded common traits.

- **Past Success:** If the recruiter could spot a pattern of success, they reasoned that the chances were great the candidate would repeat that performance throughout their career. (Grades *are* important.)

- **Extracurricular Activities:** Outside commitments such as a job, intercollegiate sports, volunteer work, or student government are all important. The recruiter looked for a well-rounded individual that balanced outside commitments with their schoolwork. If there were two or more equal candidates for one position the extracurricular activities could make the difference.

  I can clearly see why recruiters wanted to know about outside interests and commitments. Recruiters find out how well each of us balanced multiple priorities, knowing the parallel in adult life of working while taking care of other commitments.

- **Interest in their Organization:** It was important the candidate exhibit a genuine interest in the organization. Each recruiter wanted to know that you wanted the job at least as much as they wanted you.

  The interview process is a two-way street. The organization is interested enough in you to take the time, so you must reciprocate and genuinely be interested in them. Be ready to tell them what you know about the organization and how you fit their style of business. Otherwise don't bother. Your lack of interest will be apparent.

  The job learning curve will be steep. Candidates who know what they are getting into are likely to be more successful. I think most of us can recall times we were really interested in something, and consequently dove right in and excelled.

- **Qualifications:** Does your field of study match the required qualifications? In other words, if you studied Botany as your college major, are you attempting to get a job as an Accountant?

  Your experience also counts – have you had an internship or job in the field in which you are interviewing? If so, you may have an edge.

- **Culture:** An area that is so important is your potential fit in the organization. For example, Disney seeks people that will understand and perform a "value" system that is customer intimate. Disney is in the hospitality business and serves "guests" not "customers". Disney goes so far as to call their workforce "cast members". On the other hand, a company like Costco will hire people that fit the profile to perform an "operationally efficient" value system.[19]

CHAPTER TWO: GETTING STARTED

Your personality will be probed and scrutinized. Will you be a team player? How well will you perform independently? What has been your experience in group projects? What are your likes and dislikes?

There are any number of reasons why an organization will look closely at your fit in their culture. One big reason is that you are the one that will be required to make the adjustment to the organization's culture – they are unlikely to adjust their culture for you.

Lesson #3: Work Ethic
Many of the recruiters represented organizations that had little if any business in our geographic area. My curiosity led me to ask what it was about our university that had attracted them?

Some responded that their organization perceived value in recruiting at a college that had a higher population of less fortunate students. Most of us were raised near our university, products of families that were predominately lower or middle class. Quite a few of us were in college because parents pushed us to build a better life through education. Our parents were hard working people, in most cases holding blue collar jobs. The culture of hard work we grew up in was a major positive. Recruiters knew that most of us already possessed a strong work ethic.

Be ready to show you too have a strong work ethic. Organizations want people that work both hard and smart.

Early Preparation Warning
I have met many people who never thought to consider their pre-career path, college, and outside activities, to be important. They assumed the use of fancy words or jargon would demonstrate their intelligence and capabilities. They had little to show for their performance at work or in school. You know what? I am not gullible – neither are the recruiters. Never assume that words or promises are enough. A regular pattern of success is the best indicator of future performance. Lacking past success and asking for a chance is not usually enough. Especially in a career job. Don't assume anything in your career will be given to you. Only those that earn the job or promotion will get there and stay there.

WIDE-EYED WISDOM

Recruiting: The chip is in the bag…another true story

In 1980, good entry level jobs were few, most college students were not hired in their chosen careers right out of school. Fortunately, I prepared well, and received multiple job offers.

One of those offers was from Frito Lay. Frito Lay had invested heavily in a management development program. Their management development program was a commitment by the organization to find and hire the right candidates that would grow with the company. Frito Lay intended to develop enough talent to stock their company from within through a "farm" system approach (much like how a major league baseball team develops talent). Once hired, the company rotated each management trainee through various jobs to gain knowledge, understanding and experience. The first position in the rotation was as a supervisor in a plant that manufactured a variety of Frito Lay chips. Once the supervisory training was finished, the work would be in other first-line positions at the Frito Lay offices.

I was interviewed at my university career center. Successful in the initial interview, Frito Lay invited me to travel first class from central California to Dallas, Texas as part of a large group of second interviewees. Being included as part of a select group of students was an honor. I met students from Penn State, Michigan, Ohio State…you name it.

My travel would take me to Los Angeles, and then to Dallas/Fort Worth. My first flight left Fresno, CA early Friday morning in late April. Arriving in plenty of time in Los Angeles, I soon discovered that my flight to Dallas was canceled. Uh oh, that was a big problem! The potential to miss the biggest career opportunity of my life was a very real possibility. The only thing I could do was to calmly work with airline representatives to get on a flight with another airline. Mission accomplished. I was able to get on a later flight to DFW arriving in time to attend the evening dinner event. From Los Angeles, I called the National Director of Recruiting for Frito Lay. Unbeknownst to me, at that very moment, he was attending a meeting in Dallas with all the leaders of the national recruiting program. I calmly explained the situation, and how I had resolved the problem.

His name was Keith L. Keith went on to tell me that I would miss the assessment testing that was scheduled for late afternoon. I let him know that if they approved, after dinner I would take the tests back to my hotel room and work late until finished. He was impressed, and I found out later the whole room was impressed. At that moment, the hiring team marked my name as a must hire.

By the way, have you ever heard of Braniff Airlines? I hadn't either. After boarding the Braniff Airlines plane, the man next to me said the airline was in financial trouble. I asked why. He said they had invested in bad equipment. Uh Oh!

CHAPTER TWO: GETTING STARTED

The reason I tell this story is because stuff happens. What is important is how you respond – how you work through the problems and still accomplish goals for your organization and yourself.

In this case, working through the situation calmly, solving my own problem, communicating effectively, and doing what it took to complete the tasks late into the night, was impressive to the Frito Lay leadership team. Especially when the one taking care of the situation was just 21-years old.

The lesson – just about anything can be dealt with if you are prepared, calm, methodical and willing to put in what it takes to make the organization and your team successful.

Enter the Real World – Time to Make Money

Money/Compensation

At the age of 21 and now in my first career job, I was taught that money – compensation at work – would take care of itself. That philosophy would be true if I took care of my company and performed to the best of my abilities. In my case that money lesson turned out to be true.

My short-term career goals were to be the best at my position and be a great teammate. If I achieved those goals, I would be able to take care of my family and progress in my career.

Of course, there were misses. But for the most part, year in and year out our team and my individual results were excellent. As I progressed there were consistent raises. It took a few years for the raises to grow into sizeable amounts. I am sure the increases in my paycheck had to do with my professional growth and increasing importance to the organization.

Over the years, promotions and bonus plans paid off handsomely. Fortunately for many of you, today many organizations offer performance bonuses and stock from day one. Other organizations combine your salary with commissions and shares of stock. Almost all organizations have 401(k) programs. Capitalize on all of it.

If you can truly-say the organization is not compensating you for your success, it is probably time to look for an opportunity elsewhere. When judging your professional results, be honest with yourself.

WIDE-EYED WISDOM

If your judgment differs from what you hear in a performance review, ask questions. You must find out what areas need improvement, or if you are judging yourself too easily or too harshly.

Take care of your responsibilities, contribute at a high level, and compensation will follow.

Doing Your Job Gets You a Paycheck

For a team to be successful, it is important that all team members do their jobs consistently well. Everyone on the team must perform. Most members of a team possess unrealized potential – potential they may never tap.

You must excel, to get the promotion you seek. It will be no different if you own a business. Being consistently excellent will beat your competitors and offer you the best chance to be successful.

I have had countless conversations with associates who could not understand why they were passed over for promotions year after year. The conversation usually started out with something like, "I've done my job and have been here 12-years, but I haven't been promoted". Since I love to teach, these conversations always gave me an opportunity to discuss the importance of excelling to achieve career goals. Just showing up for work was not enough.

If you have your sights set on a promotion, make sure you are the best at what you do. As you are performing your job you must increase your knowledge and skills, so that you are the best choice for a future promotion. Please do not convince yourself that the organization just needs to give you a chance. Use the opportunity to perform and develop every day at work – be ready when the time comes.

Advancement – Promoted On-time, Not Ahead of Schedule

One of the best things that can happen to you is to be promoted (if you want that) when you are more than ready. You will know when you are more than ready, and your leader will know too. When you are promoted on-time you will be confident, and well prepared for the next challenge.

One of the worst things that can happen to you is to be promoted into a position that you don't want or are unprepared to perform. I have dealt with

CHAPTER TWO: GETTING STARTED

people that took jobs they did not want and others that were unprepared to take on additional responsibilities. Rarely do either of these situations end well.

Communicate your career goals to your leader. Leaders cannot read your mind, so don't leave them guessing, they want to know what interests you – they want you to be successful.

Do not rush yourself or the organization to place you in a position that you are not ready to perform. A well-thought-out job stretch is good, but without the strengths and skills, an overburdened move is a major disruptor. It is best for you and the organization that you are more than ready to take the next step.

Promotions and Open Interviews
Many organizations require an open interview process, even if they have someone that is ready to be promoted. You will no doubt run into this same process in your career. Make sure the interview is over before it starts – and that you are <u>the</u> best candidate.

It always puzzled me to interview people, after six or seven years in their jobs, who were no closer to taking on a more responsible position than the first day they were hired. These people always wanted to sell me on the idea that they were capable of doing the job and that they could learn it. They just needed to be given the chance.

On the other hand, I had folks that learned as much as possible about their desired position. These individuals worked continuously to sharpen their skills and knowledge. We all knew they were right for the position and confident in the outcome before the interview began. Promotions usually go to the people that have committed to lifelong learning, constantly excel, are team players, and achieve great results. In short, these folks consistently exhibited what was necessary to be ready for the next step. They were not asking to be given anything, they earned the promotion.

CHAPTER THREE
LET'S GET PERSONAL – YOUR MONEY

OVERVIEW

Everyone's favorite subject – MONEY! In this chapter you are going to learn the basics. Money is not a difficult subject, but you must put your knowledge into action – getting started is the hardest part. Start now, or you will find it difficult to set yourself up for a life of financial freedom and personal wealth. As you become literate in basic personal finance (and act as early as you can) your chances of achieving your life plan increase. Take your time, this chapter is packed with valuable information – so I have broken it down into sections to make each piece easier to digest.

Section 1: **Personal Finance**

Section 2: **The Plan**
Learn what a budget is, why you need one now, and how to create and follow a plan.

Section 3: **The Play**
Show me the money! Learn how to spend wisely and invest in your future.

Section 4: **The Long Game**
Learn a wise approach to large purchases.

Section 5: **The Tools**
Understand the tools available to you – cash, credit cards and loans.

SECTION 1
PERSONAL FINANCE

If there is anything that can derail a great life plan, it is MONEY. Money can be the ultimate reality check – does your life plan include a tree-lined suburban neighborhood, children, family vacations and farmers markets on the weekend? Dreamy. How are you going to pay for it? Or maybe your life plan includes the hustle and bustle of a big city – living in a converted loft, with amazing restaurants around the corner and access to a major transportation hub for exciting travel around the globe. Fabulous…how are you going to pay for it? Or perhaps a breathtaking waterfront villa in Lake Como, a la George Clooney…how are you going to pay for it? By now you are probably thinking, "Stop harshin' my dreams man!"

Years of consulting with business owners taught me the importance of starting with the end in mind. I like to ask an owner to describe a visual picture of the finish line for their business… their *exit strategy*. From this self-stated finish line, we work backward to formulate the plan, strategies and tactics required to make it successfully to her or his exit. The exit strategy concept will work for your personal life. You can start with the end in mind and work your way back, all the way to today. This process will give you a great idea of what you need to do and money you must have in the bank (within a plus or minus range), in order to arrive at or near your life plan. (You already started this process with your vision, values, and life plan draft from Chapter 1.)

I know, I know, I sound just like your parent(s). If your mom and/or dad are challenging you on this subject, they may well be spot on! Life requires money, lots of it. Remember earlier when we agreed that **you are responsible for yourself, your life, your future**? Well that means you are also responsible for your bank account. Don't count on anyone else to provide for you – I know, major let down. Except for the predestined few with fat trust funds, the rest of us ordinary folk must figure it out on our own. I assume that you will manage your own finances. If you are thinking about leaving financial decisions to someone else, think otherwise. We hear about high paid athletes and entertainers that have been taken advantage of and are now broke. Going from

CHAPTER THREE: LET'S GET PERSONAL – YOUR MONEY

flush with cash to finding out your cash has been flushed can happen to regular people, just like us. Make the choice to be committed to understanding and managing your finances.

Personal financial literacy is important to all of us – literacy coupled with wisdom will be indispensable as you plan and live your life journey. All too often we wait until we are in trouble, then we want to learn about finance, if we learn anything at all. Learning some bits of financial wisdom now will help you plan for your future and make smart decisions early and throughout your journey. After all, successful navigation of finances, are almost certain to include lots of minor course adjustments. Get ahead of the issue by learning early and reap the benefits of decades of good financial decisions.

"If you don't make a conscious effort to control your focus and decide in advance which things you're going to focus on, you'll be so pulled by the demands of the world that you will soon find yourself living in reaction rather than living a life plan you've designed for yourself."[20]

Tony Robbins
Life and Business Strategist

The world runs on money – you will have plenty of opportunities to make it and spend it. Keep in mind that money is harder to make than it is to spend, so be thoughtful about how you spend your hard-earned money.

Are you ready to get started? Now I am going to let you in on the greatest secret to a life of financial bliss. Somehow, millions and millions of people have missed out on this – but don't worry, you are one of the lucky ones. If you take this lesson to heart, and truly live by it, you will be vastly more prepared to pursue and achieve the meaningful life of your dreams. You will certainly know more than most of your peers. Okay, let's see if we can cover this in the next five hours, I mean seconds. Ready…go!

Do not spend more money than you make.

Whoa…mind blown! Seriously…did you know that?

WIDE-EYED WISDOM

Please excuse the dripping sarcasm. Unfortunately, this basic concept is lost on millions in the U.S. I want you to use that wisdom as your start, there is so much that you can do in your financial life to help you plan for, achieve, and enjoy the richness and fullness of life. Remember, **money is a tool**. Money is not an end all. Money is not evil. To use money to your advantage you must learn, practice, and enact financial wisdom – the earlier in life you do this, the more benefits you will reap. If you are already in your 30's, 40's, 50's or beyond, don't despair – the best time to begin managing your money is today.

Financial Literacy – The Basics

Money will impact all aspects of your life – from the food you eat, where you live, your healthcare, relationships, leisure time, investments, and work. **Take control** of your financial life before it takes control of you. For those of you that have kids or expect to start a family, you need to learn personal finance as soon as possible, and once you have learned the basics, teach your kids. Our grandchildren started learning about money when they were each about four years old.

Empower yourself by learning everything you can, as early as you can about finances. Do not wait. Before you have time to make excuses, let's dive in. We are going to invest in your personal financial literacy right now, so pay attention. Fortunately, this is a book, so if necessary, you can read it over and over (I know, you will be tempted to keep it under your pillow).

Financial Literacy

The ability to understand how money works in the world: how someone manages to earn or make it, how that person manages it, how he/she invests it (turns it into more) and how that person donates it to help others.[21]

Many people are only concerned with making and spending, and in fact put so much emphasis on spending, that they could never make enough money to keep up with their personal wants. They create an ongoing debt cycle. This cycle can start out small – perhaps carrying a small balance on a credit card and buying a few things here and there that they realistically can't afford. But as

CHAPTER THREE: LET'S GET PERSONAL – YOUR MONEY

years go by and the demands of life grow, so does spending. Hopefully, career opportunities and income increase as well. But if they haven't taken the time to learn about finances, and lack self-discipline, the debt cycle will grow and grow. They will be unable to break away from debt. Doesn't that look like a hamster wheel to you? **Don't be the hamster.**

We are going to develop a healthier perspective about money. Money can work for you, support your life plan, and allow you to be generous with others. But money can only do those things if you have a plan and the self-discipline to follow it. Stay ahead of the game – don't get caught on the hamster wheel. That is why before we talk about anything else regarding finances, we are going to tackle how to *be prepared* to deal with your money, and that is with a budget.

SECTION 2
THE PLAN

Budgeting

Budgeting is the process to understand the inflow and outflow of money and **Plan** how to use your funds so that you can responsibly meet your obligations, and work toward your future goals. Does everyone have a budget? No. But they should. At the most basic level, think of a budget as the plan to make this equation work:

$$Spending + Saving + Investments = Income$$

My wife and I learned to budget right away. Our income was limited, and we no longer had a parental safety net. Once we were out of the house, we were on our own. We learned to:
- Share the financial load and discuss in a caring way
- Commit to a common goal
- Budget what we earned
- Identify and document spending
- Adjust habits as needed
- Save for large purchases
- Invest for our future
- Celebrate our achievements

Budget What You Earn

My wife and I committed to live within our means. We did not buy anything that we couldn't pay cash for at the time. When the budget was spent for a specific category there might not be more spending on that category for the month. What did we do if we spent our total budget on an item before month end?!? (Which did happen.) Sometimes even with careful planning, there just didn't seem to be enough money. If our Food budget was exhausted, we cut

CHAPTER THREE: LET'S GET PERSONAL – YOUR MONEY

expenses in other areas. If the Entertainment budget was spent, we stayed home. We worked together and stuck to our plan. Neither of us made unplanned purchases. We shared responsibilities and were both committed to live within our means.

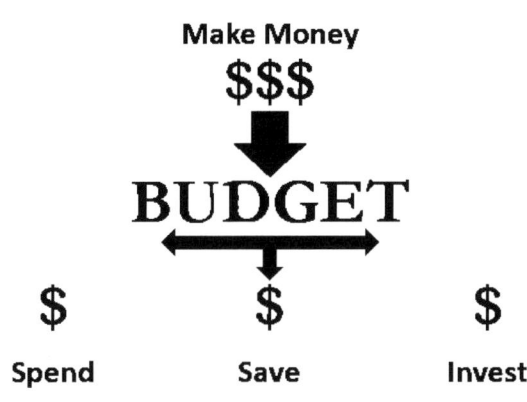

If you have few obligations, and a small income stream, this is the perfect time to learn. If you are a few (or many) more years down the road and have racked up debt, loans, etc., this process is more complex, but it is *essential* to take control of your financial life. There are a myriad of online tools, books, and bank apps to help you, but a good ol' piece of paper and pencil or spreadsheet will do the trick.

If I had a limitless income stream, I would not be too worried about any of this, but I don't have an unlimited flow of cash and I bet you don't either. Even folks making millions can (and often do) fail to live within their means. Ever hear of a Lottery winner or high paid celebrity declaring bankruptcy? Yikes – it happens. As I said earlier, as income increases, generally expenses do too. Your basic budget goal is to make sure that the outflow does not exceed the inflow. By developing smart money habits, when your income increases, or you receive a cash windfall, you will opt to save and invest larger amounts.

There is a lot to cover in this section, so let's look at where we are headed:
- **Budgeting Step-by-Step:** Learn the "ideal" budget allocation (high-level guideline for where to allocate your budgeted spending). Drill down using a hypothetical example so you can see how the process works from beginning to end.
- **The Details:** Valuable discussion and tactics to help you jump on your life plan path and stay there.

WIDE-EYED WISDOM

Gather up your bills, bank, and credit card statements – let's get started. We are going to PLAN how to use your income. (If you research Budgeting online, you will find different recommendations/methods. Don't get so hung up on the different budget approaches that you fail to get started.)

Budgeting - Step 1: *Ideal Allocation*

As a general rule, allocate 50% of your take home income to your NEEDS (minimum living expenses), 30% to your WANTS (the "nice to haves"), and 20% for the FUTURE (5% saving/15% investing).[22] Let's identify the ideal allocation for your monthly income, and then see how it stacks up to your actual spending.

Target Budget Allocation

50% NEEDS	+	30% WANTS	+	20% FUTURE
Housing		Subscriptions		Savings
Utilities		Entertainment		Investments
Home Insurance		Eating Out		
Car Insurance		Clothes		
Food		Incidentals		
Medical		Travel		
Transportation		Gifts		
Loan Payments		Home Improvements		
Charitable Giving		Home/Personal Services		
		Large Purchase Accruals		

For example, with the above guidance in mind and a $60,000 annual take home salary (assume that taxes have already been taken out of your paycheck), a high-level budget would look like this:

Example: Target Budget Allocation - $5,000 per Month

50% NEEDS	+	30% WANTS	+	20% FUTURE
$2,500		$1,500		$1,000

CHAPTER THREE: LET'S GET PERSONAL – YOUR MONEY

Okay, now it's your turn. Make sure to use your after-tax monthly income:

Fill-In: Your Budget Allocation - $ per Month

50% NEEDS	+	30% WANTS	+	20% FUTURE
$ _____		$ _____		$ _____

Budgeting - Step 2: Identify Actual Current Expenses

Step 1 was simple enough, right? Awesome, let's move on because it gets more challenging. Now we are going to comb through your *actual* spending and carefully record the cost of each monthly expenditure – be honest and get ready for a reality check. Do you have expenses/spends that don't fit in one of the categories below? No problem – make this a living document and add-to it as needed to suit your own situation. **(See Resources: Exhibit 2, p. 241)**

Example: Current Monthly Spending

NEEDS		WANTS		FUTURE	
Housing	$1,100	Subscriptions	$150	Savings	$150
Utilities	$250	Entertainment	$200	Investments	$0
Home Insurance	$50	Eating Out	$250		
Car Insurance	$200	Clothes	$150		
Food	$500	Incidentals	$350		
Medical	$150	Travel	$150		
Transportation	$400	Gifts	$50		
Loan Payments	$200	Home Improvements	$50		
Charitable Giving	$100	H/P Services	$250		
		Lrg. Purch. Accruals	$300		
TOTAL	$2,950		$1,900		$150
ALLOCATION	59%		38%		3%

Budgeting - Step 3: Compare Actual to Ideal Spending Budget

I suspect that your actual spending surpasses your ideal budgeted amounts – this means you are left with little (if anything) to save and invest and might even be living (spending) well beyond your means. Now is the time to get real about this whole Budget thing – you will need to make tough choices to implement smart financial decisions today, and for your future. Identify where you stand with your "Actual" versus "Ideal" spend.

Example: Ideal vs. Actual Monthly Spending

	NEEDS	WANTS	FUTURE
Ideal	50%	30%	20%
$5,000=	$2,500	$1,500	$1,000
Actual	59%	38%	3%
$5,000=	$2,950	$1,900	$150

Budgeting - Step 4: Rebalance and Recommit

I bet that right now many of you are already underwater and can't afford your monthly expenses. You are living beyond your means (which by the way is not sustainable). At this point you either need to make some major cuts to your spending or figure out how to increase your income (or BOTH!).

Now is the time to make decisions about how to rebalance your current spending. Must your budget strictly adhere to the 50%/30%/20% guideline? No. It would be impossible within these short pages to account for every variation and unique requirement. The key to any allocation is that your Future (savings and investments) not be lost. If you find yourself spending everything that you have in the day-to-day, or consistently splurging instead of planning for your future, then you are off course.

Do everything you can to hold sacred the 20% (at a minimum) for Saving and Investments (if you haven't started this early in adulthood, you will need to ramp up the savings rate). If you can allocate more than 20% towards your future – do it! Don't wait! You are in an incredible position. On the other hand, if you are just barely scraping by, and despite incredible discipline do not have the funds to set aside for your future, hang in there. By working through this exercise, you will gain knowledge that will stay with you as you continue to grow. As you advance in your career you will reach higher income levels. Keep these lessons with you and make a commitment to hold your expenses steady while you ramp up the contributions to your future.

CHAPTER THREE: LET'S GET PERSONAL – YOUR MONEY

Before you move along and say that **you just don't have enough** – I'm going to challenge you, because you do have more control over your monthly spending than you realize. If your budget is out of whack, identify where you can cut back or shift funds to cover your living expenses and invest. If you are truly committed to living within your means and planning for your future, you may need to make some tough and uncomfortable choices. Maybe you will sell your gas guzzling car (on which you are making payments) and pay cash for an economical, no frills vehicle. Perhaps your home lease expires soon, and you can find something less expensive or get a roommate. Or maybe you eat lunch out every day – guess what, you can brown bag it! Try a clothes swap with a friend instead of buying new. The point is, with creativity, *everyone* can adjust spending. Where you spend your money should be driven by your life plan and values – do your current expenditures reflect that?

Example: Rebalanced Monthly Spending

NEEDS			WANTS			FUTURE		
Housing		$1,100	Subscriptions	$150	$50	Savings	$150	$250
Utilities	$250	$200	Entertainment	$200	$100	Investments	$0	$750
Home Insurance		$50	Eating Out	$250	$150			
Car Insurance		$200	Clothes	$150	$100			
Food	$500	$400	Incidentals	$350	$300			
Medical		$150	Travel	$150	$100			
Transportation	$400	$250	Gifts		$50			
Loan Payments		$200	Home Improvements		$50			
Charitable Giving		$100	H/P Services	$250	$150			
			Lrg. Purch. Accruals		$300			
TOTAL		$2,650			$1,350			$1,000
ALLOCATION		53%			27%			20%

Budgeting - Step 5: *Track and Adjust*

The work you just did is **worthless**…unless you *track your actual spending and make course corrections designed to achieve your plan.* The minute that you stop being intentional with your actions is the minute that you fail to meet your goals. This is not a one-and-done exercise. Tracking requires self-discipline and a commitment to follow through. Accept this as a personal challenge and take control. Most of you won't do this – and will be less likely to hit your budget targets regularly, if at all. Please don't skip this step, it is **too** valuable to miss.

WIDE-EYED WISDOM

Invest the time (it really doesn't take that much) and effort (don't worry – it's easy). You will be more successful at taking control of your financial future. You can do it!

There are plenty of apps and online tools available, or you can use a simple Excel spreadsheet. You can design an expense tracking sheet in a number of different ways, here's just one suggestion – list the expense categories (remember to look back at your Budget and customize to your specific categories) down the left side and add days of the month across the top. Record each transaction. Let me say that again, **account for every amount you spend**, and keep a running total to see how your actual spending tracks with your budget. Take a few minutes each day to record all expenditures.

		Track Your Spending							
		Day of the Month					Budget	Spent	Balance
		1	2	3	4	5-31			
NEEDS	Housing	1,100					$1,100	1,100	0
	Utilities					195	$200	195	5
	Home Insurance	50					$50	50	0
	Car Insurance					200	$200	200	0
	Food		90		25	275	$400	390	10
	Medical				30	80	$150	110	40
	Transportation		40			220	$250	260	(10)
	Loan Payments	200					$200	200	0
	Charitable Giving			25		75	$100	100	0
WANTS	Subscriptions	13			12	25	$50	50	0
	Entertainment			20		49	$100	69	31
	Eating Out				20	130	$150	150	0
	Clothes					89	$100	89	11
	Incidentals	4	7		58	186	$300	255	45
	Travel						$100	0	100
	Gifts			40			$50	40	10
	Home Improvements					35	$50	35	15
	H/P Services		110			60	$150	170	(20)
	Lrg. Purch. Accruals	300					$300	300	0
FUTURE	Savings	250					$250	250	0
	Investments	750					$750	750	0

Change Your Habits

Items like house payment, rent, car payment, insurance, tuition, and property tax are all fixed and predictable. You may not be able to adjust these in the

CHAPTER THREE: LET'S GET PERSONAL – YOUR MONEY

short-term, although I would look closely at potential expense adjustments. You may be spending too much for rent, over bought on a home, perhaps the car is too extravagant, or you should look for lower insurance rates.

Here is where you can gain some traction – variable expenses like food, utilities, incidentals, entertainment, gas, etc. are usually areas where you can make the easiest and most substantial adjustments. Get into the details. For example: do you take your dog to the groomer and drop a cool $60 or more? Instead, buy some clippers and groom your dog yourself. Do you regularly throw out food that has gone bad? Make more frequent yet smaller trips to the grocery store. Are your home lights always ablaze? Make a habit to only use what you need and at least turn lights off when you leave a room. Or install motion sensors. Nothing here is rocket science. Some adjustments will yield a bigger return than others. You are in charge, so you get to decide what is most important to you and what you can modify or do without.

Your budget may need to be adjusted if you have underestimated or overestimated a spending category. If you share a household, discuss each spending category, and talk about ways to make your money go further. There are tactical spending adjustments you can make, such as buying store brands rather than national brands. Clip coupons and channel the dollar savings to another category.

Once you have the right balance to your budget, focus on your future (savings and investments). At a minimum you need cash socked away to cover six months of living expenses. Once that is fully funded, save more money for investments (more on that later). Your expense review is a great time to ensure that you are setting aside money for your next large purchase/expenditure – car, painting the house, roof, appliances, furniture – you get the idea. Great budget planning will make it easier to buy large items or prepare for major expenses since you will have the cash in advance. You also gain negotiating leverage when you are ready to buy, with cash in-hand. You avoid loans and sizeable interest charges, leaving more money for investments.

SECTION 3
THE PLAY

In the last section we developed a plan – your budget – so that you use your money intentionally to support the lifestyle that you can afford and build toward your desired life plan. Now that you have the plan, let's dive into what to actually do with your money. We will start with saving and investments, then move on to what you are already *really* familiar with – spending.

SAVING

Disclaimer – I must admit, Saving and Investing do not sound nearly as exciting as Spending. Spending can have a psychological impact – creating an immediate endorphin rush. It *feels good* to buy new clothes, the latest technology, eat out at restaurants and drive a new car. It *feels good* to fill up a cart load at Target, pull out the shiny plastic, and take home a bundle of new stuff that you *just can't live without.* You know what doesn't feel good? Receiving credit card bills that you can't pay. Credit card fees and interest pile up and grow into an unmanageable mountain of debt. It doesn't feel good to know that if you had an emergency medical situation, you couldn't pay for it. It doesn't feel good to fight with your partner because you can't pay your bills or do not share the same financial goals. It doesn't feel good to overextend yourself to bring new stuff through the front door, and cart it to the garbage or donation pile once its novelty or usefulness has worn off.

Wow – I just depressed myself…think happy thoughts…Allow me to make the case for why you should pay attention, manage spending, and put your excess cash to work for you by saving and investing. You just worked through an exercise to identify your monthly obligations. Hopefully when you compare the total monthly expense to your monthly income, you still have

CHAPTER THREE: LET'S GET PERSONAL – YOUR MONEY

something left over for your Future. Remember – a financially wise and proactive person is saving *and* investing to achieve their life plan.

When you save and invest, you are proactively planning for your future. The earlier in life that you save and invest, the greater opportunity you will have to grow personal financial wealth.

The world runs on money, remember? This will be no-less true in 20-, 30- or 50-years than it is today. And **you are responsible for yourself, your life, your future.** That means that you must figure out how to get out of the hamster wheel and avoid living beyond your means, now. Don't let the undisciplined and unplanned temptations of today, derail your life plan. After all, isn't that why you are investing in yourself and your career – to pursue a meaningful life under your own terms?

Saving money will have major impacts on your financial health. This is where your self-discipline will place you ahead of major expenses, and help you prepare for your coming needs (and wants). In SAVING we shift to longer-term plans. Think of saving as a proactive way for you to allocate money for investments, buy a large expensive item or an experience in your life that isn't covered by your monthly budget (such as saving for a new car, house down payment or luxurious vacation). You must also accumulate an Emergency Fund (6+ months of wages) in the event of a lost job or major unexpected expense. (The Coronavirus Pandemic of 2020 has made it crystal clear why an Emergency Fund is a must! We are experiencing the beginning of new and mutated virus epidemics and pandemics. Prepare yourself, now is the time.)

Our daughter maintains several Savings accounts, each with its own specific purpose. She sets up automatic monthly transfers into these accounts to accumulate funds based on the goal of each account. When the time comes, instead of scrambling or stressing for money, or overextending on credit, she has the cash in-hand. She accomplishes the task by saving months or years in advance. For example, we plan to take a big family trip to Disneyworld next year with our grandkids. She funneled a tax rebate from last year, plus automatic monthly savings of $250 into a "Vacation" savings account to accrue for the trip. Now, as she has begun to book airline flights, and buy park tickets, the money is earmarked and available. Plus, the money saved has been working for her, earning interest, all this time.

WIDE-EYED WISDOM

As you budget for the SAVINGS category, think about some of the goals and experiences that are part of your life plan. Do you want to own a home? Take a trip around the world? Prepare for a home remodel? Buy a car? Retire at 40? Whatever is important to you and motivates you, plan for it, commit, and take-action. Choose to take control, start with a plan, begin saving and investing, and achieve your life plan.

The following table exhibits how you can structure your savings in advance to fund major purchases, emergency fund, and investments. Estimate when you need the money, how much you need and save fixed and windfall amounts to reach your goals.

	Category	Total Goal	Monthly Saving	Notes	Annual Savings Target	Years to Goal
SAVING	EMERGENCY FUND	30,000	700	*6 months of income	8,400	3.57
	CASH, other…	3,000	125		1,500	2.00
	LONG TERM GOALS					
	Car:	20,000	250	*save to pay cash in full	3,000	6.67
	House Down Payment:	75,000	500	*20% down payment	6,000	12.50
	College Fund:	24,000	200	*for yourself or your kids	2,400	10.00
	Vacation:	3,600	150		1,800	2.00
	Gifts:	1,200	75	*Christmas & Birthdays	900	1.33
	TOTAL		$2,000		$24,000	

INVESTMENTS

Creating a quality budget takes work, and it can be tough to be transparent and honest with yourself – but this is how you will understand your financial reality. Being educated and aware is far better than sticking your head in the sand.

Do you allocate dollars for investment purposes? INVESTING is how most of us build our personal wealth and satisfy long-term financial goals. Choosing the right investments fuels growth in personal wealth. Sound investments enriched with additional deposits and allowed to grow will multiply, as earnings and growth compound over time. The earlier you invest, the more powerful and sizeable your investment portfolio will become.

Remember that millions of people are living paycheck to paycheck with no savings and few if any investments? They have allowed short-term wants and material status symbols to cannibalize their income. As seniors, with no savings

CHAPTER THREE: LET'S GET PERSONAL – YOUR MONEY

or investment portfolios, how will they pay their living expenses? The answer... they either can't retire, they rely on their kids, or ask for assistance.

There may be a time in your life when you just don't have the money to sock away for a future goal. Especially when you have very real, tangible needs, right now. I get that. A young couple adjusting to the responsibilities of adulthood and beginning a career or finishing school may not have the bandwidth to maximize contributions to a 401(k) or make regular investments.

While you may be surprised to hear that I'll support a "pass" for a short period, the longer you wait, the less prepared, and more difficult it will be to develop the habit to put investment money aside. You won't be on the path to personal security or wealth. As early as you can, make the tough decisions and spending sacrifices to prepare for your future.

Take a step now and grow. Your knowledge about finance and the requirements to be prepared for your future, will increase. And, best of all, your income will increase. Be prepared to hold your expenses, needs, wants and spending at bay, so that when your income increases, you know just where to send it – INVESTMENTS. Don't be too concerned just yet with exactly what you will **Invest** in. First, develop the self-discipline to put money aside. You won't miss the money. Those regular investment statements showing your deposits, and employer deposits and earnings become an important tool in tracking progress toward your life plan.

INVESTMENTS	Category	Component	Invest
	Personal Wealth	Stock Market	$
		CD/Bonds	
		Other...	
	Retirement	401K	
		Roth IRA	
		Annuity	
		Mutual Fund	
		Other...	
		TOTAL	$

WIDE-EYED WISDOM

Many employers offer a match on a 401(k) – this is the first place to start! At a minimum, establish your 401(k) deposit/payroll deduction that will capture the maximum employer contribution. Get those automatic contributions started today.

Spending

Trust me – you do not need help figuring out *how* to spend – you are already a pro. But let's dig a bit deeper into common money habits. Learn how to control this beast so that you spend on what you need and what you value, while making wise choices along the way to avoid the debt trap.

Impulse Purchases

Impulse is defined as: A sudden strong unreflective urge or desire to act.[23] Impulsivity is perhaps the most dangerous emotion when it comes to achieving your life plan. Control your sudden urges to spend, and the odds of achieving your life plan grows exponentially.

When faced with an impulse to buy, put the decision off for a minimum of 48-hours. Chances are after two days you will decide you don't really want to part with your hard-earned cash. Be careful when merchants give you a limited time to act. Merchants know full well that urgency plus impulse will drive increased purchases (especially on large items).

Impulses can become bad habits. For example, you become regularly concerned about how to keep up with the people next door or you justify the purchase because it will "make your life easier". Consider the following…

The People Next Door

Don't try to keep up with the people next door. Those folks are living beyond their means competing with some other family that is living beyond their means competing with another family living beyond their means – you get the picture. You don't know most, if any of those people. While picture-perfect may be the norm on Facebook or Instagram, the reality is most of the families have sizeable credit card debt, car debt, house debt, personal debt, and are financially illiterate. They owe everyone, live paycheck to paycheck, are not

CHAPTER THREE: LET'S GET PERSONAL – YOUR MONEY

happy, have little or no investments and no realistic path to achieve their life plan if they have a life plan. (They really needed the Covid bailout money.)

You will be much happier and sleep better when you build your own life plan and control your spending based on your value system. Be intentional, make your own educated decisions to control your financial future. Don't let peer pressure make decisions for you. You are smarter than that.

When I see someone with a depreciating item such as a boat or flashy car, instead of envy I feel good knowing I *could* easily buy it, but I feel better knowing that I choose not to buy that stuff because investing the money is more important to achieve my long-term goals. My buying decisions are not whether I *could* buy, but whether I *should* buy.

Keep the money you earn so you can reach your goals! Don't give your money to someone else so they reach their goals, at your expense.

Make Life Easier - To bake or not to bake …a true story:
For years, our eldest son gave me a hard time about buying take-n-bake pizza. I happen to like the fresh ingredients and baking our own pizza was fine. I've learned how to cook great pizza. The other thing I liked about take-n-bake pizza was the price. We could buy a freshly made pizza for about $10 less than the comparable cooked product. Plus, we avoided the cost of the delivery fee and tip when we picked up the pizza ourselves. With a growing family, take-n-bake pizza fit our budget well.

Our eldest son would always say, "Dad you can afford to buy the 'good' pizza, and have it delivered". He was right. Buying a baked and delivered pizza would not have dented our checking account too much. But we consciously made monetary decisions (even the 'small' ones) that would keep moving us toward our financial goals and teach our kids to question their purchase decisions and the consequences. My question to our son was, "Why should we pay so much more?" Even today when we want pizza, it is almost always take-n-bake.

Fast forward to a few days after our son got married. Not long after their honeymoon, we met with our son and his new bride, to give them a wedding gift. I asked our son to remember all of those take-n-bake pizzas we brought home and cooked ourselves. Then I asked him, "Do you remember telling me that we had the money to pay for a cooked and delivered pizza?"

Of course, he remembered it all. Then I told them both, as a wedding gift, we banked the pizza savings (plus earnings) to pay off the remaining debt on his truck (he still owed a few thousand dollars). I think my lesson was driven home.

WIDE-EYED WISDOM

Consumer Behavior/Confidence

We live in an economy that is driven by consumption. Consumption is interwoven into the fabric of our culture. Consumer sentiment drives our economy and the financial health of a multitude of businesses that depend on consumption. When consumers feel good, they buy more. Our government, financial markets and businesses pay close attention to consumer sentiment. You can bet that when the consumer mood turns sour, the press will be all over the story and a dip in the economy will be just around the corner.

Try this out. Make yourself keenly aware of when you are feeling your best (in other words, gauge your mood). If you are like most people, when you are in a good mood you feel like spending. You can come up with all kinds of reasons why you want to buy "stuff". You will probably entertain more often and frequent restaurants on a regular basis. Your optimistic mood encourages you to spend. Couple your mood with undisciplined decision making and you develop unhealthy financial habits. In my case, I've noticed that a good mood and confident demeanor will allow me to consider and at times buy large ticket items. For some reason, when I feel good, I am ready to give my money to someone else – in large amounts.

"Bad mood" buying occurs in some people when they are not feeling well. They need a "pick-me up" – and hope to feel better by buying something new. Unfortunately, the feelings of well-being that come with buying are short-lived, and the debt cycle (ie. mounting credit card bills) often created by undisciplined spending will prolong and exacerbate their negative emotions.

Monitor your mood and confidence and see how it impacts your buying habits. Knowing why you make buying decisions is important. Once you have a better understanding of your personal consumer dynamics, you will have a better idea of how to control your spending and live within your budget.

Depreciating Items

If by now your eyes are glazing over, take a deep breath and return your focus because this message is important: **consumer goods depreciate immediately upon purchase**. That means you spend more for the item than you could ever hope to recoup. Let's discuss the dangers of buying *stuff*.

It is one thing to buy a small item by mistake and regret it later, but the size of a purchase mistake will be magnified when buying large consumer

CHAPTER THREE: LET'S GET PERSONAL – YOUR MONEY

goods like autos, RV's, boats, furniture, appliances, and jewelry. Accept the fact that buying the aforementioned items is not an investment. You will not sell the item for anything close to what you paid for it.

With use and exposure to the elements, autos and boats depreciate and eventually wear out. There is additional expense required for insurance, routine maintenance, and major fixes. There is nothing wrong with owning automobiles or boats – but you should consider all factors before purchasing. And of course, do not live beyond your means. The purchase must fit your budget in the short and long-term. Even with careful planning, large purchases tend to cost more than you originally anticipated, so go into this purchase with eyes wide open.

Jewelry is an interesting subject – glitter and glamour are important to quite a few people. Maybe it is the idea of showing off to friends and family? Or maybe just the personal enjoyment of all that sparkles. At any rate, jewelry is a common gift and can be an important symbol. Our daughter for one cannot pass a jewelry store window without thoroughly looking over (and enjoying) each glittering piece inside. If jewelry is important to you or someone you love, educate yourself on the reality of what you are buying. Don't kid yourself to think that jewelry is an investment or that you could ever sell it for anything close to what you paid. While a similar investment in your retirement account would be leaps and bounds more valuable to you, reality tells me you will either give or receive a fair amount of jewelry. Know that you are buying a look and a feeling, not an investment. Never take on debt to make a jewelry purchase.

Furniture is not an investment. I chuckle when someone says, "that dining set is worth thousands of dollars". What they really should have said is, "I paid thousands of my hard-earned cash for those sticks of furniture". If you have ever tried to sell used furniture you know what I mean. You won't get much for a used dining set, couch or chair. There are times when your only option is to pay someone to take the furniture away.

Unfortunately, consumers in the U.S. focus their spending on stuff that depreciates immediately. Take a tour of lower- and middle-class neighborhoods. You will see garages, driveways and backyards filled with stuff that was purchased with someone's hard earned money and is now virtually worthless. Millions of people are locked into giving their earnings away for stuff they think they can't live without.

WIDE-EYED WISDOM

> "If you buy things you don't need, soon you will have to sell things you need."[24]
>
> *Warren Buffet*

Surf the net and look for personal storage businesses in your area. There are a lot of them. In addition to all the stuff you see in the neighborhoods, those same people from your tour are paying monthly fees to store even more stuff they could not live without. Spending on depreciating items and paying storage fees is a double bust.

If you aren't careful you will become one of the folks that brings tens of thousands of dollars of new stuff through your front door. Later, you will rent storage, and donate or throw the stuff away.

You might be thinking that most purchases are small. True enough, but when you accumulate these items, the total will surprise you. Think twice or three times before you spend on items that depreciate – "less" is truly more.

Budget Busters

When you are reviewing your spending look no further than this list of Budget Busters – some of which may be near and dear to your heart. Some spending on these items may be necessary, but excessive spending – giving away your earnings spending – is ridiculous. Why would you want to give your money to someone else?

Prepare your budget, then eliminate the stuff where your earnings/income are wasted. When you are living within your means and preparing for your future each of these items should be on your radar as an expense that can and should be managed.

Be blatantly honest and commit to be disciplined about how you use your money on every one of these items. You may be throwing away your financial future by spending too much. Before you say, "But I have to" spend on utilities, remember that how you use power, water, phone, and gas is the issue. There are items on this list that with care can be minimized. There are other items that swallow your funds and should be cut or eliminated

CHAPTER THREE: LET'S GET PERSONAL – YOUR MONEY

Budget Busters

Shopping	Lifestyle	Dwelling
Designer Brands	Eating Out	Oversized Home
Clothing	Subscriptions	Utilities
Jewelry	Vacation Home	Home Improvements
Souvenirs/Trinkets	Travel	Furnishings
National Brands	Entertainment	Décor
Full-price goods		
	Habits	**Personal Care**
Transportation	Coffee	Haircuts
Extravagant Vehicle	Gambling	Manicure/Pedicure
Car Repairs	Cigarettes	Massage
Gas	Drugs	Dental/Medical Care
	Alcohol	Tattoos
Services	Convenience Stores	Piercings
House Cleaner		
Yard Maintenance	**Financial**	
Delivery Fees	Consumer Interest	
Storage Fees	Bank Fees	
	Credit Card Fees	
	Insurance	

I get that you are not going to live a totally austere life. After all, money is a tool. Use the tool wisely. Your goal should be to find the right balance of income and expense so that you are able to enjoy life while staying on-track to achieve your life plan.

If you and I took a critical eye to this expense list, we would find many items that all of us could live without. I am not asking you to do that. Arm yourself with the knowledge of what you *can* live without – you may need to make major cuts in the future, so applying a critical eye now is important.

Just for kicks, I calculated the investment returns on $150 per month over 40-years. If, instead of buying cable tv, we invested the same $150 at an after-tax return of 6%, in 40-years we would have about a quarter of a million dollars. Just think, all those people that could not live without cable tv, and are now broke at retirement, could have had $250,000 in investments. (Yes, I know there are much less costly ways to enjoy television shows. Take advantage of the honest ideas and share those tactics with your friends and family.)

A real-world example of the need to cut out what you can live without, is a 47-year old woman I know. When she was in her early 20's she started buying coffee drinks each day for her and two kids. She gambled each week, drank alcohol on a regular basis, and unfortunately developed an addiction to cigarettes. She spent an average of $730 per month on these habits. If she had invested the $730 per month, from the time she developed the coffee/gamble/alcohol/cigarette spending habits, at an after-tax return of 6%, she would have over a half million dollars in investments as of today. If she continued to invest the $730 per month until she retired at 65, her investments would be worth about $1.9 million.

By the way, she could have used a 401(k) contribution, plus employer matching funds, and her wealth would end-up far greater than $1.9 million. Probably over $3 million. There is no question that you need to live your life and enjoy certain pleasures. You have earned them. Take the time to figure out which pleasures you enjoy and are worth the cost and missed investment opportunity. Do the math. You might find ways to adjust your spending, enhance your investments and still enjoy regular pleasures. (I have included a spreadsheet in **Resources: Exhibit 3, p. 242** that shows what could have happened if the $730 went into investments with a 6% return.)

"The well is dry" – A true story…

Many years ago, I led a personal finance class for couples in their late 30's and early 40's. These folks were hard working people – the majority were two income families. In just about every case, teenage children lived in the home.

We discussed the need for an emergency fund equal to six months of living expenses. This subject struck a nerve with a few couples. They talked about the "need" to buy things for their kids. The kids had to have certain types of clothing, and other items, so they would fit in at school. Reading between the lines, I surmised it was the parents not the kids that thought they should buy these items, so that others wouldn't know they were barely getting by.

> **"Too many people spend money they haven't earned, to buy things they don't want, to impress people they don't like."**[71]
>
> Will Rogers

CHAPTER THREE: LET'S GET PERSONAL – YOUR MONEY

A woman came up to me after class. She was clearly nervous about what she had heard. She and her husband were two of the people that said they spent their money to make sure the kids had the right kinds of clothes and status items. She told me that she wished they had a couple of hundred dollars between checking and savings, much less six months of living expenses.

Until that class, I did not realize the depth of struggle that couples experienced with the most basic money issues. Those families really needed the financial counsel. I hope some of the couples learned skills that have made a positive difference in their lives.

Giving

You have already read about not giving your hard-earned money away. What I have been referring to is living beyond your means by buying depreciating stuff that you think you can't live without.

Let's look at when you *should* consider giving your money away. Giving may already be important to you to support the causes you believe in. Without you and people just like you, the many great causes and help provided to those in need would cease to exist.

I consider giving a privilege, and a personal investment in our world. "A privilege," you might ask? Yes, as you experience success, and practice sound money management, your overall earnings and monetary wealth should increase. The fact that we live in the most powerful country with the most vibrant economy in the world, is enough to assume we have been very blessed to be here. Imagine if you had been born in a third-world country where clean drinking water and food were your two highest priorities. When was the last time you worried about food and clean water?

Your community needs a portion of your resources – whether that be financial or your time/expertise.

Most of us have causes that are near and dear to us. Perhaps a family member has been impacted by cancer, and you are touched to help in some way. You may want to give money toward the eventual cure for this dreaded disease. Or, you have a heart for children and want to contribute toward the education and life needs of kids in your country or around the world.

Involve your family in giving decisions. In addition to our regular giving, we spend time each year with our grandchildren to discuss and participate in giving to poor families living in third world countries. Through a trusted organization we buy farm animals, vegetable seeds, fruit trees, bicycles, Bibles, water purification equipment, safety from abuse and mosquito nets. Our grandchildren help choose what we buy. It is interesting to watch the kids allocate our giving budget as they make their way through the gift catalog. They give the matter serious thought. While they learn to give back, they learn to manage a budget.

Consider it a privilege to contribute to those less fortunate. Make planned contributions a part of your budget. Choose causes that are consistent with the values you identified when building your life plan.

SECTION 4
THE LONG GAME

Spending: Plan for and Spend Wisely on Large Purchases

You don't need any pointers on finding things to buy – we are wired to spend, spend, spend – we already talked about the psychological motivators. Just walking through a grocery store with our grandkids I can see how early the wants begin ("Pop, let's buy this" as our grandson pulls me to the treat aisle).

Now that you have learned how to plan your spending (remember that simple Budget exercise?) – we are going to look at how to tackle some of the large and long-term expenses that you will eventually face. First, we will look at important preparation tactics, then jump into the nitty-gritty with two of the most common large purchases – buying a car and buying a home.

Preparing to Buy the "Big Stuff" – A Smart Tactical Approach

If you want to avoid paying someone else interest on loans, a tactic which will allow you to earn interest on your money, consider the following.

Large consumables like cars, appliances, furniture, and RV's all have a useful life. With a few minutes of research, you can estimate how long each one of these items will last.

Establish an estimated replacement date for each large item you own. Determine how many months there are between today and the replacement date. Estimate the replacement cost of the item and include that information with the replacement date on your personal calendar.

Use this formula:

$$\frac{\text{Replacement Cost}}{\text{Number of Months to Replacement}} = \$ \text{ Monthly Amount to Save}$$

Save this amount monthly. You will have enough cash (plus interest or investment earnings) to buy the replacement when the original item wears out.

WIDE-EYED WISDOM

Real Life Example: Car

You have estimated, with normal use and maintenance, your car will last 8 more years from today (96-months).

Next, do your best to estimate the purchase price of your next car. Use today's price and add inflation for potential price increases (you might want to add 2% to 3% per year to today's replacement cost). If the same car sells for $30,000 today, moderate inflation of 2% would cause the price to hit $35,000 or slightly above. Your next car (eight years from today) purchase estimate is in the range of $35,000 plus or minus.

Your savings calculation will look like this: $35,000/96 = $365 per month that you must save to have ready cash to buy your next car. With very modest interest earnings, your investment balance, when ready to buy the next car, should exceed $37,000.

Now that you can see your tactic for accruing funds in advance, over time, let's look at the basics of the first of your large purchases – buying a car.

Car Buying 101: Purchase and Payments

The purpose of a vehicle is quite simple – to get you from Point A to Point B. But the myriad of options available can make the choice overwhelming for some, and the process intimidating for those who have not done it before. There is a huge range of make, model, and options to choose from, with a wide cost spectrum. Car buying differs from many retail purchases because many of the terms are negotiable. Expect and be prepared to negotiate.

Before you step foot on a car lot, get your priorities straight. Identify your budget, and your transportation requirements. Let's look at some of the variables that will go into the car buying process, and how car dealers make their money.

With a son-in-law in the car industry, I feel the need to level-set about the potential perception that all car dealers are sleazy or dishonest. While this may certainly be the case for some dealers (trust your intuition and walk away from these situations), most dealers are not out to rip you off and will treat you professionally and with integrity. Keep in mind that as with any business, car dealers must make a profit to stay in business.

CHAPTER THREE: LET'S GET PERSONAL – YOUR MONEY

Car Buying Basics

	New	Used
Condition	Wait until the year-end model changes to take advantage of sizeable manufacturer markdowns on remaining stock.	Often more budget friendly and can be a good value for a well-maintained vehicle. Normally there is more dealer profit margin on a used car.
Price	Price is always negotiable – never pay the list amount. Internet research can help guide your expectations regarding the appropriate price. You may want to consider timing your purchase toward the end of the month when dealers and salespeople are motivated to hit month-end sales goals.	
Features	There is a huge range of features available – and they come with a price. Know your "must-have" items and be prepared to negotiate the cost of upgrade packages.	
Finance	Are you paying cash for this vehicle? That is the best way to stay within your budget and avoid finance costs. If you are financing this purchase, check car loan rates with your bank. Compare to what the dealer offers you. Dealers have access to several lenders they frequently do business with (and receive a kickback from the loans they generate). Compare, select, and negotiate the option to get the best terms for you.	
Extended Warranty	Extended warranties are generally a profit item for a dealer – if the terms of the warranty make sense for your situation, negotiate the price. Some new cars have lengthy warranties.	
Year-End Volume Incentives	Manufacturers award volume-based incentives to dealers based on number of units sold – you may be able to take advantage of discounted pricing at year-end while dealers are attempting to increase their sales volume to qualify for incentive income payments. Or, manufacturers offer large purchase incentives, watch for these.	

WIDE-EYED WISDOM

Car Buying Steps

Before you get too invested in the process, I want to remind you that there are millions of cars on the road. There will always be another car for sale that meets your needs. Don't get so emotionally wrapped up in a car that you make an uneducated or impulsive decision. With Wide-Eyed Wisdom, use incredible self-discipline.

STEP 1: **Determine if you really <u>need</u> a car**
Will your current mode of transportation suffice for today and the immediate future? If you can postpone a car purchase, set money aside monthly so that you pay cash when the time comes. If you <u>need</u> a car now, head to Step 2.

STEP 2: **Money Matters – Build your Budget**
Ideally you have included this item in your Budget and saved proactively month by month, year after year, so when it is time to buy, you are ready to pay cash! If you have not saved money in advance, evaluate how much money you can truly afford to spend – don't forget the insurance, maintenance, and fuel costs. Use self-discipline – stick within an affordable budget. You may need to sacrifice some bells and whistles. Focus on the reason to buy a car, safely getting from Point A to Point B. Spending more than you can truly afford will jeopardize your financial future, life plan.

STEP 3: **Do your Research**
Figure out what type of vehicle will meet your requirements. Minivan or sedan? Cross-over or SUV? You have a lot of options, filter those by the following:
- *Safety:* I will not put myself or my family in an unsafe vehicle. Death and injuries from car crashes are devastating. If I can reduce injury or death risk by buying a five-star safety rated vehicle, I will and hope you will too. I have friends that are alive today because they chose wisely and fared well in serious crashes.
- *Operating Costs:* Research vehicle reliability. Mechanical problems equal maintenance costs. Compare gas mileage too – this is a very real, daily cost differentiator.
- *Insurance Costs*: Once you have narrowed your vehicle preferences to a couple different options, get multiple insurance quotes and compare. Insurance rates vary by make and model.

CHAPTER THREE: LET'S GET PERSONAL – YOUR MONEY

- **Residual Value:** Chances are you will not keep your vehicle through the entirety of its useful life. If you plan to trade it in or sell at some point down the road, be aware that the Residual Value (what your vehicle is worth, "X" years down the road) will differ based on make and model. Vehicle age, popularity, mileage, and exterior and interior condition have a major impact on residual value.
- **Used or New:** You may have a strong personal preference on whether to buy Used (average cost $20,000*) or New (average cost $37,000*). Many new vehicles have excellent warranties. There is peace of mind knowing repairs for the first few years will be on the manufacturer's dime. Keep in mind that a new car depreciates the moment it is driven off the lot – the vehicle status change from new to used equals a sizeable loss of resale value. A used vehicle that has been properly cared for (make sure to have an inspection at a reputable dealer and review Carfax reports prior to purchasing) can provide an excellent value, often allowing you to get more upgrades at a price you can afford.

  Average cost in April 2020 according to US News & World Report[26]

STEP 4: Double Check Your Priorities

At this point you should have a solid understanding of what you intend to buy. You may have even located a few cars that fit the bill, either through personal online listings or a reputable local dealership. Before you head out to look at cars, be sure to review your finances again. Be realistic and committed to stick to your budget.

STEP 5: Test Drive

You have done the hard work – now is the time to have some fun. Test drive your preferred vehicles. If the vehicles you researched are disappointing after the test drive, ask for a recommendation. Your car should be a long-term purchase, so take your time. There will always be another car for sale.

STEP 6: Negotiate the Purchase

Once you have settled on a vehicle, it is time to negotiate! (See Chapter 8 for Negotiation Tactics.) As the buyer, remember, you have the power and leverage – be prepared with negotiation tactics (along with the big stuff like price, think out of the box – cosmetic blemishes to fix, car washes, oil changes, full tank of gas, etc.). During negotiations be honest, firm, and fair.

STEP 7: **Enjoy!**
Enjoy your new vehicle and be sure to keep up with regular maintenance. With regular maintenance you have a better chance of avoiding major costly repairs and will help maintain the value of your vehicle. Look to the future and prepare for your next car purchase - remember our tactics for making large purchases. Start saving now for the next vehicle, so that over time you will be able to build enough funds to pay in cash. (Plus, earn on your savings/investment dollars.)

Car Loans
Would you be surprised that in 2019, over 85% of vehicle purchases were financed? Given the pervasive debt in our country, this isn't too surprising. The cost of interest on a car loan will greatly impact the overall cost of the vehicle. And the greatest impact on the interest cost is credit score. If you have done an excellent job managing your finances and using credit responsibly, this is where it will pay off. With a great credit score you will pay less interest than someone who has done an average or sub-standard job managing their credit.

Auto Loan Rates by Credit Score – April 2020[26]

Credit Score	New Car	Used Car
750+	4.97%	5.22%
700 - 749	5.02%	5.27%
600 - 699	11.12%	11.37%
451 - 599	17.93%	18.18%
450 or Lower	Don't bother – take the bus	

Let's look at what personal credit score means to you, with a couple different scenarios using the current average new car cost of $37,000. (Walk through this exercise using a calculator or online loan tool. You will need purchase price, interest rate, and loan term.) **(See Resources: Exhibits 4 and 5, p. 244-245)**

CHAPTER THREE: LET'S GET PERSONAL – YOUR MONEY

Example 1: **New Car Purchase** **EXCELLENT** **Credit Score (750+)**		*Example 2:* **New Car Purchase** **MODERATE** **Credit Score (600 - 699)**	
Purchase Price	$37,000	Purchase Price	$37,000
Less: 20% Down	($7,400)	Less: 20% Down	($7,400)
Loan Term	60-months	Loan Term	60-months
Interest Rate	4.97%	Interest Rate	11.37%
Car Loan	$29,600	Car Loan	$29,600
Monthly Payment	$558	Monthly Payment	$649
Total Payments	$33,491	Total Payments	$38,943
Total Interest	$3,891	Total Interest	$9,343
Down Payment +	$7,400 +$33,491	Down Payment +	$7,400 + $38,943
Loan Payments	=	Loan Payments	=
Total Cost	**$40,891**	**Total Cost**	**$46,343**
Excellent credit gives you negotiating leverage. Before you take out a loan, compare rates among several lenders. Lenders compete aggressively for loans to high credit rated individuals.		There are numerous borrowing options for those with poor credit. As we discussed earlier, it is best to save your money so that you pay cash for your car. To repair a poor credit score, have the cash in-hand, secure a small loan, then quickly pay the loan off in full.	
(*Payments have been rounded.)			

**The increased interest cost for the person with Moderate credit was over $5,000 more than the person with excellent credit. I don't know about you, but I'd rather keep my five-grand.

Summary:
Borrowing can be expensive. If you are prepared for a large purchase, by saving in advance and using self-discipline in your car selection, chances are that you

will make a great buy. You should also have accrued earnings on your savings. Taking the above steps will allow you to work your plan on your terms.

HOME Buying 101: Purchase and Payments

Likely the largest purchase you will ever make is a home. Home buying can be an exciting, yet daunting and stressful event. My wife and I have bought and sold eleven homes (primary residence, vacation, investment properties) to date.

As you have probably gathered, we have always been careful with our finances, which certainly has extended to our choice in homes. There should be a lot of careful thought and consideration that goes into buying a home. Home buying is a long-term purchase with serious financial implications. Arm yourself with thorough knowledge and understanding about the home buying process. Consider your life plan during the process.

There are plenty of available resources to walk you through the home buying process. I'm going to focus on the financial piece of the puzzle. Before you get too caught up dreaming about the countless number of homes you find on Zillow, come to realistic terms about how much you can truly afford.

As you are getting started building your future, be careful not to reach so far up the ladder that you lose your grip and fall flat on your face. Behind your monthly mortgage payment is a hulking beast of a loan with a mountain of interest that you will pay over decades. Once you have made strides in your career and have a sturdy handle on your financial health, there will be plenty of time and opportunity to move up the home buying ladder.

In advance of the million-dollar question – how much home you can afford – let's set the groundwork with some basic home-buying terminology.

CHAPTER THREE: LET'S GET PERSONAL – YOUR MONEY

Home Buying Basics

List Price	Amount the seller is asking for their home and a starting point for negotiations. Depending on the market, some sell for more than List Price (think bidding war), while others sell for less.
Offer	This is a legal document that you will submit (usually via a realtor) with your proposed Purchase Price and any special conditions. Don't be so emotionally attached to a home that you pay more than it is worth, or you overlook major issues.
Purchase Price	Mutually agreed upon sales price between the seller and buyer.
Earnest Money	Typically, about 1 – 2% of the purchase price, held in Escrow and applied at closing.
Escrow	A neutral third party that holds financial obligations from both the buyer and seller after an accepted offer and through closing.
Down Payment	Amount of cash paid at closing to reduce the loan principal. Typically, 20% is a minimum to avoid paying Private Mortgage Insurance. Lenders require a certain amount of money as a down payment to qualify you for a loan. The more money you put down, the lower the home loan payment.
Loan Principal	Amount of the Purchase Price financed via a financial institution – the Sales price, plus closing costs, minus down payment.
Interest Rate	Cost of money – lower for excellent credit, higher percentage rate for marginal credit. Interest cost as a % of payment is highest during the first several years of the loan.
Term	Usually a 30-year period. A shorter period (20/15/10-year) increases monthly payment and decreases interest cost.
Private Mortgage Insurance (PMI)	Fee for buyers with less than a 20% down payment. If a buyer stops making loan payments the Private Mortgage Insurance protects the lender.
Closing Costs	Fees in addition to the Purchase Price of a home, related to securing a mortgage and making sure the property title is clear. Application fee, appraisal fee, title search, title insurance… Expect to pay 2 – 5% of the loan principal. You may be able to negotiate with the seller to cover part or all the Closing Costs.
Property Tax	Annual tax payable to the County where your home is located, based on a property's Assessed Value. Depending on how your mortgage is structured, may be collected monthly and paid on your behalf. Property taxes vary county to county.
Utilities	Costs associated with gas (propane or natural gas), water, sewer, garbage, electricity, cable, internet, Home-Owners Association (HOA) dues, etcetera…
Maintenance	Maintaining the condition of home, repairs, and improvements – if it breaks, you have got to fix it!

WIDE-EYED WISDOM

Equity	This is the difference between the market value (ie. selling price) of a home and the outstanding loan balance. (Also… subtract closing fees and commissions to arrive at Net Equity)
Realtor Commission	These are the fees, paid by the seller, to handle the home sale marketing, paperwork, and commissions to broker and individual realtors. Fees are negotiable. Normal rates are usually 5% to 6% of the home purchase price. The sales commission is split between buyer's representative and seller's representative.

Back to, "What can I afford?" That is the million-dollar question, isn't it? A quick search on, "How much home can I afford," yields a commonly shared guideline. Your total housing cost should be no more than 28% of your gross income (pre-tax).[27] I've done the math and for many of you just getting started out, that's not going to pencil. Instead, I want to use what we already *know* about your expenses and spending, then work backward to identify how much home you can truly afford. Buy a home and your other expenses aren't going to just magically disappear – usually those expenses will increase.

If you have significant debt like student loans, credit card debt or car payments, the bucket of money remaining may be small or nonexistent. Bottom line – until you have your "financial house" in order, you have no business jumping into a home purchase. Sorry. Once you have reduced (or eliminated!) your debt payments, and developed self-discipline in your spending, you will be ready to start looking at a home purchase.

Keep in mind that when you buy a home, there are more monthly expenses than just your mortgage payment. Such as:
- Private Mortgage Insurance (if your down payment is less than 20%)
- Property Tax (rates vary widely by location)
- Utilities (could increase from your current)
- Maintenance (when you buy a home, you own all fixes and upkeep)
- Homeowners Insurance (more expensive than Renters Insurance)

If you created a real and working Budget, it is going to be easy to hone-in on how much you can truly afford. Here is the basic logic: what you can afford to spend on housing is how much you have left over after you have paid for everything else.

Do you remember the 50/30/20 Rule? Allocate 50% of your take home income to your NEEDS, 30% to your WANTS, and 20% for the FUTURE.

CHAPTER THREE: LET'S GET PERSONAL – YOUR MONEY

Housing falls into your NEEDS category, so for the sake of simplicity we are going to set aside the WANTS and FUTURE buckets.

I'm going to work through a basic example to explain the process. Let's look back at our sample budget from earlier with a $60,000 net income. Remember, we re-balanced and got as close as we could to our 50/30/20 guideline. Many monthly expenditures are not impacted by the purchase of a home – we are stuck with those expenses regardless of where we live.

Example: Housing Funds

NEEDS		
Housing	$1,100 *	*This is the bucket of money available for monthly Housing Costs
Utilities	$200 *	
Home Insurance	$50 *	
Car Insurance	$200	
Food	$400	
Medical	$150	
Transportation	$250	
Loan Payments	$200	
Charitable Giving	$100	
TOTAL	**$2,650**	
ALLOCATION	**53%**	

In this example, there is $1,350 available to cover recurring monthly home costs. A wise financial steward will avoid paying PMI with a minimum down payment of 20%. We can devote these funds to: the mortgage payment, property tax, utilities, and insurance. Rates for all of these vary widely depending on where you live. Do some homework to investigate rates and averages in your area. A trusted realtor can provide a lot of this information.

Okay – still working backwards – let's put the pieces of the puzzle together to find out how much of a monthly mortgage payment we can afford.

Housing Funds	-	Private Mortgage Insurance	-	Property Tax	-	Utilities	-	Home Owners Insurance	=	Monthly Mortgage Capacity
$1,350	-	0	-	250	-	200	-	50	=	$850

You can use an online mortgage calculator with current interest rates to plug-in your available monthly mortgage capacity to find out the total loan amount.

WIDE-EYED WISDOM

At the time of this writing, interest rates for 30-yr fixed mortgages are quite low – about 3%. That would give us a **$200,000 loan**.

The loan amount plus saved down payment equal the maximum home purchase price!

You can enhance your home purchasing power by increasing the down payment or increasing your income. The more you earn or save, the more you can buy! Use unexpected windfalls like a tax rebate, work bonus, inheritance, side hustle, or DIY savings to sock away towards a down payment. Coupled with what you have been saving monthly (remember the large purchase accruals in your budget) – little by little, over time – you will be able to accumulate a significant chunk of money.

If you find that the homes you can afford don't fit your needs or wants, it's up to you to decide whether you want to compromise your wish list to buy now, or if you want to wait and continue to save to be able to afford more.

Credit Score Impact on Home Loans

I have included a home purchase scenario which compares the same transaction for a buyer with excellent credit versus a moderate credit buyer.

Take a close look at the difference and manage your credit carefully. Just like the car purchase example, loan interest rates translate to big dollars. Stay on top of your credit score – you own it. Credit score will have big implications on your purchasing power.

CHAPTER THREE: LET'S GET PERSONAL – YOUR MONEY

Example 1: **Home Purchase EXCELLENT Credit Score (750+)**		*Example 2:* **Home Purchase MODERATE Credit Score (650 - 699)**	
Purchase Price	$250,000	Purchase Price	$250,000
Less: 20% Down	($50,000)	Less: 20% Down	($50,000)
Loan Term	30-yr fixed	Loan Term	30-yr fixed
Interest Rate	3.00%	Interest Rate	5.00%
Home Loan	$200,000	Home Loan	$200,000
Mortgage Pymt.	$843	Mortgage Pymt.	$1,074
Total Payments	$303,480	Total Payments	$386,640
Total Interest	$103,480	Total Interest	$186,640
Down Payment +	$50,000 +	Down Payment +	$50,000 +
Loan Payments =	$303,480 =	Loan Payments =	$386,640 =
Total Cost	**$353,480**	**Total Cost**	**$436,640**

Note: The difference in the two examples is the Interest Rate. Interest Rate is driven by your credit score. For this modest home, the buyer with moderate credit will pay **over $83,000 more** to borrow the same amount of money. Your financial discipline *does* matter!

Conversely, if you look at the purchasing power of the two buyers, for the moderate credit buyer to pay $843 per month, their total loan capacity is only **$157,000**. That means the buyer with a moderate credit score will have $43,000 less to spend on a home than the buyer with excellent credit.

Buying a Home – The Total Cost

Well done – now you have answered the "million-dollar question" and know how much home you can afford. If you aren't in the market right now, this will help you think through the process, plan ahead, save your money, and be prepared for when you *are* ready to make that commitment.

WIDE-EYED WISDOM

But before we move on, there is one more cost I want to circle back and call your attention to – translation – you need a bit more cash on hand (Or, increase your home loan amount), separate from the down payment, to complete the transaction. There will also be:

- **Closing Costs** (typically 2% to 5% of the purchase price). This covers the cost to facilitate the transaction. A selection of fees is listed below.
    - Loan fees
    - Appraisal fee
    - Credit report fee
    - Inspection cost
    - Title fees
    - Escrow payment

Congratulations! Now that you are a land baron or baroness, enjoy your new home!

SECTION 5
THE TOOLS

So far, we have looked at how to align your spending and saving habits with your income, the importance of saving and investing for your future, and tactics to prepare for and make large purchases. We are wrapping up the basics of Personal Finance with a look at some financial tools that you will use in your life journey – namely, credit, credit cards, and loans.

Credit

As of fall 2019, people that live in the U.S. owe about $14 trillion.[28] This debt is made of all types of loans. (Student loans, car loans, home loans, home equity loans, credit cards, personal loans/lines of credit, consumer loans…)

This debt is a double whammy for borrowers. Here is why:
1. Interest cost on $14 trillion, is paid by borrowers. ($840 billion)
2. Lost investment income opportunity, the result of paying $840 billion in interest, is borne by borrowers. ($50 billion+)

Although it is difficult to estimate the impact on the economy, the total cost to borrowers at a 6% average interest cost and loss of 6% after tax investment income, is nearly $900 billion annually.

While it is almost impossible to avoid some debt, your goal should be to minimize what you owe. Always seek to minimize interest payments. While you minimize your cost of debt, aim to maximize your investment earnings.

Individual Credit Score

The three major consumer Credit Rating Bureaus[29] in the United States are:
- Equifax
- TransUnion
- Experian

The purpose of the credit rating bureaus is to compile information about your credit history and create a credit score.

WIDE-EYED WISDOM

Your credit score is called a FICO score.[29] FICO represents "Fair Isaac Corporation". This is the largest and best known of the companies that provide software for calculating credit scores. Ask your friends if they know what FICO stands for – you will probably be the only one in your circle that can answer the question.

In the most widely used credit score modeling, a perfect credit score is 850 and the lowest score is 300.[30] According to Lending Tree the consumers that fall in the range of 720 to 850 will get the best lending rates. Close to half of all consumers fall in the 720 to 850 range.

Credit bureaus collect information regarding your payment history, available credit, amounts owed, bankruptcy, payment default, liens, and number of times your credit history has been checked. The information is used to build your credit score. This information is readily available. Nothing about your payment history will be hidden from credit bureaus.

Credit scores are used by lenders (banks, credit card issuers, etc.) to make a lending decision. If lenders decide to lend to you, the interest rate and credit limit will be dependent upon your credit score. The better the score the lower the interest rate.

Recently, businesses, such as insurance companies have begun to check credit scores. High credit score individuals are likely to be offered lower cost insurance coverage. There is a correlation between credit scores and insurance claims. (Perhaps the result of self-discipline?) Consult your insurance company for information regarding credit score impact on insurance premiums.

Consumers also have access to credit scores. Check your credit score periodically to ensure accuracy and to guard against identity theft.

To secure the best FICO score, pay all obligations on-time and in full, and avoid carrying credit card balances. Rating bureaus like to see a regular history of timely loan and bill payments and unused credit capacity. (An example of unused credit capacity is a credit card with a $10,000 limit and a zero balance.)

Credit Cards

Credit cards are ubiquitous today – if you don't have one yet, you will – probably several. Credit cards are convenient and offer many benefits. However, that little piece of plastic is one of the most dangerous items in your financial arsenal. Reckless use can derail a life of financial peace.

CHAPTER THREE: LET'S GET PERSONAL – YOUR MONEY

How do credit cards work? The credit card issuer reviews your application (including legal name, social security number and annual salary). Based on your income (and checking your credit score), you may be approved for a credit limit – the pool of money that you can spend and pay back later. Here is where it gets tricky for you. The dollar amount of your credit limit will be more than you are able to pay back in a monthly billing cycle. When you are unable to pay the total balance on your card at the time the statement is due (credit cards have a one-month cycle), you will be charged interest on the unpaid amount.

The first rule of using credit cards is to **pay every credit card bill in full** when you receive the bill. In other words, **do not buy anything that you are unable to pay for immediately**. Violating this rule to buy stuff that you can't live without will put you in a costly and dangerous consumption trap.

There are five major issuers and a gazillion other businesses and retailers that issue credit cards (think Target, Costco, Nordstrom, Home Depot, Macy's, Best Buy…just to name a few). The top five credit card companies: Visa, Mastercard, Chase, American Express, and Discover have issued almost 800 million credit cards in the United States.[31]

Americans owe $1.07 trillion[32] to credit card issuers – that is trillion, with a "T". As of March 2020, this debt has an average annualized interest rate anywhere between 16-21% (creditcards.com and thebalance.com). Did you catch that? I think my heart just skipped a beat thinking about the annual interest cost of buying depreciating stuff.

However, the use of credit cards can enhance your financial health. The key here is *proper* and *disciplined* use of credit cards.

Understanding the Credit Card Game

Credit card companies fill the role of payment administrator. The credit card companies are the link between consumers and merchants. Credit card companies assume payment risk (ie. a consumer defaulting on payments) in exchange for merchant transaction fees, consumer interest, fees, and penalties.

A credit card balance is an unsecured loan to a consumer. (The credit card issuer does not hold consumer collateral to secure the short-term loan.) Consumers pay significant costs when balances are not paid in full each month.

WIDE-EYED WISDOM

I have provided financial information on four of the major credit card issuers. This will give you an idea of the scale of credit card company profits and market value (as of April 2020).

Major Credit Card Issuer Financial Position[33]

Company	Share Price (April 2020)	2019 Net Income	Market Cap.*
VISA	$160	$11.6 billion	$359 billion
American Express	$88	$6.6 billion	$67 billion
MasterCard	$265	$8.1 billion	$257 billion
Discover	$40	$2.9 billion	$11 billion

Market Cap. = Number of stock shares outstanding times share price. In other words, the market value of the company based on the current stock price.

Cash vs. Credit Transactions[34]

Do you use cash or credit for most transactions? The use of cash in the U.S. represents about 31% of all purchase transactions. Credit cards and electronic payments make up 69% of all purchase transactions. While cash may never be totally obsolete, the use of plastic and electronic payments continues to increase while cash use continues to decline.

- As of 2018 the AVERAGE purchase transaction was: $84
- The average CASH purchase transaction: $22
- The average CREDIT CARD purchase transaction: $112

As you can see, credit card transaction size is five times higher than cash transaction size. Merchants love large transactions, so they encourage the use of credit. Very few merchants will not accept credit cards. Those that don't accept credit are missing opportunity and may be flirting with business failure. As more companies have issued credit cards, competition has stiffened. To compete effectively, credit card issuers are sharing a piece of their income as incentives to consumers. We are bombarded by reward deals, either on television, online, in person or through the mail. Credit cards are here to stay, so let's look at the benefits, and understand the dangers.

CHAPTER THREE: LET'S GET PERSONAL – YOUR MONEY

The Good – Why I Am a Fan of Credit Cards

Easy access to credit	When used wisely the ease at which an individual can secure a credit card is a great strength. Most people will secure a credit card with even the most modest earnings. If you need credit and universal acceptance, a credit card will provide both.
Build credit history/ credit score	Credit cards are a great way to build your credit score. Quite often you will be unable to secure a loan without a good payment history/credit score. Credit card companies offer programs to establish credit, giving borrowers the opportunity to establish loan payment history and a credit score.
Emergencies	There will eventually be a situation in your life, when you must make a quick payment, and the credit card will be the most useful item in your wallet or purse. If you have not yet had an emergency requiring immediate payment, eventually you will.
Rewards	There seems to be no end to the types of reward cards available. Take advantage of using regular everyday purchases to get cash back, gift cards, merchandise, hotel stays, airline tickets, you name it. Using credit cards for regular everyday purchases can help build rewards without an increase in spending.
Convenience	There have been countless times that I have been away from the house and needed gas or food and did not have cash in my pocket. My credit card made it fast and easy to buy what I needed. You can even use a credit card, with a limit, to help manage a child's spending and needs while away at college. If you carry credit cards, make sure you store the issuing credit card phone number in a safe place, just in case your card is lost or stolen. Major credit card companies develop sophisticated purchase profiles for their customers. If a credit purchase/charge does not fit your profile, the credit card companies will usually disable the card and contact you.

Travel	If you travel, a credit card is a splendid form of payment. Credit cards are widely accepted in just about every country on earth. When traveling abroad, notify your credit card company in advance of your trip. A foreign purchase using your credit card could set off alarm bells and your card may be disabled at the wrong time. Currency exchange rates are an issue in foreign countries. If you use cash, you must be able to understand exchange rates, or risk being taken advantage of. Many merchants in foreign countries know they will never see you again, so they will err on their side of the exchange. Let the bank do the exchange. You might pay a small fee, but you will know that the currency exchange is fair and equitable for both parties.
Managing a Budget	By now you should have created a budget. When using a credit card, you will be able to easily categorize and view your spending online, at any time. These records will help you stay on track with your budget and identify any areas where you need to adjust purchase habits.

For the many strengths and benefits of credit cards, there are also great weaknesses. Now read the reasons why I am not a fan of credit cards.

The Bad – Why I Am NOT a Fan of Credit Cards

Easy Access to Credit	Just about anyone can get a credit card. There are regular offers, some right at the store register, with discounts off your purchase if you "sign up today". The merchant accepts the risk, knowing the potential upside (increased purchases, interest, and fees) of your ongoing business. Buying can easily spiral into excessive spending, a maxed-out card, minimum payments, interest, fees, and eventually payment default.

CHAPTER THREE: LET'S GET PERSONAL – YOUR MONEY

Access to a Cash Advance	A cash advance is a convenient method of expensive borrowing. Cash advances sound like a great idea until you pay the interest costs. In April of 2020, the best interest rates ranged from 19% to 22%, plus a possible 3% transfer fee.[35] Pause and think two or three times if you are considering the use of a cash advance. Don't put yourself in a position of using a cash advance to live beyond your means. You are digging your personal financial hole deeper. Like I tell our kids, "put the shovel down".
Balance Transfers	A balance transfer is a high interest loan. Credit card companies promise low or no fees for a period because they know that over time, you will pay handsome interest and fees on the balance transfer. You may receive several months interest free, but after the initial 0%, the best interest charges will likely be between 13% and 23% annually. There could be an additional transfer fee of 3% to 5%.[36]
Enables Large Purchases	Now you know that people with credit cards spend almost five times more per transaction than those that pay in cash. Why? There is a feeling of empowerment in having a $5,000 or more credit card limit which can almost certainly lead to a lost perspective on what you can really afford. Your ability to buy has been increased without regard to your ability to pay. As a test, put your credit cards away and use cash exclusively for 90-days. Force yourself to pull cash out of your wallet when you buy or consider buying. Better yet, limit the amount of cash in your wallet or purse. Without the money in your hand or credit line, you will be forced to plan for and make better buying decisions, particularly on impulse purchases.

WIDE-EYED WISDOM

Fees: Interest, Late Pay, and Annual

Set a goal for yourself and your family to never pay interest, late or annual fees again. I've included the payment information from an actual credit card statement. The original $1,726.56 credit card charge was comprised of gas, groceries, pet food, aquarium admission, home repairs, an airline ticket, sporting goods and eating out. Someone who falls into the minimum payment trap would more than double the original purchase price by paying interest costs.

New Balance:	$1,726.56
Minimum Payment Due:	$25.00
Payment Due Date:	7/21/20
Annual Percentage Rate:	19.24%

Late Payment Warning: If we do not receive your minimum payment by the date listed above, you may have to pay a late fee of up to $38.00 and your APR may be increased up to the Penalty APR of 29.99%.

Minimum Payment Warning: If you make only the minimum payment each period, you will pay more in interest and it will take you longer to pay off your balance.

If you make no additional charges using this card and each month you pay…	You will pay off the balance shown on this statement in about…	And you will end up paying an estimated total of…
Minimum payment of $25.00	10 years	$3,527

Bankruptcy

The ease at which a person can rack-up credit card debt is alarming. He buys more and more then realizes that he can only pay part of the balance or risk not having enough money for rent, food, and other essentials. Credit card companies gladly oblige this dilemma, for a fee of course… Lacking discipline, he repeats the cycle month after month, even adding new credit cards to the mix. Pretty soon he can't make the minimum payments and debt collectors are now hounding him.

Bankruptcy is always an option and is likely to wipe out the credit card debt. The problem is the bankruptcy will be on his credit record for years. Now an established credit risk, he is unable to qualify for a mortgage or car loan (or if he does the interest rates are high). If this sounds like you, seek a credit counselor to work through ways to pay off debt and save your financial future.

CHAPTER THREE: LET'S GET PERSONAL – YOUR MONEY

Managing Your Budget	Without self-discipline and careful monitoring, unabated spending can blow your budget – and your financial future – all with the simple swipe of a card. Remember your life plan.
Theft or Loss	What do you think would happen if your credit card became lost or was stolen?
	Losing control of your card can result in credit damage that can take months or years to repair.
	To guard yourself against lost or stolen credit cards, make sure you have the customer service phone numbers readily available. When you discover loss or theft of a credit card, freeze accounts as quickly as you can and report fraudulent activity to the credit card company.

Summary

- Credit cards can play a positive personal financial management role.
- Used wisely, credit cards can help build an excellent credit score.
- Never buy so much that you are forced to pay fees or interest.
- Be disciplined…planned purchases and regular bill payment are best. (If you don't have the money in the bank and item in your budget, walk away.)
- Store credit card company phone numbers in a safe place, just in case cards are lost or stolen.
- Never use your credit card as an ATM.
- Credit card balance transfers should be avoided.
- Pay off credit card debt as quickly as possible.
- Whether travel is local or international, a credit card is an excellent form of payment.
- Wise use of credit cards can help you gain rewards.

WIDE-EYED WISDOM

Loans

Thomas Jefferson once said, "Never spend money before you have earned it."[37] Our government and our country, (beginning with those we elect), could learn something from him. Our country operated into the middle of the twentieth century as if Mr. Jefferson controlled the business of the U.S. In the early 1940's there was no national debt. Today, in 2020 the national debt stands at more than $24 trillion.[38] Our national debt continues to climb and is estimated to reach $27 trillion by 2023.[39] Our elected leaders are spending money we do not have. Interest payments on the national debt are staggering and the United States of America is living beyond its means. (Recent payments due to the COVID pandemic will increase the national debt even higher.)

For the few of you that already live by Jefferson's message, congratulations! For the rest of you, take the words of Thomas Jefferson to heart. Focus on yourself and your future – set a goal to buy only when you have the money in-hand. This will force you to develop self-discipline, limit wastefulness, save yourself financial grief and help you achieve your life plan. Loans in this country allow a person or family to live well beyond their means. Countless Americans are deep in debt, at the expense of their future. You have already read that Americans owe over $14 trillion[40] on all types of loans.

I'm not saying all loans are bad. To the contrary, if you are financially savvy and disciplined enough, quite often you can borrow money at rates below what you could earn on a quality investment.

Don't jump headlong into borrowing until you have studied the consequences and understand the impact of your decision. Financial disaster can strike when your lack of knowledge is coupled with a strong desire for instant gratification. Too often our must haves cloud our judgment and test our self-discipline. We spend and borrow beyond our means, then are unable to keep up with the payments – this results in a loan default – consequences of which will haunt you for years. Many families have been ruined by financial problems. Just because you can borrow money does not mean you should. Resist giving your money away. Take pride in going your own way, avoid the herd mentality. The herd is headed to slaughter.

Loans are a huge source of profits for financial institutions. A bank uses customer cash deposits as one source of funds for lending. The bank may pay the depositor .2% and then loan the money at 4%. The financial return on the loan is astronomical. If you have ever wondered how banks make money, now you have a partial answer.

Loans also create significant risk for the lender. To mitigate this risk, lenders rely on credit scores and collateral to secure loans. There are always a certain number of delinquent loans and loan defaults which drive loan expense, reducing the lending net profit. Even so, lending is good business. When lending to those with less than excellent credit, banks plan for a certain number of loan defaults. Interest rates are increased to cover the losses, ensuring a handsome profit.

The loan interest you pay is front-loaded. In other words, you pay significantly more interest in the early months or years of the loan term and small amounts of loan principal (the amount you borrowed). As your loan term matures, an increasingly larger share of your payment will be directed toward reducing the principle, until the loan is fully paid. For an example of a home loan payment schedule, **See Resources: Exhibit 6, p. 246**.

To avoid interest costs, it is best to pay extra toward the principal early in the life of the loan. Paying principal early in the loan term will reduce your total interest cost and pay the loan off earlier. So, if you have a loan, plan to pay more than the monthly payment on a regular basis toward the principal. (Make sure you tell the lender when you are paying extra toward the loan principal. Without your direction, the lender may apply your extra payment incorrectly.)

Common Loan Types

There are many different loan types, some more desirable than others. The various options available will depend upon loan purpose. We will look at each type, including benefits and what to watch out for.

Common Loan Types

Acceptable	Least Desirable
Home Loan	Borrow from a family member or friend
Home Equity Loan	Consumer Loan: deferred payments
Car Loan	Credit Card
Lease	Payday Loans
Personal Line of Credit	Online Installment Loans

WIDE-EYED WISDOM

Home Loan

For some people, buying a home yields their only tangible net worth (or at least most of it). In the past, homes appreciated in value over a period of years — eventually the homeowner built valuable home equity.

Buying a home requires self-discipline. Discipline is required to save money for the down payment, closing costs, insurance, property taxes, maintain the property and make the monthly mortgage payments.

There are many types of home loans. The most common home loan is a 30-year term with a fixed interest rate. You can get fixed rates on other home loan terms. I suggest most home buyers stick with a fixed rate loan. History tells us that variable interest rate loans become an invitation to buy beyond our means. Eventually interest rates go up, monthly payments rise and loan defaults increase. Too good to be true, that palace you bought will be lost.

Some folks suggest stretching yourself to buy as expensive of a house as you can. I suspect they are banking on rising markets where you might achieve a high rate of home appreciation. They are also betting that your income will rise significantly during that time. What they don't anticipate is a major real estate crash, like what happened just over a decade ago which resulted in huge amounts of foreclosures and negative home equity situations all over our great country. Our newlywed daughter and her husband had just purchased their first home the year before the crash – resulting in over $150,000 of lost equity as the market bottomed out. Ouch!

My suggestion is simple, don't live beyond your means. Just because you can make a payment does not mean that you can afford the home or the payment, or that you *should* stretch to buy at that level. Appreciating home values are not a guarantee – balance your optimism with a realistic view of your financial situation and what it will take to achieve your life plan. Keep living costs within your means and channel your income increases into investments.

Make sure that your expenses, including regular home maintenance and investments fit into your budget. And please, don't neglect funding your retirement and investment portfolios so you can buy a house. Stay within your budget, using your life plan as your guide.

CHAPTER THREE: LET'S GET PERSONAL – YOUR MONEY

Home Equity Loan

These loans are used to finance a home improvement or at times a large consumer goods purchase.

Banks market this loan type to customers with excellent credit. The banks believe you have home equity to tap into and this loan type is billed as a method to make improvements, thereby increasing your property value. Lenders want you to believe the loan will pay off in the long run (when you sell your home).

Remember – if you are keeping your property up to date you should spend as you go…don't find yourself spending a huge chunk of money at once forcing you to borrow. Hint, hint – for those of you that are in warm climate areas – the swimming pool can wait until you have saved the money (look back at the tactic to save for large purchases).

What not to do: I once talked to a young man at a university orientation about home equity loans. He was an incoming freshman and was bragging about how his parents were able to buy a new car using a home equity loan. He went on to say how cheap the payments were. I'm certain he didn't have any financial schooling, nor did his parents. They took out a $40,000 loan secured by their home equity. That car will have little or no value in eight to ten years. They didn't understand the true cost of buying a depreciating item with a long-term home equity loan.

Their 15-year home equity loan at 4.5% allowed the family to get $40,000 using their home equity as collateral. Their monthly payment was $306 over 180-months. Assuming they use the full 180-months to pay off the home equity loan, the final cost of the new car will be over $55,000. They will pay over $15,000 in interest. The car will be worn out in eight to ten years and the family will still be making payments for 5 to 7 more years.

No consumer goods purchases: Bottom Line – do not use home equity loans to buy consumer goods. Don't mortgage your home and put a dent in your wealth to buy a depreciating item. You will never get off the hamster wheel and will be giving your money away.

WIDE-EYED WISDOM

Car Loan

Most of us will get a car loan at one time or another. Quite often this loan might be the first you use – me included. A car loan is one of the quickest ways to establish credit…for better or worse.

If you are a credit newbie, here are my suggestions:
- In advance of your purchase, estimate the amount of money it will take to buy the car (check out the section on purchasing a car). Let's say the car is $15,000.
- Use my savings tactic for large purchases, bank enough cash to buy the car – Yes, I mean have all the cash in hand to buy the car.
- As part of your research get pre-approved for an auto loan from the best source you can find (pay attention to the rate, terms, etc.).
- Once you have negotiated the price of the car, ask the dealer for a small auto loan.
- Negotiate the loan rate and terms with the car dealer. Dealers have various sources of auto loans, so they can shop and find a competitive loan from a legitimate lender.
    - Remember, the car dealer does not want you to leave without the car. They will match or beat your best loan rate.
    - Finance a portion of the car – say $2,000 to $3,000 (remember, you have this money already).
    - Over the next 90-days, pay off the loan balance in full.
- The result: You have just established excellent credit.

If you find yourself unprepared…you have not saved the total purchase price of the car and you really do need a vehicle, do your best to exercise self-discipline when buying. Stick with what you need, avoid going overboard. (You have heard about the tragedies when people on cruise ships fall overboard. The same word picture can be used to illustrate the consequences of overspending.)

Lease

A car lease is a loan. You will go through information disclosure and credit checks to qualify for a lease. Understand the elements of a car lease before you

CHAPTER THREE: LET'S GET PERSONAL – YOUR MONEY

go to the dealer – do your homework and prepare to negotiate. (First off, most experts believe it is best to buy, rather than lease a car.)

Capitalized cost: You will hear the term capitalized cost which does not necessarily equal the car sticker price. The capitalized cost is the amount the dealer/manufacturer uses as the value of the vehicle when calculating the lease payments. Capitalized cost is negotiable (in many cases capitalized cost will be the sticker price). Negotiate a capitalized cost below sticker price, just as you would when buying.

Interest rate: The interest rate on the lease is also negotiable. The percentage rate will not necessarily be the same cost to borrow money if you were to buy the car. Compare interest rates between competing dealers and negotiate the best deal.

Buyout price at lease end: Buyout price is an estimate of the value of the vehicle at retail when the lease expires. The manufacturer bases a portion of your monthly lease payment to offset vehicle depreciation. If there is a chance you will buy the vehicle at the end of the lease, prepare to negotiate.

Mileage: You may be able to negotiate your lease payment downward if you plan to drive fewer miles than the original offer. Keep in mind that you will pay high mileage fees if you exceed the allowed mileage cap.

Personal Line of Credit

The select few with a great credit history may have the opportunity to open a personal line of credit. Personal credit lines are usually unsecured, which means that there is no collateral pledged in the event of payment default.

The borrowing rate on the line of credit usually varies with a benchmark rate. Banks charge a fixed amount of percentage points over a benchmark rate. As our economy slid into recession years ago, most banks reduced their offer of personal lines of credit. Recently there appears to be a bit of a comeback with some banks advertising personal lines of credit to select customers.

WIDE-EYED WISDOM

Borrow from Family Members or Friends

I am not a fan of borrowing money from family members or friends. Too many things can go wrong, and financial problems derail even the best of relationships. Most of the time there are no written terms or consequences, to mitigate late or non-payment. Quite often one party or the other will forget terms of the verbal agreement. Or the agreement terms or promises are stretched beyond what was originally intended.

Many children borrow from their parents and then don't pay the money back. Do not be one of those people. Your parents have their own life plan. Take pride in treating your parents with love and respect. Honor your parents by keeping them out of *your* financial problems.

You need to plan properly for what you buy. Save until you have the money to buy. Stand on your own two feet with advance planning and preparation. Yes, it is work! And it requires self-discipline! Don't put your friends or family and yourself in the awkward lender/debtor relationship.

Credit Card

Discussed in detail earlier – credit card use is a type of loan. If you are undisciplined, the fees and interest payments will eat at your finances until gone. Beware the easy source of credit!

Consumer Loan with Deferred Payments

For the most part, these loans are a selling tactic in high-margin retail businesses like furniture and mattress stores. How often have you seen the advertisements? "Buy now and make no payments for 48-months, pay no interest payment for years…pay principle payments only."

The gross margin (the profit a company makes on a sale) on furniture and mattress purchases is so high that the merchant can borrow money, extend credit to you, and still make a huge profit. There is credit risk, which is a small price to pay, to fatten their profits.

Do not buy unless you need the item and have money in-hand. Remember to save monthly, in advance, so that you can pay cash when it is time to buy. Resist the temptation to buy based on want.

If you plan to buy something that has a no-interest payment offer, and you have the cash in-hand, consider the following…

CHAPTER THREE: LET'S GET PERSONAL – YOUR MONEY

- Calculate the interest costs of borrowing money for the months or years the merchant is willing to extend payment credit.
- Negotiate a discount for cash payment now, at least equal to the borrowing cost the merchant will pay to carry a no-interest loan.
- If you choose to use the no-interest payment option, make certain you invest your money, do not spend it. Make payments on-time so that you do not trigger an accrued interest penalty.

Payday Loans

Payday loans are used as a bridge to get money a few days prior to receiving your paycheck. If you need a payday loan as a bridge from the point you want to spend, to when you receive your paycheck, you are either living beyond your means or you don't earn enough to survive.

Using a payday loan may mean you are in a downward financial spiral. Payday loans will accelerate the spiral. You become a slave to fees and interest costs. Eventually the fees will consume your whole paycheck.

If you find yourself considering Payday loans (or Pawn Shops), get help from a professional counselor. You need career, budget, and financial counsel. There are plenty of agencies, some free, that can help you with budgeting and career counsel. Listen to what they say, learn, establish, and practice new habits.

On-Line Installment Loans

This is the newest loan of the bunch, and a spin-off of Payday loans (with the rates and terms to prove it). I suspect this loan type was created for the digital "natives" and those digital "immigrants" with money problems.

Within a few minutes you can complete an on-line application, and in many cases, have the money in about 24-hours. Sounds great until you review the loan rates and terms – lending rates range from mid-20% to over 1,000%. Yes, over 1,000%.

Manage your spending so that you never consider borrowing money this way. If you find yourself in a situation where you are considering this type of loan, stop and get professional financial counsel right away.

WIDE-EYED WISDOM

Tactical Money Management

Proactive money management means regular expense review. Money decisions are one area that you control – don't be the hamster. Taking ownership of your finances will directly impact the quality of your life – what you are able to achieve, experiences you are able to enjoy and the goals you are able to reach.

Don't give your money away – periodically review your expenses to see what you can reduce or cut. Redirect the expense savings to what will impact your financial well-being and future (pay down debt, invest). As you eliminate debt and invest, you will create financial flexibility. (Remember your life plan.)

When you practice awesome expense control, at some point reducing expenses will become challenging. There is only so deep a person can cut expenses and still live. Remember to enjoy the journey (by the way, this is not an excuse to throw caution – and money – to the wind). Here are some thoughts on how to approach cost cutting/expense control.

When you must reduce expenses...
- Reference your budget.
- Confirm your spending against planned spending in all categories.
- Decide what you can do without (coffee, shopping spree, new car).
- Decide what you can reduce.
- Adjust your plan and spending habits.
- Talk with your family and share thoughts and ideas so that you are all on the same page.
  - Make expense savings a game you all get to play.
- Measure your results and celebrate your success!

As you reduce spending, fill your emergency fund, savings, and investments. It is very satisfying to watch your money grow.

When you have diligently reeled in your spending/expense habits, turn your focus to increasing earnings to make the biggest difference in your financial future.

I have included a short expense check-up exercise. Use this to help you visualize what expenses can be better managed and how you can use the savings to your advantage.

CHAPTER THREE: LET'S GET PERSONAL – YOUR MONEY

Self-Reflection

What items are consuming too much of your hard-earned cash (include the amount)?

	Item	Amount
1.	_____	_____
2.	_____	_____
3.	_____	_____
4.	_____	_____
5.	_____	_____

What could you do with that money instead?

Make a positive change! You can do it!

CHAPTER FOUR
MOVING ON UP

Up to this point, we have covered the foundation for your life plan (guided by your vision and values), career choices, financial basics and now it is time to focus on a rewarding career.

But why do you have to work anyway? I mean come on, my personal life goals involve copious amounts of toes in the sand with a drink in my hand (iced tea, by the way)! When you drink your iced tea, if you want to splurge on a simple pleasure, buy some flavored syrups and turn the plain brewed tea into a gourmet drink. Restaurants charge $3 or $4 for something similar. You can make great flavored iced-tea for pennies – trust me, it is delicious.

Back to the subject at hand. In case you haven't memorized this already, here is another reminder: **<u>you</u> are responsible for yourself, your life, your future**…and this includes your career (the most likely way that you will fund your life plan)! Do not play victim or the blame game, you make the decisions and there are amazing opportunities just waiting for you. This chapter is full of wisdom about how to get the most out of your career.

Learn the good habits to repeat and the bad habits to avoid. Discover ways to make yourself more effective, how to increase your value to your organization, and how to open your mind. Each tip is a small snippet. Read them over and over. Internalize what each lesson means to you and your career. Observe others in your organization, how they behave and what drives them. Then *do something* with your new knowledge and understanding.

WIDE-EYED WISDOM

Develop a Career Mindset

Career Ownership

You own your development. Yep, you. It is nearly impossible to stay in the same spot on the learning curve. You either grow or stagnate. If you fall behind, don't blame it on the organization, the boss or the guy around the corner. The person staring back at you from the mirror each morning – yes that familiar looking one – owns your career development.

If you don't invest in your growth, your skills will become outdated, you won't be competitive, and you will flatline. Learn continuously and you won't need to worry about raises and promotions. Those will just happen.

You are the proud owner of your career, so invest in yourself continuously and enjoy the ride. Your ceiling (and earning potential) will rise with each new bit of knowledge and understanding you gain.

Empowerment

Organizations want to hand control to their best people. Think about traveling by commercial jet. Do you want a pilot with a spotless safety record with thousands of hours of commercial and fighter jet flying experience? Or would you like to turn over the controls to the guy that practices flying a biplane on a World War I video game? *But he shot down the Red Baron.*

I have often heard from confused colleagues, griping that they were not "empowered by management." Most of them failed to realize the link between empowerment and their personal knowledge and understanding. Fill up your tank and you will find that empowerment is in your hands. Develop your knowledge and understanding and you will be the pilot sooner than you think.

Industry Knowledge

Hopefully, you have joined or will join, an organization that you love. If you turn out to be one of the few that really loves your work, the journey will be much more interesting. Regardless of the organization, I can't stress enough how important it is to learn as much as you can about your industry.

Knowing the history and future potential of your industry, what works and what doesn't will be invaluable as you learn, perform your role, and progress in your career. This will also give you opportunities to look outside your organization for other roles in your chosen career field. Commit to become an industry expert.

Performance Reviews

Performance Reviews are an opportunity to gauge your professional growth. Reviews can be quite valuable when you are prepared, engaged, and ask good questions. Use your performance review as an opportunity to ask about the path to the next promotion or next raise, as well as identify ways you and the organization can support your development (new project opportunities, classes, etc.). Document the performance review discussion and use it as your guide. If your organization mandates one review per year and no more, ask your leader for an interim review, especially when you have made significant progress in your development. Your genuine interest in your leader's professional assessment will demonstrate that you are actively committed to develop yourself and increase your worth to the organization.

Be wary if your organization crams all employee reviews into a short amount of time. Don't allow yourself to be short-changed. Be your own advocate. If you need it, ask for more review time. If you have a quality leader at the helm, they will appreciate your interest in your own development and be supportive of discussing your strengths and opportunities for growth.

Understand your Organization's Mission, Vision and Value Systems

Organizations spend a boatload of time and money developing mission, vision, and value statements only to shove the document into the dark reaches of a drawer or cabinet. After a quick review of mission, vision and values, the focus turns back to running the business. In other words, leadership and employees go right back to work taking care of what they are rewarded for doing and may ignore organizational priorities while selfishly looking out for their own pocketbooks.

In 2019 Wells Fargo found out the hard way. Leadership structured a bonus plan that was unintentionally a reward for dishonesty. The plan was certainly not in alignment with Wells Fargo's mission, vision, and values. What happened? Thousands of new accounts were set-up in the names of unsuspecting customers, all without customer knowledge. To make matters worse, program oversight was lacking. A single phone call/tip from a Wells Fargo branch employee to the L.A. Times triggered an investigation that ultimately exposed the practice. Wells Fargo was fined $185 million by the U.S. Consumer Financial Protection Bureau and over 5,000 employees lost their jobs, including many highly compensated executives. Wells Fargo has their hands full with attempting to repair their image with customers, regulatory agencies, and investors.[41]

Be the exception and set yourself apart from others – learn, understand, and mold your work to the organization's mission, vision, and values.

Mission Statement: A mission statement is a description of why an organization exists. It is created to identify the overall goal of an organization with regards to the product or service it provides, its primary customers (or market), and its geographical region of operation. It may include a short statement of fundamental matters like the organization's values or philosophies, a business's main competitive advantages, or a desired future state—the "vision".[42]

Vision Statement: A vision statement is a declaration of an organization's objectives, intended to guide its internal decision-making. A vision statement is not limited to business organizations and may also be used by non-profit or governmental entities.[43]

The vision statement may also emphasize a desired future organizational state that is a stretch, believable, and attainable.

Organizational Values: "The operating philosophies or principles that guide how an organization is to conduct themselves, as well as its relationship with its customers, partners, and shareholders."[44]

Values are paramount to understand and guide how you and the organization will make decisions.

Summary: Mission, vision and values are necessary, so that each person has the roadmap to understand how and why their position and work is important to the success of the organization. Knowing each of the three is also essential

CHAPTER FOUR: MOVING ON UP

to design meaningful position descriptions and an effective organization structure.

Once you know and understand mission, vision, and values you will be more comfortable with the tasks you perform daily. It is comforting to know that you are on track. There will not always be someone available to tell you that you did your job well each day. By knowing and understanding mission, vision, and values, you will truly be the best judge of your work success.

Skills

Solve Complex Problems

> "Every complex problem has a simple solution that doesn't work."[45]
>
> H.L. Mencken

I think Mencken is saying that complex problems almost always require complex solutions and a diverse team to join in the solution process.

According to Scott E. Page, a professor of complex systems, political science, and economics at the University of Michigan, diverse groups of problem solvers outperformed groups of the most intelligent individuals, at solving complex problems. The reason: the diverse groups got stuck less often than the smart individuals, who tended to think similarly.[46]

A diverse group stands a better chance of coming up with a good solution than a single individual or a group of like individuals. Never underestimate your value or value of those around you to deal with complex problems. You may be better equipped than the most intelligent person in the room.

Negotiations

You already know the basics of how to negotiate. Early in life, most children and their parents practiced various forms of negotiations. Any meal with our grandchildren will include a round of negotiations from each of the three kids attempting to pin down the number of bites of dinner required to score dessert, watch television, etc. And do you know why they are often successful? First, they are unafraid to ask/engage, and second, they move on quickly from a "no" to a different tactic.

Effective negotiators are few and extremely valuable to their organization. Take formal negotiations classes as soon as you can, and then **practice** the skills on a regular basis. Make no mistake, you will have plenty of opportunities to negotiate in both your personal and professional lives.

Learning effective "win – win" negotiations will save you money, make you money, and help you get ahead in your career and your personal dealings. Become an expert negotiator and raise your professional ceiling.

Skills Development

Many companies train the skills necessary to do the job. However, you must improve and refine your skills so that you are the best at what you do – that is your responsibility. Look at it this way – the training function within your organization (if even available) will be limited to broad appeal training material – attempting to reach as many people with any given course, as possible.

Figure out what you must learn to develop your expertise beyond just the tasks to do your job. Identify your own education needs, present those to your leaders, and ask for their support. If they won't help fund your development, don't let that stop you. Drive skills development yourself. (If "no" is the response, ask yourself if you are with the right organization.)

Growth and development of the #1 resource in any organization – human capital – is essential to success.

Add Arrows to Your Quiver

What do I mean by this? A quiver holds arrows for the bowman. A professional bowman can be especially deadly when possessing a quiver full of sharp arrows. Professional arrows are specialized skills, abilities, knowledge, understanding, professional networks, mentors/coaches and advanced experience.

Add more arrows to your quiver by taking advantage of as many learning opportunities as possible. The more arrows you own, the more you will be recognized and tapped for your expertise. You may also develop a reputation for being able to handle anything that comes your way – talk about value.

Keep Skills, Knowledge and Understanding Relevant

Keeping skills, knowledge and understanding current should be your never-ending quest. Technological advances have caused positions and industries to

CHAPTER FOUR: MOVING ON UP

change at a revolutionary pace. Whole companies can lose relevancy in a few short years. Some examples of "leader to bust": Kodak, Blockbuster, Nokia, Xerox, Blackberry, JC Penney, and Sears. These companies did not keep up with industry advances and were left in the dust.

Whether you own a business or work for an organization you must keep your skills, knowledge and understanding current and relevant. Having many years of experience is great if your skills, knowledge, and understanding are up to date. Just consider, the person that says, "But I have 30-years of experience." The experience of that person is how to build a Conestoga wagon. Don't lean on past experience too much. (Think about the implications of "past".)

You own your career and must seek regular opportunities to develop new and/or updated skills and abilities. Don't wait for your organization to find development opportunities for you. When development opportunities are available, your organization will likely support you, but it is your job to identify the resources that will fill your intelligence tank.

I have used various means to strengthen skills and gain more knowledge and understanding. Here are my favorites:

Read: There are thousands of great books on just about any subject you can imagine. Some books are better than others. Ask for recommendations and read reviews and you will find the books that are best for you. Compare and contrast what you read with what you experience at work and in life. You will raise your career ceiling by being an avid reader.

Book Groups: Ask colleagues to join you in a book group. I usually had a subject and a book in mind when I asked my colleagues. Certain people were always interested in learning. One way or another, the people committed to learning seem to find one another.

The optimal size group in our sessions was usually six to eight people. If a group is too large some folks will not give input. Smaller groups are more comfortable with one another and will share readily.

Once the group and book are established, schedule a one-hour recurring appointment in the morning, one day per week. People seem to be fresher early in the day and ready to discuss the material.

WIDE-EYED WISDOM

The leader should prepare an outline and lead the first discussion. Rotate book group leadership going forward. Every participant should be encouraged to join in the discussion. If someone is not taking part in the discussion, ask them questions so they get the idea you want and expect them to be involved. Everyone will get the idea that their participation is important, wanted, and necessary.

Consult the meeting rules document in the Resources section at the back of the book for ideas on how to structure your book reviews. Many of the same guidelines apply. **(See Exhibit 9: Meeting Rules, p. 249)**

Audio Books: If you are on a plane, commute, or have down time, audio books work great. Title selection continues to increase, and the price is less than buying a traditional book. There are subscription services that make it even easier – you can listen in your car or at home while you are making dinner or out for a run.

Seminars: Be serious about seminars and outside educational opportunities. Yes, you are away from your workplace, but the program is work and career related. And by the way, seminars are usually paid for by your organization. If there is prep work, make sure to complete the assignment – your advance preparation will ensure your best learning opportunity.

The best way for an adult to learn is to listen and take notes as they view the presentation. Listen intently, take notes, and ask questions.

If your organization sponsored your seminar attendance, afterward prepare a synopsis of what you learned. Your synopsis will help you be an active learner and become more accountable. Plus, you will establish a high standard for the individuals and teams in your organization.

Coach or Mentor: Allow yourself to be coached and mentored. Be o.k. with the idea that you may not always like what you hear. Good coaches and mentors will stretch you – and what is discussed might "hurt". You will improve as you are pushed and stretched. A good coach or mentor will make sure that you are challenged and will be a cheerleader pushing you to do your best along the way.

CHAPTER FOUR: MOVING ON UP

Please keep in mind that leaders from your organization are there to support you. If you are willing and sincere, people will move heaven and earth to give you the best chance to succeed. Make sure that you take advantage of their support and act on their challenges. The most frustrating experience for a coach or mentor is when time and effort are expended with a mentee and that person does not perform. The mentee may revert to making excuses. That won't fly. Mentors and coaches are in high demand, their time is valuable.

On the Job: On the job training is usually a mixed bag. In my experience, organizations are all over the board on how they train and educate new and long-time associates. Don't be surprised if the training is sink or swim.

That said, no matter what, when an education or training program is available, take advantage of it. Don't miss out on opportunities. Colleagues have consistently remarked that they learned something valuable even when attending a training session on a subject in which they were already an expert.

Become a subject matter expert. At a young age I was able to travel to other company locations quite often, all because I had become an expert in our company systems and processes. The exposure was great for my career and my confidence. I met leaders throughout the company and became well known, which helped me to garner promotions and salary increases. By becoming the subject matter expert, people gravitated to me for learning opportunities and to fix problems.

Open your mind and become inquisitive. Seek to understand why things work a certain way. Don't settle for just the "how." Understanding "why" will allow you to connect the dots and become more knowledgeable and develop keen understanding.

You will become an adept problem solver when you know what, how and why – which will make your job more interesting, raise your value to the organization and keep you steps ahead of those competing with you.

WIDE-EYED WISDOM

Habits for Success

Under Promise and Over Deliver

Being overly optimistic can get you into trouble. Unrealistic promises can lead to negative reviews. Be realistic and never overpromise.

> "If you will promise less and do more, your boss will eventually put your name on the door."[47]
>
> *Anonymous*

You will have a good idea of what it takes to finish a task. Nailing down an exact date can be difficult. When asked for a timeline, present a range of optimistic to pessimistic. If there are dependencies or resources required to meet the due date, make those known as you are estimating the completion date range. Give an honest estimate of what resources are needed to deliver on your task. When something unexpected stands in your way of delivery, raise the issue. Don't wait until the last minute. (Do your best to solve the issue, or at a minimum make a recommendation.)

Be on Time

Get to work and to scheduled meetings on-time. Whether you are in an office, or work remotely, your colleagues need to know they can count on you. Habitual tardiness can be interpreted as a lack of respect for your team members and a disregard for the importance of your work.

If for some reason you can't make it on-time let your team know in advance. Granted, when you are always on-time you may be alone for a few minutes in the meeting room. Better to be early than late.

Be Prepared: *Bankers – another true story*

Years ago, the CEO of our company gave me a great gift. He enrolled me in an Executive Management College program conducted by Stanford University. It was a week-long program that was packed solid from early morning to late evening.

There were full-day segments in Finance, Operations, Marketing, Human Resources, and business cases galore. Advance preparations were intense. We were given 90-days to complete three textbooks and about a dozen business cases. I studied everything carefully and completed the entire assignment on-time.

CHAPTER FOUR: MOVING ON UP

There were approximately 50 students in attendance. It appeared that two or three of the 50 people spent the time and effort to prepare on all subjects. My advance preparations enabled me to understand everything the professors presented. During the Finance class segment, I participated in an excellent discussion one-on-one with the finance professor. The evening of the finance class, I was approached by a group of Vice Presidents from a major California bank, asking me to explain net present values to them. Wait – what? My background is in marketing and business operations. Yes, these bank VP's asked me to explain net present values. So, I did. Advance preparation is powerful!

That story aside, do not attempt to fake your way through meetings, or your work. Make sure you are always well prepared. There are teammates, customers and other stakeholders counting on you. Besides, others can tell when you aren't prepared. Don't insult their intelligence with some lame excuse.

When you are prepared the whole team will be better prepared. Your preparation will create positive peer pressure among colleagues. All team members will learn that they must be well prepared.

If you are in school, make advance preparation your personal commitment. Call it the "term of commitment." Commit to complete every assignment and/or study preparation, ahead of the due date. If you are asked to read, make it a priority to read the assignment right away. If you are asked to answer questions do them right away. If you have a paper due, make sure it is finished ahead of the due date. Complete assigned material on time and engage with your professors during class.

Your scores will improve, and finals prep will likely be short reviews, instead of all-night information cramming. There will be no unfinished work hanging over your head. An uncluttered mind equals excellent play.

Check for Clarity and Understanding

Miscommunication occurs often in organizations and will plunder valuable time and resources. We think we hear something correctly and go in a direction, only to find out there was a misunderstanding. If only we understood the first time. I bet you have plenty of examples of miscommunication.

Take time to clarify what was said or written. Be courageous enough to summarize in your own words, and repeat back, what you heard or read. Especially if that means speaking up in a meeting. It is better to repeat the command in your own words and know the direction is clear. Chances are, there are others that want clarification but are too afraid to ask.

Devour Your Work
When you let things pile up several things happen:
- Pressure mounts
- The job becomes more stressful
- Work quality diminishes
- Work is not as enjoyable
- The feeling of accomplishment dissipates
- People that depend on you lose trust
- Performance reviews become problematic
- You leave your job or are asked to leave

When you have something to do, get it done. Don't wait. When you get things done on time or ahead of schedule you will be known for being a highly productive associate.

Devouring work is common to high achievers. The best and brightest devour their work. Each one of them stays focused and finishes consistently, with excellence. Being ahead of the workload gives them opportunities and free time to develop additional skills and abilities – placing them ahead of their peers. Leaders place a high value on their achievers and will reward them with extras, such as working from home, taking time off or flexing the workday.

Perform work on time, accurately and efficiently, because you never know what tomorrow will bring. At the same time, raise your ceiling and separate yourself from your peers.

"Give it a Whirl"
Never decline an opportunity by telling a customer, colleague, or leader, "that's not my job." In my view, that individual just rehearsed how to slam the door on their career.

There were times when I was asked to perform roles or create new functions without prior experience. Some of the subjects I had barely read about. When asked to step into something brand new to me, I had to learn quickly and always discovered that I *could* do the job. New challenges will stretch you and cause you to think in ways that you had never considered. You will become less opinionated and learn that there is a lot more going on in the world than what you see on the surface.

If you are asked to do something new for the organization, even if you have never done it before, give it a whirl. There is nothing like a little bit of pressure to be challenged to learn something new. You will discover how much more you are capable of, help your organization and yourself. It takes courage to jump into something new. Find your courage. You may experience a few bumps and bruises, but you will eventually succeed.

Leaders really appreciate, and value the people they can count on. Be one of those people that take the risk to learn something new. Your new experience builds your value. No one can ever take that experience away. Remember the bowman? Give it a whirl and you will add professional arrows to your quiver.

Set Realistic Stretch Goals

Set goals that will stretch your professional knowledge, understanding, and capabilities. You will grow and develop as you set stretch goals and achieve them. Chances are you will grow even if you miss your stretch goals. After all, those goals are a "stretch."

My goal setting focus was usually twofold, learning and performance. The learning goals were usually achieved on my personal time. (At home, my family would tease me about reading so many business and leadership books.)

Performance goals were linked directly to my work and our team's work. Performance goals were usually a combination of the organization's goals and how to build and develop my team members.

Set goals, measure your results, and you will raise your ceiling yet again.

Say Thank You

Be genuine and thank others. A personal thank you might be the only bit of good news a person receives at work or at home. Believe me, long after the work is finished and career completed, your colleagues will remember the people that really appreciated them.

A simple handwritten note, card, small gift, recognition lunch, e-mail, personal visit, or any number of other ideas can work wonders. By recognizing people for their work, you will form strong bonds and develop relationships that will help you, your team, and your organization.

Make sure you take advantage of all opportunities to thank your team. You will stand out from the crowd when you are genuinely thankful.

Take Ownership – *the "three stooges"* …another true story

Early in the third year of my first career job, there was an incident at our office with three company associates. The events of the afternoon and evening of that fateful workday are indelibly etched in my memory. Now, looking back, what happened is comic, but at the time it was not so amusing.

I was part of a small buying team that officed in Oakland, CA. We bought frozen and deli food products for distribution to independent supermarkets up and down the west coast. Our office housed a small population of about 15, including people that worked in our data center and a small fresh meat buying operation. We worked at a fast pace and days passed quickly. We had to stay ahead of job demands or risk getting run over by the work.

At the time, profits were under plan, so our senior leaders gave the directive to reduce labor. One of the positions being eliminated was held by a woman in our Oakland office. She supported the accountant stationed in Oakland and would occasionally take overflow work from our buying office staff.

It was Wednesday about noon. (Wednesday was Ad Meeting day at our Fremont, CA office.) The leader of our office traveled to Fremont each Wednesday and would be in the Ad meeting from noon through the end of the day. (Creating a weekly food advertisement for independently owned grocery stores.)

Our company controller had arrived from the Fremont office. He came to Oakland to take the two assistants to lunch, as a farewell to the woman losing her position. His visit was a nice gesture.

Anyway, one o'clock rolled around and there was no sign of the controller or the two assistants. Pretty soon it was two o'clock and still no controller or assistants.

After a long afternoon of waiting and wondering where the two assistants and the controller might be, we finally had our answer at about 6 p.m., when in strolls (I mean, stumbles) the now, three stooges.

It was obvious from their conditions that we had a problem on our hands. In fact, not only did we have "a" problem, we had three problems. Fortunately for the three "problems", the boss left before they went to lunch and would not be back until Thursday morning.

CHAPTER FOUR: MOVING ON UP

Problem #1: *The controller was a "sleepy" drunk, so he went into the break room, found a couch, and went to sleep. We were a bit lucky with this one. Our attention turned to the remaining two.*

Problem #2: *The woman losing her job was a "happy drunk". She was trying her best to sit on the lap of one of the two buyers. (That would be me. I did my level best to avoid her and keep her in the chair opposite my desk.)*

Problem #3: *The woman with a go-forward position in our buying office was a "mean drunk" (ironically, also the one that hummed, "If I only had a brain", on a regular basis).*

I don't drink alcohol. I can't stand the taste. When we were at a function, I would always capture the car keys when others planned to drink. I have heard that people can be very different when they are drunk. Man, did I have proof that Wednesday evening. In alcohol terms, 200 proof.

The question at hand was how to get each of them home safely. During the commotion that followed, we lost track of the sleepy drunk. Fortunately, he was able to make it home without incident. To this day I don't know if he got a ride or drove himself home. I would like to believe he got a ride home.

My buyer colleague and I kept telling the two women that we would take them home safely and get them to work on-time in the morning if they would only let us help. Pleading with them to follow us to our cars, we promised that each of us would drive one of them home. We asked for cooperation, and home addresses. I'm sure you can guess – neither cooperated.

The happy drunk kept doing her thing which wasn't really causing a major problem. I just had to keep her at arms-length. The mean drunk became increasingly surly, then the foul language started. Her favorite phrase became, "F… you." She wouldn't cooperate with either of us. After several rounds of pleading and hearing her response of "F… you", my counterpart and I were running low on ideas and it was getting late. The designated driver role only works if the drunk will tell you their home address, get in the car, fasten their seat belt, and sit still while you drive them home.

Once the foul language started, the situation spiraled further out of control. The accountant stationed in our building stepped out of his office to see what the commotion was all about. After a heavy office stapler hit the doorway next to his head, he decided to retreat to the safety of his office, swiftly closing the door behind him. (Coward!) I can still see the next move by our mean drunk, as she took a swing at the nose of my colleague, the other buyer. At 6'5" tall, he bent in the middle to avoid her roundhouse right. Thank goodness she wasn't the picture of quickness or she might have dropped him right there.

Finally, the lightbulb went on. The mean drunk's boyfriend happened to be a truck driver for our company (and as luck would have it, had just arrived at our facility from his daily route). Let's call him! A quick call to dispatch and he was on his way from the transportation office, up the stairs to our buying office.

The other buyer and I were relieved to see the boyfriend step into our office and hoped to hand over ownership of problem #3, mean drunk, aka his girlfriend. Upon seeing his girlfriend sloppy drunk he looked right into the eyes of my office colleague and I, then blurted out, "Well, who is responsible for this?". I was in disbelief. What do you mean who is responsible for this? (And we trust this guy to drive a loaded 53' semi-truck in heavy traffic in the bay area of Northern California?) Do you think someone held her down and poured whiskey down her throat?

There is always someone else to blame. The person that owns the problem is shielded by friends and family, or by themselves as they finger point or throw an unsuspecting person under the bus.

Own up to what is your responsibility. Resist the temptation to pass the blame to others. People will respect you for taking responsibility for your mistakes. You will also be forgiven.

Oh, by the way, we were able to get the two ladies to their homes safely. They both made it back to the office on-time the next morning. Obviously, they had to answer for their actions with H.R. and our office leader.

> "A man may make mistakes, but he isn't a failure until he starts blaming someone else."[48]
>
> *John Wooden*

Offer Solutions

Solving problems is risky. Everyone you meet in any organization is very capable of pointing out problems (and they do – often very loudly).

I have found that while everyone is pointing out problems, only a few people are committed to providing solutions. Most people just don't have the courage to put a solution in place. Somehow implementing solutions is not worth the risk. Or maybe they are waiting for permission or are hoping someone else will take care of it.

CHAPTER FOUR: MOVING ON UP

It takes courage to be right or wrong. Learning to step up and solve problems is worth the risk. There is nothing like a messy situation or complex problem that sparks initiative. Problem solving also provides opportunities for budding leaders to rise to the occasion.

> "Courage is not living without fear. Courage is being scared to death and doing the right thing anyway."[49]
>
> Chae Richardson

If you want to succeed, be courageous enough to implement solutions, and succeed or fail. Chances are you know exactly what to do and you will succeed. If you fail, learn from the experience, and get right back in the game on the next problem.

Another tidbit of wisdom…if you are pointing out a problem to someone else, make a recommendation or two on how to solve it. Or solve the problem, and then inform others.

For Leaders: If your team brings you problems but no solutions, try the following…
- Ask yourself if you are performing as a manager or a leader. (Read on for my definition.)
- Ask the bringer of the problem to recommend a potential solution or multiple solutions.
    - If their solution sounds like it will solve the issue, then…
        - Ask them to put the solution in motion.
        - Be careful not to shoot down their idea unless it would be a disaster.
    - If you hope to develop the person, and their solution is not optimal, but will work, then maybe their idea *is* fine for now. (Later as the associate is more comfortable and confident with problem solving, offer counsel to help them improve.)

Leaders and managers differ in their approach to problem solving. The manager may think she/he must solve every problem. The manager's office is problem central, and the door seems to revolve one problem (I mean, person) after another. On the other hand, the leader listens carefully to the issue, asks pertinent questions, delegates problem solving, approves an implementation plan, and timeline. If necessary, a follow-up meeting is scheduled. Leaders operate on a Plan, Implement, Control methodology.

Think for Yourself
Don't believe everything you read or hear. There is constant misinformation that clouds the truth. Some of the misinformation is intentional. But, quite often, what has been reported incorrectly, is unintentional. Misinformation can be the result of carelessness caused by poor listening skills, fear of challenging what has been communicated or someone's effort to dramatize the situation. The pressure to perform may also send us down the wrong path. Or sometimes, stuff just happens.

Take the time to clarify as much as possible. Do not assume. Assumptions can lead to bad decisions. If something doesn't smell or sound right to you, ask questions and listen carefully. Once you have learned as much as you can, think for yourself. Don't follow blindly.

Trustworthiness – to Gain and to Lose
To be a highly valued colleague, people must trust you in all situations. Trust enables you to carve out your place as a high integrity associate and valuable organizational asset. Organizations lean on the most valuable and trusted associates. The only people invited to confidential meetings are those that can be trusted with privileged information. As you develop awesome trust, you will be tapped to help solve the most serious problems, as well as to discuss and consider major opportunities.

> "You can have a compelling vision, a rock-solid strategy, excellent communication skills, innovative insight, and a skilled team, but if people don't trust you, you will never get the results you want."[50]
>
> *David Horsager*

If something is confidential keep it that way. Some people hear something confidential and can't wait to tell others, probably to "look" important. If you are trusted with confidential information, don't discuss it with anyone else.

I made it a priority to keep confidential items a secret. I wouldn't share confidential information with my wife or family. To this day, my family will tell

CHAPTER FOUR: MOVING ON UP

you that I didn't talk about work very much. The fact that I could keep privileged information secret, made me a trusted colleague. I am proud to say that at all levels I never betrayed the trust of the organization or my colleagues.

- **Rule #1:** Trust may take years to build. Begin to build trust with all stakeholders, and never stop.
- **Rule #2:** You can lose trust during a momentary lapse in judgment. Once trust is lost, there is a good chance you will never gain it back.

(These points apply to your personal life too. Put yourself in the position of the person that has been betrayed. Think about how you would feel. Could you ever trust the betrayer again?)

Coaches and Mentors

Mentors and coaches help you develop professionally and personally. A **coach** is someone that will help you improve your skills. A **mentor** is someone who will hold you accountable and challenge you. Ever heard of tough love? If so, that is what a mentor will bring.

Don't expect coaches and mentors to give you all the answers. Each are likely to ask you questions, lots of them. Be prepared to be challenged to reach your own solutions. Find one or more skilled professionals that are willing to help you develop. I once had six mentors simultaneously. My mentors had different backgrounds, skills, and perspectives. It was up to me to ask the right questions and use what they taught me within the framework of my own style.

Mentors and coaches must be trustworthy. Be careful not to ask just anyone to be a mentor or coach.

- Don't ask the people that will tell you want you want to hear. They will just confuse you.
- Don't choose your friends. You need candid feedback, not happy talk.
- Choose a trusted expert that is willing to take time to help you.

Have Fun

One colleague would gauge the temperature of his team by asking if they were still having fun. The responses he received gave him a great idea of how his team was doing. His approach was refreshing and pretty darn successful.

WIDE-EYED WISDOM

Work play is priceless. I recall many times when we had fun at the office. We had one office that armed themselves with Nerf dart guns. A short war would break out at least once a day. The mood of the office was playful, but each person performed their work at a high-level.

Each workplace needs an instigator that will help the others have a good time while they are working. Make sure that your instigator is playing in good taste. Monitor the situation so others don't ruin a high-quality work culture.

Be sure to balance fun with work – after all, no one is paying you to be a Nerf war champion. Work and fun can be mixed to create a healthy and productive work culture. There is nothing like feeling positive energy and excitement, ready to get to work and win together!

Do It Right One Time – The First Time

The speed at which we find ourselves operating these days often leads to the creation of more problems and rework. The old saying, "do it right the first time," is true.

Imagine how many people it would take to run an organization if there were no problems. If work were performed perfectly the first time, most organizations would probably need half the staff. Customers would be much happier (not to mention the employees).

Take an extra beat to stop and understand before generating subpar deliverables. Despite all best efforts, mistakes will happen. Mistakes due to poor time management or lazy effort should never be acceptable.

Be the Best

> "If you are not the lead dog, the view never changes."[51]
>
> *Robert Benchley*

There will always be demand for the best people. Commit yourself to perform at the highest level. You will always have a job and will be highly valued. Plus, knowing that you are the best will give you a great sense of satisfaction and confidence, not to mention a scenic and pleasurable view from your lead position.

When you are the best at what you do, opportunities will find you.

CHAPTER FOUR: MOVING ON UP

Sleep on It – A Cautionary True Story…

I am sure that we have all been in situations where some bad news or a confrontation throttles us toward an immediate and explosive reaction. In the workplace, as in relationships, serious damage can occur from ill-conceived, knee-jerk reactions. Here is a real-life example of sleep on it before you react…

Our company was in a growth by acquisition mode. It seemed like every few months there was another acquisition announcement. Across the country, our Midwest-based organization was buying. The company set a goal to operate our supply chain in every state in the U.S. With sales of about $4 billion when I started, within three or four years we had passed the $10 billion mark. Most of the sales gains were from acquisitions.

One of the most recent acquisitions was in our region and my team was assigned responsibility for another distribution center in our area. Just after we completed the latest distribution center project, our company announced yet another acquisition in California. The company bought a local competitor that was about three times the size of our bay area division.

As you spend time in an industry, you will come to know many other players, including competitors. The new acquisition, being so close to our offices and with faces we knew, generated an immediate rivalry among several staff members. And by this time, we had all grown accustomed to the fact that acquisitions meant some amount of duplicate labor – which resulted in the elimination of some positions. Both staffs felt threatened and wondered what would happen to their jobs.

A good friend of mine, we will call him Mr. D, was the leader of one of the most important divisions of the company. Mr. D was a very friendly guy, high energy, positive, fun loving and one of the most successful people in our division.

One day not long after the acquisition of our bay area competitor, Mr. D received what I will call a "nasty gram" in the mail. The letter was from his counterpart, Mr. J, of the acquired company. Mr. J's letter was an attack about how bad things were at our company – openly critical of Mr. D and his business unit. That letter (now a permanent record), informed Mr. D what would change when Mr. J took over. What precipitated the letter I will never know, but Mr. J even copied our national vice president (who happened to have tremendous respect for Mr. D). Wow – that's guts, or something else…

Mr. D was livid. He had no idea why someone would write something like that. He hadn't talked with Mr. J in months. Mr. D's initial reaction was to write a letter in response, a letter that would be complete by afternoon and sent in the interoffice mail the same evening.

WIDE-EYED WISDOM

Once Mr. D completed his reply nasty gram, he asked me to read it and make edits. Mr. D's retort was not nice, in fact, "vile" might be a good term to use. I read the letter. Mr. D asked me what I thought. I told him it was probably an accurate takedown in response. Then I told him not to send that letter in the evening interoffice mail. Instead, I advised him to put it in his desk drawer, sleep on it and we would talk in the morning.

Early the next morning a very apologetic Mr. J was on the phone to Mr. D., having just received a "dressing down" from our national vice president about his unprofessional conduct. Mr. J was in serious hot water with the acquiring company leadership.

Mr. D came to my office and told me that he had just received a personal apology. He went on to thank me for telling him not to mail the nasty response. You see, the letter would have been in the interoffice mail and delivered to Mr. J the afternoon after the apology call. (Besides, a return nasty gram was not the best way to handle the situation.)

Embarrassment averted we both learned some powerful lessons.
1. It pays to take the high road.
2. Take time to decompress (and even sleep) on an emotional response.
3. Don't respond to every bit of criticism lobbed your way.
4. Once something is put in writing, it becomes a permanent record.

Don't Assume – *There is Almost Always More to the Story*

I have learned time and time again to take extra care when making judgements about others. Better yet, don't judge people. There is almost always more to the story than what is readily visible. Somewhere below the surface are facts that must become known to fully understand the situation.

Picture yourself with me, at a men's league softball game many years ago. It was late June in the Willamette Valley. The summer evening was warm, and the smell of the fresh cut grass was sweet. Prior to game time our softball team would stretch, throw, and run as we prepared to play. This baseball diamond didn't have banks of lights, but that didn't matter since there would be plenty of light for our game. The sun was still high in the sky, hours from the horizon. At 6 p.m., in early summer, darkness is still about 3 hours away. Even by 9:00 p.m. there is still twilight for another 20-minutes or so.

Temperatures were in the low eighties and it just felt wonderful to be on the field. Playing softball makes me feel like a kid again, even if it is just slow pitch. There was nervous energy all around, as each of us prepared to play.

CHAPTER FOUR: MOVING ON UP

I played the outfield. (One of those alignments with four outfielders.) I was stationed in left-center field. There was always lots of action in the area I covered. I ran well and if the batted ball was airborne, and I got there, the hitter would be out.

In sports, one thing I did well was catch. I could catch just about anything. For me, playing defense was more fun than hitting. There was nothing better than snuffing out the hopes of the other team by running down what looked like a sure hit and recording an out. There was less pressure playing defense. The real pressure was standing at home plate with everyone's eyes in the park fixed on you.

On the adjoining field a girls fastpitch softball game was in the works. It is amazing how fast and under control 11 and 12-year old kids can throw a pitch. I'm not sure the men on our team could hit anything those girls would have thrown to us. It was obvious that they had been playing softball most of their lives. Some probably had a bat, ball, and glove from the time they could walk.

During our game and in-between pitches, I would sneak a glance over at the girl's field to see how things were going. The scene was alive – not only the game, but unfortunately some controversy stirred up by spectators (about 25 to 30 people in the stands at game-time). I assume the spectators were mostly parents. Some folks were there to encourage their daughters while others were there to watch their kids win.

Rather than cheer and encourage, some parents seemed to think the only thing that mattered was the Win. Perhaps in some sad way, the parents own self-esteem was intrinsically tied to the outcome of their kid's game. Or maybe they watched too many games on television with a growing confidence in critiquing the officials – who knows the true motivation, but what I do know, is it created an incredible scene.

As skilled as those young softball players were, it was unlikely (if not impossible) that any of the girls would ever play professional softball. There are other things you can hope to learn or experience while playing sports... such as the love of the game, teamwork, maturity, confidence, self-discipline, new skills, friendships, fun and recreation. One or two of these young ladies might have gone on to play competitively in high school or even be fortunate enough to receive scholarship money to play in college.

I watched and listened as several parents hurled verbal abuse toward the middle-aged home plate umpire. It was difficult to tell what started the verbal onslaught. The criticism from a verbose group of people on the third base side started as the first pitch was thrown and continued for the first two or three innings. I still don't understand how the stakes of this children's game could create such intense emotions. The embarrassing actions of the parents was tough to watch, even for a bystander. If I had been playing in that game and my parents acted that way, I would have wanted to hit the exit, or hide.

The abusive behavior continued until and without warning, the home plate umpire unsnapped his chest protector, shin guards and mask, then gently laid them down on home plate. He didn't say a word to the parents, coaches or the players. The umpire made his way up the first baseline and toward the exit. He had obviously reached his limit of verbal abuse for the evening and was leaving the diamond.

One very mouthy man sitting on the third base side jumped up and yelled, "Where do you think you are going?" The umpire stopped for a moment to answer the question, but before he could say a word, another volley came from the heckler, "Why don't you get back here and do what you are getting paid to do?"

The response from the umpire was classic. In his calm matter of fact voice he said, **"I'm not getting paid. I'm a volunteer".**

You could hear a pin drop in that place. Everyone went dead quiet as the umpire made his way off the playing field and to his car, presumably on his way home, for as one would hope a much better finish to the evening. Anything had to be better than the abuse he took that evening on a field of play.

Some 30-years later my mind's eye still holds vivid pictures of the events of that evening. I can see the outfielders, the infielders, pitcher, catcher, and umpire. Of course, the "cheering" section along the third base line making total jerks of themselves is there too.

The parents of those girls should have been ashamed of themselves for verbally assaulting that man while their girls played. They couldn't see past their own obsession with winning, to recognize that he was there to help their kids develop softball skills and have some fun. I'll bet a large faction of the "fans" in attendance didn't even know the rules of the game, much less be skilled enough to critique an umpire. They brought a critical eye of ignorance, and a yapping mouth with them. The volunteer umpire took time away from his family, and perhaps other personal priorities to help those girls. A tip of the baseball cap to him for making the sacrifice, and how he handled the situation.

Let's run through some of the lessons this experience teaches about judging and reacting, especially without all of the facts:
- Be ladies and gentlemen in all situations – always treat others with respect and kindness.
- There is almost always more to the story, so do not make hasty assumptions. Incomplete knowledge does not excuse bad behavior.

CHAPTER FOUR: MOVING ON UP

- Show grace, people make mistakes.
- Rush to judgment and damage can be difficult to fix or last forever.
- You don't need to voice an opinion on everything.
- It is better to be the voice of reason.
- If your friends or family become part of a mob scene, do your best to reel them in, immediately.
- Listening, learning, and understanding is powerful, yet rare.
- When your mouth is closed, it is impossible to stick your foot in it.

The People that Make the (Work) World Go 'Round

Group Projects

Hopefully, you learned a lot in school about how to work successfully as a team, on group projects. If you haven't learned how to work as a team you'd better get going. At work, you will be involved as a team member or leader of group projects more than you may realize. Some projects will be cross-functional, and you may be working with people you don't know.

A limited amount of work is "solo", brush up on your group project skills.

Teamwork

You won't win alone. The most satisfying success you will experience is with your team. Find and use resources that will help you understand how to be the most effective teammate you can be.

The best thing you can do for your team is do your job to the best of your ability. You must be **trustworthy and reliable,** day in and day out. (As an example, if you happen to play basketball and are the top 3-point shooter, you better be in the right position when your play is called, because that ball is coming your way. It will be difficult for you to explain why the ball sailed untouched into the stands.)

Respect Others

Always treat people with respect, even if you don't like them. Think about how you felt the last time someone was rude to you. You certainly felt wronged and devalued. In the future you may steer clear of that person or experience lingering bad blood.

Often, when faced with a major purchase decision, my wife and I will discuss our needs, wants, and questions in advance of our shopping trip. She is usually the researcher, armed with questions and seeking information. While shopping, at times salespeople devalue Cindy by ignoring her and focusing their attention on me. That lack of respect is at their peril. What they don't know and haven't taken the opportunity to learn, is that she is <u>the</u> primary decision maker. I'm usually just along for the ride and there to support her decision. As the expert decision maker, she has the prerogative to take her buying power elsewhere and when disrespected, that is exactly what she does.

Treating people with respect pays big dividends. People naturally gravitate to those they trust, respect and can count on. When trusted, you are approachable and safe to your colleagues. Your kind attitude and manner, even in tough situations, draws people to you.

Share Information

Some people believe that it is advantageous to withhold information. That could not be further from the truth. If there is information, a system, process, or tool that will help others do a better job, share it. Be a key resource by helping your colleagues improve. When they improve the team will improve.

When you are known for being a key resource, your "expert" power quotient is building. As an expert you can influence in ways that you never dreamed of. Of course, if the information is confidential keep it that way.

Relationships

Your professional network can either be priceless or worthless. I've worked with colleagues that were masters at building relationships. Some of my colleagues benefitted personally by millions of dollars. Those personal benefits were in part, due to awesome professional relationships. The reason: people work closely with people they know, like and trust.

Hang out with the right people. Surround yourself with people smarter than you. Develop as many friends and trusted contacts as you can. Learn from them. Upwardly mobile people create a wave-action that can be ridden, much

CHAPTER FOUR: MOVING ON UP

like riding a breaking ocean wave. You can learn from those folks and ride their wave until you are able to create your own.

Don't ever make enemies or harbor grudges. You can't run an effective organization if people are fighting with each other. The drama created by infighting will drain the life out of you and the organization.

Know Your Colleagues

Everyone is important to the success of the team. Make it a practice to get to know everyone at your office. Or, in larger operations get to know as many people as you can – from the receptionist, the janitor, operations teams, the IT developer, to the president.

Make an honest effort to engage beyond a superficial manner. When a team cares about one another, they are more likely to perform at an optimal level. When a colleague knows that you really care about them, they will go through fire for you.

Work With, Not For

Have you ever heard this phrase, "So and so works for me"? My antenna goes up every time I hear that comment. To me, that comment points to an antiquated, hierarchical structure and focus on "self" rather than the "team". The more modern, appropriate, and effective view of the work relationship is that leaders and their team both work *for* our organization. We work *with* one another. We don't work *for* the leader.

When you are in the leader position, you work *with* the team you lead. Do what it takes so the team works *with* you. The team will decide whether they want to follow where you want to lead them. By the way, **the leader is there to serve** the organization, customers, and team. Not the other way around.

Step-Up/Volunteer

Leaders want and need team members who will step-up when a volunteer is necessary. When crickets are the answer to a solicitation for volunteers, you can bet your leaders are taking stock of the situation. Silence is not golden.

Step forward when volunteers are needed. Stretch, learn, develop, and increase your value to your organization.

WIDE-EYED WISDOM

You won't be able to be in on everything, so encourage coworkers to get in the game too. Share the load as a team and experience success together.

Just Win, Don't Worry About Who Receives Credit

Teamwork is at its best when no one on the team cares who receives individual credit. Most of my career has been spent in high-pressure, fast-paced jobs. Our buying office team at each location had to stay steps ahead of customer demand for tens of thousands of items. We dealt with all types of shipping problems and customer demands. (You would not believe the stories.) Our job was to anticipate sales demand on our assigned food products, buy in advance, keep the product fresh and meet an order fill-rate of 97%+. Customers ordered today for delivery tomorrow and we better have product ready and the food better be fresh. Trust me, a food buying office is for you if you thrive on intense pressure and fast pace.

> "It is amazing how much can be accomplished if no one cares who gets credit."[52]
>
> *John Wooden*

As the leader, I would frequently tell our team that our buying office performance reminded me of sports officials. If the game is played and the referees or umpires go unnoticed, they must have performed well. Our work team did our best to make work "uneventful", which meant we had done a good job and went unnoticed. If our customers or executives noticed our buying team, that meant we had some serious problems.

Don't worry about getting credit. Do your job to the best of your ability. If you perform your role well, you will be doing your part for the team. When all team members collectively do their best, you can accomplish what you once viewed as impossible.

Celebrate

People get wrapped up in today's demands and they forget to celebrate success. Consider taking on the role of head-cheerleader and initiate celebrations.

Regular celebrations help the organization, team, and you in many ways:
- Build teamwork

CHAPTER FOUR: MOVING ON UP

- Increase trust and morale
- Increase positive motivation
- Rewards flow
- Encourage high-quality work
- Stakeholder satisfaction improves
- You get the most important projects
- Build top organizations
- Achieve personal goals
- Become recession proof
- Others aspire to join your team

Beware – Drama

Nothing in my college courses prepared me for dealing with personal issues at work. There are times when you must help a team member with a serious problem. I understand that responsibility and will always help a teammate.

On the other hand, I have never been able to reconcile how ridiculous, petty issues made it into work. Each inflicted so much damage. I can only guess why some people seemed to need attention. Team spirit, morale, and performance are compromised by people that create drama at work. By drama, I mean gossip, inuendo, threats, bad jokes, harassment…you get the picture.

Leave that stuff out of the organization. There is no place for it. If you bring, create, or participate in any of the above you will find yourself in serious discussions with your leaders and Human Resources.

Believe me when I say that all the people in the organization have better things to do than deal with drama. You never want to draw that type of attention to yourself.

Communication

Meetings

In almost every instance, meetings are a colossal waste of time. I am convinced that organizations waste billions of dollars on unproductive meeting babble. The root of the "meeting problem" is that very few leaders know when a meeting is truly warranted. And if a meeting is warranted most don't know how to lead the session. Think twice about calling meetings. Do you really need to meet, or would a quick phone call and discussion take care of the issue?

When a meeting is called, people are late, unprepared, don't understand the meeting purpose, meet without an agenda, and go off track by telling stories that don't relate to the issue at hand. Without purpose, organization and leadership, meetings are doomed. Some meetings even turn into a session where the participants talk themselves out of necessary action.

Many decisions can be made quickly and efficiently, without expending the resources that are incinerated in a meeting. If the right decision can be made without the masses, do the team a favor and make the decision.

For those committed to successful meeting outcomes, develop a meeting culture starting with a meeting rules document. Meeting rules will create important structure and standards in your organization.

If your organization does not have a meeting rules document, develop one. Look in **Resources Exhibit 9: Meeting Rules. P. 249.**

Face to Face or Phone

The digital age has enabled people to avoid one another. Technology has hatched generations of hermits by enabling people to take up permanent residency inside their smartphone and/or computer. More and more people don't know how to relate to one another on a personal level. Next time you are at a restaurant, look around you. What do you see? How many people are peering into their smart phones instead of talking with their table mate(s)?

Or how many times have you tried to contact an organization through their website or by phone and never heard back. Treating customers that way is pathetic and unacceptable.

Endless e-mail trails seem to be the rule at many workplaces. Most issues could be solved immediately, if one person got up from their desk and went to see the other person (or picked up the phone to talk).

Make sure you treat customers and colleagues with respect by personally engaging them as much as possible. People aren't likely to remember all outcomes of your dealings, but they will remember how they felt when dealing with you. Be more engaging and become the person others prefer to deal with.

CHAPTER FOUR: MOVING ON UP

E-mail

A former colleague, a vice president in our company, would regularly write 1,000 plus word e-mails. She sent regular late evening dissertations via-email on a regular basis. I won't say she was the *leader* of her team, but she was in the leadership position. She managed her subordinates through e-mail. (Notice I didn't say she *led* her subordinates.) Her example is an unbelievable misuse of e-mail and a terribly ineffective attempt to lead. Her leadership attempt was chaotic, resulting in poor morale and substandard operating performance.

There is no way the people in her department would read her e-mails. The sheer number of words was far too much to digest. No one, not even direct reports would read what she sent.

I met with her and recommended that she keep her messages crisp with few bullet points, no more than what will fit on one screen shot.

Important/Urgent Items

Important/urgent items deserve personal attention. If time is of the essence or the subject is important, it is counterintuitive to fire off an e-mail, buried amongst countless other messages.

When you are working on an important item, the wrong answer is, "but I sent them an e-mail".

If you have something that is urgent/important, pick up the phone or go visit the other party face to face.

My Preferred E-mail Message Types

Keep your message content manageable. If the message won't fit on one screen shot, it is too long. Never ask the reader to scroll to read your message, most will not take the time.

Good Uses for E-mail:
- Quick updates/Organizational announcement/Information sharing
- Distribute documents
- Meeting invitation
- A thank you message or to recognize someone (although if geography permits, in person is better to say "thank you" or "job well done")

WIDE-EYED WISDOM

E-mail Wisdom
- Ask yourself if you should call or meet face to face (the most effective way to solve something is one-time, in person).
- Don't use e-mail to assign work to others – talk to your colleague when you need to hand-off work.
- Don't copy the masses.
- E-mail is not a CYA tool.
- Write short crisp e-mails in simple language.
- You don't need a read receipt on everything you send.
- Be judicious about the use of priority – if something is "URGENT", pick up the phone instead.
- Stay current – read, respond, and use a filing system to move messages out of your inbox.
- Schedule meetings using your office calendar tool.
- Spell check and proof language.
- If you are upset about something, sit on it – you will regret a quick emotional response.

Follow-up

There aren't many things that irritate customers and colleagues more than someone who doesn't follow-up. Ignoring another person is disrespectful. Instead, be known as the person that always follows up on-time, every time. If you have not yet resolved an issue requiring follow-up, update the person that inquired.

Great follow-up is a positive habit you carry with you everywhere you go. When it is time to be considered for another position or promotion, your dependability will be a key factor in the decision.

Answer Your Office Phone

I have visited office after office and one thing I see just about everywhere is that phone message lights are lit up like Christmas trees. Apparently, few people answer their phones. If someone is calling, it is probably important, so pick up the phone. When you answer the phone, you get opportunities to develop positive relationships, help colleagues, and customers.

CHAPTER FOUR: MOVING ON UP

Hibernation is for Bears

Don't treat your office or cube space as your private cave. Come out into the office and show yourself on a regular basis. It is best if you get up and walk around from time to time. You will be happier, healthier, and more productive.

Your colleagues need to see your face, there is nothing like personal contact. Leave hibernation to the real bears.

Leadership

Highly effective leaders are tough to find. In the formative years of the United States of America, our population was but a few million people. Despite the low population, our country was blessed with a long list of great leaders.

Look at the state of political leadership in our country today. In 2020 the United States has a population of 330 million people. Yet we cannot seem to find honest, high integrity leaders to handle our domestic and world affairs. We have a divided country begging for genuine leaders to bring people together into the "United" States of America. There are few leaders evident that appear to be up to the task. Why is this?

Leaders are not born…**Leaders are made**

History is filled with individuals considered "great" leaders. History also tells us that most great leaders didn't go looking for a major world crisis or catastrophe. They happened to be at the place and time when it was "sink or swim". Circumstances created the platform for history and leaders to be made. As a result of being dropped into sometimes dire circumstances, leaders rose to the occasion. While it is true that many made mistakes along the way, their vision, desire, and commitment transformed them into unmistakably powerful forces. Forced to lead, they overcame monumental hurdles. I'll bet that if you could talk with any one of the great leaders, they would tell you that they weren't sure they would make it past the crisis, and were probably worn out by the end, yet afterward were more confident than ever.

WIDE-EYED WISDOM

Your Leadership Path

Crisis situations aside, people can spend years developing – learning more year after year and steadily moving toward leadership proficiency. Before you know it, these people have developed a bank of great leadership skills. They weren't necessarily the top raw talent, but they took the time to invest in themselves. Their leadership skills were developed and then honed through disciplined study, hard work and practice.

You already have a well-defined personality. Is leadership something that you seek? Or will leadership find you regardless of your interest? If so, embrace who you are and smooth the rough edges to further develop your leadership style. Do your best to learn as much as possible, as early as possible. Refine your leadership qualities as you progress. Be careful to refine your style rather than be something you are not.

One method of refining your style is to watch other leaders. You can learn a tremendous amount by tuning in to how leaders conduct themselves. Watch for both good and bad habits and learn from both. As you learn, study how others respond. Note how you feel and respond. You will remember what actions created various feelings and responses.

I invested countless hours watching, listening, and learning from leaders in the organizations that I served. I learned from some of the best and some of the worst. The key is to observe carefully, ask questions, listen, and learn. Take plenty of quiet time to think about what you have learned and how you would translate that lesson into your own sphere.

All too often, people are promoted into leadership positions with little clue as to how to truly lead. (That person will hopefully learn on the job without too much damage to their team and/or themselves.) Void of the appropriate mentors and leadership education, chances are these new "leaders" will plateau quickly and potentially fail. Their leadership days may be lost forever.

Instead, tap into a variety of available resources to learn about effective leadership. Continually develop your skills throughout your life.

Develop People

Early in my career one of our middle managers taught me that the most important job of a leader is to develop people. I never forgot that lesson and spent many hours teaching, coaching, and mentoring team members. I learned

CHAPTER FOUR: MOVING ON UP

that people are very capable and want to do the right thing. If you develop the people around you, you will be able to relinquish control to others. As a result, you and your team will become more powerful.

A development focused organization has many advantages, from attracting talented people to assuring the long-term future of the organization. You can never attract and retain enough talent. Those that are continual students of the business, combining "work smart" with "work hard" will succeed.

For those of you that aspire to be a leader, make sure you remember to invest in associate development. Once you and your team develop, you will *gain* control by *giving up* control to your team.

Don't Forget the Personal

Work/Life Balance

Let's address this long debated and idealistic concept. Do you buy into "work/life balance"? I don't and here's why. To me, work and life are a series of complex tradeoffs. There are multiple choices you will weigh against one another. You aren't going to be able to balance the two. You will give up something in one area to get something in the other.

Remember back to your vision and values that drive your life plan? Let those shape how you prioritize work and personal life. Do your best to align commitments to your values. If you do, you will feel more settled and at peace with your work and life decisions. If you overcommit yourself, unfortunately you may experience negative consequences later in life with your family, significant other and/or yourself.

When our daughter was a new mom, working full-time with a toddler at home, she attended a Project Management class. This topic was up for discussion. Until her daughter was born, it seemed altogether possible to balance it all, after all she was extremely organized and driven. But while discussing the work/life balance topic, a lightbulb went on and she recognized that she could *not* have it all. She enjoyed her career but realized that she would need to sacrifice some career choices (projects, travel, promotions) to have precious time with her daughter. Just realizing and accepting that the work/life balance notion was unrealistic, (and voicing it to the group) did wonders to help her prioritize and feel confident in her choices.

It is imperative to address the work/life tradeoff issue early, to make sure the requirements of your chosen career are consistent with your life plan. You can enjoy a fulfilling personal life while still experiencing a rewarding career but be realistic and plan for trade-offs.

Take Care of Yourself

For those who listen during pre-flight safety instructions, you are familiar with – *in case of emergency, put your oxygen mask on first before assisting others*. The same is true for life. Take care of yourself first so that you can then take care of others.

You are not a machine. You only have one mind and one body. Your body and mind require exercise and rest. Recreation is an important source of rejuvenation for your body and mind. Look at the root of recreation. The active part of the word recreation is *re-create*.

> **The origin verb: to refresh by means of relaxation and enjoyment, as restore physically or mentally.**[53]

Take time off, play regularly, develop hobbies, make friends, entertain, be entertained, and take advantage of rest and downtime. Plan for recreation as a critical piece of "work/life tradeoffs".

I learned a valuable lesson from our 9-year old son Matt. I am still not sure why I asked a 9-year old this question, but his reply was genuine and resonates with me today, nearly 28-years later.

> "If you watch a game, it is fun. If you play it, it's recreation. If you work it, it's called golf."[54]
>
> *Bob Hope*

After a particularly tough day at work, I walked in the front door and I looked at our son and asked, "Matt when you have a tough day at school, what do you do when you get home?"

Without hesitation he looked at me and said, "I go play." Within moments he left the room and was out the door to resume his play time. The words of wisdom that came out of our 9-year old's mouth is something everyone should hear, understand, and practice.

CHAPTER FOUR: MOVING ON UP

Be careful not to turn your recreation into a project – I think most of my former colleagues exercised just to keep their heart going. There might have been a short-term endorphin rush from a gym visit or a run, but I don't think they really relaxed or enjoyed the activity.

Other colleagues played in competitive baseball, softball, golf, and hockey leagues. In those cases, it appeared to me that those folks enjoyed the games and the competition. They each played a game they loved. The result of their play – exercise *and* relaxation.

Let your 9-year old self take over. Choose something you really enjoy that will benefit your physical and mental health. Allow yourself to name the time and place and rediscover the kid inside of you.

Vacation, a Novel Concept

Let's talk about what happens in the organizational world of vacations – harken back to our discussion regarding work/life balance. It will be up to you to guard personal breaks for yourself and your family. While many modern progressive organizations have keyed into the needs of their employees, it seems many others have little, if any clue about why quality time-off is necessary to attract and maintain a healthy, vibrant workforce.

Many of your organizations may have this same culture. It will be up to you to ensure that your vacation is your opportunity to rest, recreate, and recharge. Don't let someone else intrude on your vacation. It may take guts, but you can leave your work phone at home. You can leave your laptop at work. You can unplug, and in doing so, recharge.

Vacation or personal time off is one of those areas to keep front of mind as you examine your fit into organizational culture. If your organization or one you are considering has an antiquated approach to their workforce, take a hard look to see if the career fit is consistent with your life plan.

Another Mai Tai, anyone? Or, in my case, another mango iced tea?

CHAPTER FIVE
HURRY UP AND FAIL

Do you ever feel like you are going to be discovered as a fraud? A miserable failure that is really masquerading as a capable human being. If you have had these thoughts – read carefully. Misplaced thoughts like these go through the minds of a lot of people. Those failure thoughts are just momentary distractions from you and your future. Don't let these thoughts take over. Remember, you are **intelligent** and **capable**.

Regarding the U.S. involvement in World War II, Franklin D. Roosevelt said, "The only thing we have to **fear** is **fear** itself." What FDR said during WWII applies to our fear of failure. If we fear failure, it distracts from what we need to do, making the goal more difficult to achieve. We, locked in our own minds, become our own worst enemy.

At times you may still feel overwhelmed. Understand, *failure* may be our best teacher. Failure is just one step in the process of achieving success. Don't stop. Keep putting one foot in front of the other until you reach your goal.

> "You never fail until you stop trying."[55]
>
> Albert Einstein

How else would we be stretched to the point of achieving so many great things? You must stretch to learn – failure will stretch you, and if you don't quit, increased understanding and confidence will be your reward.

WIDE-EYED WISDOM

For goodness sake don't fail at something the first time and quit. Or worse yet, quit before you start. I've done both. The road seems a bit rocky, the going gets tough and the easy way out is to quit. Try explaining to others why you quit, especially to a loved one. There are times when you are ever so close to success and cannot see the finish line. Quite often you are within reach of the finish and don't know it – so think twice about quitting.

> "Ninety percent of all failures result from people quitting too soon."[56]
>
> *Anonymous*

Sometimes you may feel like quitting. You have had enough of trying and probably feel worn out and defeated. Success isn't close or even apparent. You have failed too many times. That is usually the point when you must recommit to the idea that you *can* accomplish what you set out to do. All of us will reach a point when we either quit or move forward. I've been there. Most of the time I chose to move forward. I regret the times when I quit too soon. As I have matured, I rarely quit and as a result, I succeed often. I can only imagine what I might have accomplished if I had possessed that wisdom at a much younger age.

I'll use my early college days as an example of a refusal to quit when discouraged. I attended a community college for two years before transferring to California State University, Fresno.

Fresh with an Associate in Science degree in Business Administration from my local community college, I was ready to make the move to a four-year university. We aren't talking about an Ivy League school, but it was a big leap all the same. C.S.U.F. has a great Agriculture program, what you might expect given its location in California's central valley. I used to joke that I got along great with Ivy Leaguer's, being a "cousin" with my Alfalfa League school. (No disrespect intended to my fellow Bulldog alumni or the university. I was blessed with a great education at Fresno State.)

One of my first classes at Fresno State was Business Law. That first Tuesday morning at about 8 a.m. our Business Law professor asked the community college transfer students to raise hands. Out of a class of 35 or so students about 8 or 9 of us raised our hands. Our professor told us that community college transfer students would perform at about a half grade worse than students that had been at Fresno State for their full education. At

CHAPTER FIVE: HURRY UP AND FAIL

first, his comment hit me hard. Initially discouraged, I could have quit right then. But instead of giving up, I got going. At the end of the semester I was able to remind the professor of his comment and that I took it as a personal challenge. I studied hard and led his class that semester. Mission accomplished. In fact, the business law professor had hoped that the transfer students would make the commitment to succeed, even though history indicated otherwise.

During my college days, I learned that I could either sit back and accept failure or I could accept the challenge to succeed. Once I figured out that I belonged and that I could compete with anyone, my confidence and capabilities grew rapidly. I've accomplished far more than anyone thought I would achieve, including myself. I believe that I still have much more to accomplish. I am capable of great things – and so are you.

Famous Failures[57]
Check out these famous folks that persevered despite experiencing more than their share of failure.

Abraham Lincoln
Abraham Lincoln was famous for being a rail splitter turned President of the United States. As President, he is best known for his work to introduce equal rights in our country. Mr. Lincoln's crowning achievement was to free the slaves and abolish slavery (in the U.S.) once and for all.

When Lincoln was 23-years old, he lost his job and lost an election for the State Legislature. At the age of 26 his wife Ann died. Three years later he lost a bid to become Speaker of the Illinois House of Representatives. In 1848 he failed in his attempt to become Commissioner of the General Land Office in Washington D.C.

Having been elected to the U.S. House of Representatives in 1846 he wrote the draft of a bill to end slavery. Then his perseverance finally began to pay off – he was elected the 16th President of the United States of America.

Had Lincoln given up early in his life, who knows how things would have turned out. His image would not be on the five-dollar bill or the penny, and the Lincoln Memorial in Washington D.C. would not exist.

WIDE-EYED WISDOM

Albert Einstein
Einstein failed to pass the entrance test into the Swiss Federal Polytechnic school. During his university career he nearly dropped out due to poor performance. At one point, Albert's father thought that he was a major failure. Eventually Einstein went to work as a door to door insurance salesman. (I can't fathom Einstein selling insurance door to door.) He also worked for the Patent Office. Of course, today he is considered to have been one of the brightest minds in modern history.

Bill Gates
Bill Gates was born in 1955 in Seattle, WA. He still lives just east of the Seattle downtown on nearby Mercer Island, in the middle of Lake Washington. In his late teens, Bill and his close friend Paul Allen built a company called Traf-O-Data. They attempted to sell their device to the traffic department of King County (Seattle), but their creation did not work when demonstrated to the supervisor in charge of the buying decision.

Later, Gates enrolled in Harvard. (He scored a near perfect on his SAT.) After only one year, he and Paul Allen dropped out of Harvard and started a new company – perhaps you have heard of it – Microsoft.

Elvis Presley
Elvis Presley was born in 1935 in Tupelo, Mississippi. He had an identical twin brother (Jesse) that was stillborn. His family was poor and moved from place to place, unable to make ends meet. As a teenager he tried multiple times to break into the music business. Twice he was turned away at Sun Records. He tried out for a quartet and was told he could not sing.

Elvis made his next career move – driving a truck. A few months later Elvis caught his big break through a friend of a friend. He went on to record "That's All Right," which caught the attention of some important people in the record business.

Elvis became the first artist to sell over a billion records worldwide. Known as the "King" of Rock n' Roll, what would the world be like if Elvis had abandoned his music for a career as a truck driver?

CHAPTER FIVE: HURRY UP AND FAIL

J.K. Rowling

When she was just 25-years old, the idea of *Harry Potter* sparked. She had her break but didn't know it at the time. It would be a few years before she was able to capitalize on her brainchild. Within a few months her mother died. After a move to Portugal, J.K. met a man and married. She gave birth to a daughter in 1993. Her marriage became rocky, due to domestic abuse, and she eventually separated and later divorced. She had only written three chapters of *Harry Potter* by 1993.

After a failed attempt to get into Oxford, failure to finish *Harry Potter*, and a failed marriage – she was left clinically depressed and suicidal. But she persevered and two years later finally managed to finish *Harry Potter and the Sorcerer's Stone*. Another year was spent working through her agent and the major publishing companies. All twelve major publishers rejected her book. (Can you imagine passing on *Harry Potter*?)

Then in 1996 a small literary house, at the direction of the owner's daughter, gave J.K. Rowling a small cash advance for her book (years after her initial idea was hatched). Many more books, movies, merchandise, and theme park rides have followed. J.K. Rowling became the first author to become a billionaire through book writing. Thank goodness she didn't quit.

Moses

Have you ever heard of Moses? He was born of Hebrew slave parents and rescued by Pharaoh's daughter who raised him as her son. He was favored inside Pharaoh's household.

Eventually Moses was exiled from Egypt. Prior to dealing with Ramses, using God's power and direction, Moses was a reluctant leader – continually questioning Authority and lacking the understanding of why he was chosen.

He stuttered so badly that his brother Aaron had to go with him to deliver messages to the Pharaoh. Even though he wanted to live his last days in the "Promised Land", he never made it there. But he did fulfill his purpose as he led the Jews out of Egypt, ending 400-years of slavery.

WIDE-EYED WISDOM

Michael Jordan

Michael Jordan, famous for his six NBA championships with the Chicago Bulls, was not always a rousing success. As a sophomore in High School, Michael did not make the Varsity basketball team. Never again to be denied a spot on the roster, Michael went on to become perhaps the best basketball player of all-time.

Michael will tell you that he missed more than 9,000 shots in his career. Many of those missed shots cost his team a win. But many of his made shots clinched wins and championships.

The former Chicago Bull took a short break from his NBA career to play minor league baseball (that experience was not a rousing success). As a player for the minor league Birmingham Barons, Michael enjoyed some level of success but returned to basketball within two years. (Side note – if you haven't seen the movie *Space Jam*, check it out. Our grandkids just watched it for the first time and loved it, despite having no reference for the fame or success of Michael Jordan or the other athletes/celebrities featured.)

Today Michael Jordan is a part-owner of the Charlotte Hornets of the NBA. So far, with Michael Jordan as an owner, the Hornets have experienced little success. Seemingly motivated by failure, Michael never gave up.

Milton Hershey

In 1911 Mr. Hershey made a deposit for a ticket on the RMS Titanic. Lucky for all of us that have a penchant for chocolate, he did not take passage on that doomed ship.

Milton Hershey never finished high school – he dropped out before his fourteenth birthday and started work as an apprentice at a print shop. At the ripe age of fourteen he was fired after an accident with one of the machines.

His list of failures included:
- Failed candy store business
- Unsuccessful venture into a candy and restaurant chain
- Failure at selling candy on the streets of New York City

CHAPTER FIVE: HURRY UP AND FAIL

Eventually Milton Hershey was able to start the Lancaster Caramel Company. After seven years in business he sold the company. With the proceeds from that sale, he started the Hershey Chocolate Company.

With his wife Katherine, they founded the Milton and Katherine Hershey School in Hershey, Pennsylvania. Today the school is the primary responsibility of the Hershey Trust, the largest shareholder of the Hershey Chocolate Company. Hershey profits are used to support the education of underprivileged and at-risk youth. I have the honor of making a visit to the Milton and Katherine Hershey School, and am blown away by what this man accomplished and how his legacy has impacted so many lives across so many generations.

Oprah Winfrey
Oprah! Ever heard of the queen of daytime talk? Of course you have heard of Oprah. She is a self-made billionaire who rose from a poor and troubled early life. Born in Mississippi in 1954 to a teenage mother, Oprah was raised by her grandmother the first few years of her life. She moved back to live with her mother when she was six years old.

As an early teen, Oprah was molested by her cousin, uncle, and a "friend" of the family. When she was 14, she was pregnant. She lost her baby shortly after birth. She eventually found a job as an intern at a radio station and then a news anchor job after college. She moved to Baltimore, Maryland as co-anchor. Later a producer in Baltimore removed her from her job as "unfit" for television. (Imagine being that guy.)

After moving to Chicago things got interesting for Oprah. Her AM Chicago show eventually turned into the Oprah Winfrey Show. As they say, the rest is history.

Walt Disney
Walt Disney, the founder of Disneyland was born in 1901. World renowned today, Disney paid his dues with early career failures. As a teenager he was hired by a newspaper in Kansas City and fired for "lacking imagination" and "having no good ideas".

WIDE-EYED WISDOM

Later, Walt Disney had some success producing cartoons to show at the beginning of movies for Newman's theaters. But his cartoons did not produce enough income for his company, resulting in bankruptcy.

Walt moved to Hollywood when he was 22. He and his brother Roy started Disney Brothers Studio, later known as Walt Disney Company. In 1928 Walt created Mickey Mouse. His company began to gain traction. Mickey was the star of "Steamboat Willie", which became a hit.

In 1955, Disneyland was opened in Anaheim, CA. When the park opened, the paint was still drying, and many rides did not operate perfectly. Undaunted by early setbacks, Walt Disney built the foundation of a company, treasured by families and now one of the most valuable businesses in the world.

Thomas Edison

Thomas Edison was born in 1847 in Milan, Ohio, one of seven siblings.

In 1877, Edison invented the phonograph. Right on the heels of his success with the phonograph, Edison began work on an incandescent lightbulb that could be used by the masses. He estimated that he failed over 10,000 times as he developed various iterations of his light bulb. Did you catch that? *Ten thousand times!!!*

Undaunted, he continued with the belief that he had not failed. He had succeeded in proof that the 10,000 iterations would not work. Finally succeeding, we have Edison to thank for the light bulb. He went on to hold 1,093 patents. Obviously, Thomas Edison did not fear failure. Instead, Edison seemed to view failure as one step closer to success.

Common Traits Shared by All of these Famous Failures:
- They believed in what they were doing.
- They had the courage to fail.
- There was no "I Quit!" in any of them.
- They each became rousing success stories.

Failure – Final Thoughts

This chapter is one that our daughter asked me to add – as a personal message for her children. The topic of failure is especially prevalent in her mind, even

CHAPTER FIVE: HURRY UP AND FAIL

to this day. Always striving for success – the pressure she puts on herself to excel and be the best also became a stumbling block – she became afraid to fail. And this fear at times prevents her from trying new things and experiences that she isn't sure she can knock out of the park or execute perfectly. Don't let the fear of the unknown or the fear of looking silly or the fear of disappointing yourself or others keep you from experiencing life or pursuing your dreams. Do your best – accept that your best is enough. Learn and move on. The real failure would be if you never get started.

The challenge for most of us is to believe enough in ourselves to continue when things look bleak. Shed the fear of failure, in fact go ahead and fail. Keep moving forward. You will eventually succeed.

Take a moment to reflect…
What is your greatest failure so far?

What did you learn from it?

How have you applied those lessons?

Armed with new knowledge, how will you approach failure and success in the future?

CHAPTER SIX
LIFE – MASTER CLASS

We have covered a lot of ground – congratulations, you stuck with it! Now that you have learned the basics, let's look at some advanced topics. In this chapter we will cover some of my favorite lessons for day-to-day life.

You will learn…
- The fundamentals of negotiations.
- How, when, and why to "do it yourself".
- How (and why) to prepare yourself and your family for a disaster.

Whether you are single, have a partner, or a family, this advanced information is important to your future. Make sure to use and practice your new skills.

Much of what you learn in the following pages will take pressure off the expense side of your budget, thereby freeing up much needed cash for savings, investments and maybe even some fun!

Negotiations

Van Spurgeon, a good friend of mine for many years, said this, "In life you don't get what you deserve, you get what you negotiate."[58]

Van has held hundreds of negotiations seminars around the world. He is an incredibly wise and shrewd businessman. He is also a great mentor and coach. There are not enough pages here to pass along all that I learned from Van. His lessons will be with me for the rest of my life. Van has retired and joined a group of volunteers that has planted thousands of trees in the Midwest. Future generations will never know who planted those trees, but they will enjoy them all the same. Van has also planted many thousands of seedlings, so to speak, in his pupils. I was lucky enough to be one of them. We will bear fruit for years to come and impact others that will also be fruitful, all to the credit of Van and people like him.

> "Society grows great when old men plant trees whose shade they know they shall never sit in."[59]
>
> *Anonymous Greek Proverb*

Today Spurgeon Management Services is led by Paul Adams of Olathe, Kansas. Paul has carried on the work Van started and is educating people in large organizations across the U.S. Make sure you attend "Win – Win" or another session on negotiations. You need the skills and the confidence that goes with them, or you won't get what you deserve.

Bargaining and Negotiations

Bargaining is used when recurring deals and relationships are not a primary motivator. Parties in bargaining are usually concerned with the short-term results of their efforts. They know they are unlikely to get a "good" deal, but don't want to settle for a "bad" deal. They work hard to get the best they can for the near-term.

Bargaining is also usually associated with one party winning and the other party losing. This happens regularly in organized labor contracts. Some labor participants refer to contract discussions between a union and organization as negotiations. Others use the term bargaining. From what I have learned, bargaining is the most appropriate term to describe labor contract talks.

Negotiations strategies and tactics are employed by folks that are concerned about the long-term. Of course, they want the best deal. They also know that relationships and positive interactions are important. Negotiations are used in business most often when both parties want to "win". Both negotiators can strike a good deal for themselves and their organizations while ensuring the other party will work with them again in the future.

CHAPTER SIX: LIFE – MASTER CLASS

Confidence

I think the number one reason people don't negotiate is fear of failure. Simply put, they don't want to be told "no". Lacking confidence, they don't ask for anything beyond opening terms.

As small children one of the first words we heard was "no", usually from an authority figure, like a parent. What's the response? Our head hangs down, lip turns under, and feelings are hurt. As a result, most of us adults are afraid to hear "no". Many years later, with that ingrained childhood experience, we don't ask for fear of getting our feelings hurt or asking a question that makes the other party think we must be stupid. Think about how you felt as a kid when you heard the word "no". How does hearing no make you feel now?

There is a smaller group of people, the strong-willed bunch, that as children, really didn't care if they were told "no". They did their thing regardless of what others said. Our grandson James is one of those fearless kids – often to our frustration. I trust this skill will serve him well as he matures. The strong-willed kids have the confidence at a young age to hear "no" without a major impact on their feelings. As adults, it is likely the strong-willed bunch will remain confident and hearing "no" means find another way to the goal.

Willingness to Negotiate

For negotiations to occur both parties must be willing to negotiate. Quite often one party or the other is stuck on initial terms and is unwilling or unable to budge or ask for a better deal. If so, negotiations will not occur. This inertia can happen with either buyer or seller. I have met plenty of buyers that accepted the list-price and terms and didn't ask for anything to enhance the deal. The seller may have been ready to negotiate but the buyer failed to ask.

Such is the case when a buyer pays list price for a vehicle, boat, or jewelry without asking for discounts or more favorable terms. I know people that have left money on the table, muzzled by their fear, negotiations never started. The best way to avoid failure to negotiate is with thorough advance preparations and practice.

WIDE-EYED WISDOM

Prepare to Negotiate

I joke quite often about how the internet "knows everything". In this case, the internet can play a valuable research role in negotiation preparations. Prior to the internet, it was difficult to ascertain a bad deal from a good deal from a great deal. For a consumer, the internet is a treasure trove of all kinds of information that will help prepare you for negotiations. This is especially true on major purchases.

As an example, car buying information is plentiful – you can compare deals that have been made in the recent past. This will provide you with the information about what you should expect to pay. Your research should also include loan interest rates (if you don't have the immediate cash), extended warranty costs and insurance.

Make a list of all the things you could negotiate, from free car washes and oil changes, extended warranty, price of the car and other extras. Document and take your notes with you as you prepare to negotiate your purchase.

Minimums and Maximums

Part of your preparation as a buyer is to determine what you are willing to pay. Or as a seller, what you are willing to accept to sell an item. If you are the buyer, you should understand the range of what the seller is likely to accept as a minimum price and the maximum that you are willing to pay. As a seller you should have a good idea of the minimum you will accept and the maximum a buyer might pay.

Minimums and maximums are critical to successful win – win negotiations. Without a min and a max, you will be lost and vulnerable.

When making a purchase offer, start by asking the seller what they want for an item. Once the seller gives you a price, a maximum has just been established. The buyer will pay no more than the price the seller quoted.

Do your best to get the seller to give their asking price first. The seller may give an asking price that is below the minimum you expected to pay. You may have just saved yourself a lot of money by asking the seller to quote a price first. And, you may have an opportunity to improve upon the deal.

If you can't get the seller to quote a price, then you will be forced to make an offer. Be careful how you make the offer. Once you have made an offer, you have established the minimum you will pay. The seller will negotiate to get a higher sales price.

Be careful when someone asks you to give your "best" deal as the first offer. In normal negotiations a best offer is a tactic to establish a minimum you will pay. Or, if you are the seller the maximum you will receive. As a buyer your best offer should be a starting point. You will be disappointed if you start with an absolute best on the first offer. The seller will always want more money.

If you are selling something, almost without exception you will get less money than your asking price. Again, conduct research so you understand the minimum and maximum market value of the item. As a seller if you lead off with the minimum you will accept, you are in for a disappointment on the amount you receive.

Gathering Information

Assume the other person is a strong negotiator – well prepared to ask questions that are designed to give them the upper hand in negotiations. It is important you ask good questions too.

You should be asking the seller plenty about the item. You need information to gauge the condition of the item, the seller's eagerness to deal and what might be open to negotiation. You may also find out what is most important to the seller and get an idea of what it will take to make a deal.

Do your absolute best to give information cautiously and gather information liberally. Quite often, open discussion prior to negotiations will yield helpful information you can use to strike the best deal.

Closed Questions

A closed question can usually be answered by a simple yes or no. Closed questions discourage open dialogue and squelch negotiation points. Use closed questions sparingly during negotiations.

Using *are you, will you, can you*…will usually be answered with one word - *yes* or *no*. For example, asking "Are you willing to discount the price" or "Are you willing to negotiate"? The seller can answer very quickly "no" and the opportunity to negotiate may be over before it starts.

WIDE-EYED WISDOM

There are other ways to phrase your questions. Smart phrases make it known that the buyer or seller realizes that you expect to negotiate. Those other phrases are usually in the form of open-ended questions.

Open-Ended Questions

Open-ended questions require more than a yes or no answer. An open-ended question will encourage discussion and potentially reveal additional negotiation points. Asking open-ended questions lets the other party know that you expect to discuss the issue openly and expect some improvement in the deal.

By rephrasing the closed question from above you can set a different tone during the negotiations process. "What type of discount are you willing to give if I buy today?" First, you are sending the message that you expect a discount. Second, you are setting the tone that you expect to negotiate price and perhaps other terms.

Depending upon the response you may be opening the door to several other points of negotiation. The wise use of open-ended questions will increase your chances of a better deal and enable a potential win-win for both parties.

"Why" Questions

Be careful when considering use of a "why" question. Remember your childhood? You might have received a scolding like, "Why did you do that?". Most of us compliant ones had that drilled into us and why was almost always asked in a stern and negative tone.

Today many years later we still don't want to be asked why. (I can still hear my mom, "Why would you do such a thing?") In other words, using a why question is in many ways accusatory. One party is accusing the other by using why. The result is usually that the person on the receiving end of the why question will immediately go on the defensive or shutdown.

In constructive dialogue it is best that neither party feel threatened nor defensive – remember, our goal is win-win.

CHAPTER SIX: LIFE – MASTER CLASS

During Negotiations

Give Information Cautiously

Imagine that you are shopping for a car. You are so excited that you can hardly contain yourself. Without thinking you blurt out to the salesperson, "I just love this car! It's perfect!" What do you suppose will be the result? You have just told the salesperson that you are emotionally attached to *that* car. Read the next few words slowly and commit them to memory. New and used cars are a dime a dozen. There is another car out there exactly like the one you are looking at, so don't get caught up in the moment. There will <u>always</u> be another deal on the same car (or even one better) somewhere else.

As you prepare, determine what you do *not* want to tell a salesperson. A couple of examples that almost always come up during a car purchase.

1. Your budget
2. Your monthly payment capacity

If you give that information, expect the salesperson and their sales manager to use it to take your mind off the total sale price of the car. They may use the information to squeeze every dollar out of you. They will "upsell" by adding more items for you to consider, all while staying within your monthly payment parameters. All it will take is to extend the length of the loan term to keep you within an affordable monthly payment while they get the biggest sale possible.

Or, if you have cash, they work you toward the biggest sale possible. (Remember to have the self-discipline to live within your means.)

Always invest your time in preparation and be certain that you understand the minimums and maximums on each of the key buying points, prior to beginning negotiations.

Negotiate One Point at a Time

If you are prepared, you should have a list of items to address during negotiations. Stay focused on the task at hand and avoid confusion by addressing and reaching agreement on one item at a time. When you reach agreement, be sure to summarize before moving to the next item. If you are not in agreement on an item, you can always put that piece on-hold and circle back toward the end of the negotiation session.

There will be give and take. Keep in mind that you may be willing to give up something on one item to get a great deal on another.

Take Notes

Prepare excellent notes prior to the negotiation session. Your prep might contain facts from your research, a list of items to negotiate and the maximum you expect to pay. These notes are for your eyes only.

During negotiations, take charge of note taking. One party to the negotiation must record the agreement. It can be easy to forget or to mischaracterize an element of the negotiation. This process will assist you and the other party to clarify each point and to identify any open issues that warrant further discussion. As you negotiate point by point, make sure you record each item and your agreement. Keeping a record of the deal will help you ensure that each party lives up to the agreement.

Bundle

To "bundle" is to identify multiple items and set a total price for the package. As the total value goes up the stakes are higher for both buyer and seller. Quite often there is extra pressure to reach a deal with a more valuable bundle.

There is a show on cable called "American Pickers". Frank and Mike are the stars. They use the bundle tactic often. Initially they may not be able to reach agreement with the seller on the price of a single item. But when they add more items and bundle, they almost always reach a deal.

For example, the next time you are at a garage sale, you could ask for a price for the whole group of items you would like to buy. In this case neither buyer nor seller are likely to get hung up on the price of a single item.

Silence

At times I have used silence to my advantage when negotiating a purchase. Because silence is uncomfortable, often salespeople feel like they must say something to fill the gap. The salesperson may offer something else that you haven't asked for, as a result of your silence. Or they might offer a bit of information that would help you negotiate the current point or the next.

As a test, I've used this tactic on conference calls quite often. If you are directing the discussion and fall silent it won't take but a few seconds for

CHAPTER SIX: LIFE – MASTER CLASS

someone to jump in. Most people are uncomfortable with silence. Try it sometime – it is interesting to see who is the first to jump and fill the void.

"What else?"

Ask "what else" multiple times during the session. Asking "what else" lets the person know that you expect more. The phrase will also help you to make sure you have uncovered as many of the negotiating points as possible. When you have reached a deal, before you close make sure to ask, "what else" three more times. Salespeople want to make a deal. If you ask, often they will add something at the last minute.

Summarize and Close

The reason for creating a summary is so that both parties perform their part and are ready and willing to deal in the future. As mentioned earlier, make sure that you summarize each point as you negotiate. Summarizing develops clarity for both parties. Once you have reached the end of negotiations, run through your notes, and give a "plain English" summary of each individual point of agreement.

Be certain to identify any follow-up items and both sign the agreement.

Follow-up/Perform

You cannot develop and maintain a win – win negotiations relationship if one or the other party does not perform as agreed. Always follow-up and perform on your part of the negotiated agreement.

Practice

What would any skill become if you did not practice? To become a skilled negotiator, you must practice every chance you get. You will find that the more you practice the more confident and comfortable you will become. Part of my practice has been as an observer during negotiations. It is much easier to pick up valuable learning when you are a casual observer. I especially enjoy sitting alongside a skilled negotiator and taking in all of what they do as they work their way through a deal.

Throughout your life journey you will have countless opportunities to negotiate. Continue to learn the finer points of negotiations and what works best in different situations. Negotiations will become second nature. Rather than viewing negotiations with apprehension, look at the experience from a different viewpoint – negotiations can be fun and rewarding. You never know what great deal may be lurking in the process.

The final word on negotiations…
TINSTAAFL

Ever heard of this? TINSTAAFL stands for, *There Is No Such Thing as A Free Lunch*.[60]

Spend some time in the world and you will find this lesson to be true. In life and in business it is rare that you receive a "free lunch". There is almost always something expected of you to enjoy that lunch. Keep this in mind as you go about your personal and professional lives. Negotiate early and often. If you fail to negotiate you will not get what you deserve.

Do it Yourself (DIY)

The DIY concept is popular today, with a multitude of shows, even whole television networks devoted to the "DIY Revolution". Do It Yourself knowledge is a valuable skill that will fill your intelligence tank and keep money in your piggy bank. Choose to pay yourself instead of paying somebody else.

Years ago, we had an outdoor drainpipe clogged with debris that would not drain. Water was coming out of the top of the drainpipe located next to the foundation of our house. I had an idea of what might be clogging the drain. A few years earlier I pulled out some small blocks of wood from the same drain. Chances were, during new home construction, some adventuresome youngsters dropped the blocks in while playing on the site. I had always wondered if the drain was totally clear. Now my answer was bubbling up much like the "black gold" or "Texas tea" that Beverly Hillbilly Jed Clampett discovered while on a hunting trip decades ago.

I called the local plumbing company. During the 30-minute visit the technician ran a camera down the pipe a grand total of about 6-feet and hit the clog in the pipe. That visit cost me about $175.

I asked the plumbing technician to estimate the cost to dig up the rough pipe, clear the clog and reinstall a new pipe section. He told me it would require

CHAPTER SIX: LIFE – MASTER CLASS

a digging crew for a full day and my cost would be about $1,000. (It always seems like the cost of a small job at home starts at $1,000 and usually goes up from there.) Let me get this straight, to dig a hole three feet deep by one foot wide by three feet long (to uncover the plastic rough pipe), cut out the clogged section and glue in a new piece was going to be $1,000. Let us not forget they'd also have to shovel dirt again to fill the hole.

No way was I going to pay that kind of money. Instead, I called on our youngest son Chad to help me do the job. Chad is always game for outdoor projects – especially when he can dig a hole. It took us two hours of digging to uncover the clogged section of pipe. Another 15 minutes and I cut out the clogged section – a 12" combination of silt, wood and rocks. We made a visit to the local Home Depot and spent about $25 for the replacement parts including a piece of rough pipe, coupling, primer, and glue. It took us another hour to measure the necessary replacement pipe, cut it to fit, clean and glue the coupling on both ends. Fifteen minutes later we had filled the hole with dirt.

> "If you want a thing done well, do it yourself."[61]
>
> *Proverb*

With the $975 savings in my pocket, Chad and I went to lunch to celebrate. We laughed about how the two of us took less than half a day to fix the drainpipe. By the way, I invested the $975 savings, now worth about $3,600.

Lesson Learned

Beyond gaining confidence and drainpipe repair knowledge, I learned that the first rule of property ownership is to keep your property up to date and in good working condition. If you fail to keep your property up to date, you will be in for an unpleasant surprise when you decide to sell. All your pent-up maintenance will cost you. Buyers will not pay top dollar for old, out of date real estate. Stay on top of both small maintenance items and the large replacement stuff like siding, exterior paint, roofs, appliances, carpet, and flooring. Regular maintenance and fixes also help you avoid major repairs.

The same goes for cars and recreational toys like boats, RV, and wave runners. Maintenance is important to avoid major repair bills. Regular scheduled maintenance will also extend useful life.

WIDE-EYED WISDOM

With that in mind, make sure to teach yourself how to perform basic tasks that accompany homes, cars, and toys. The more things you own, the more you must maintain and repair.

You Are Capable

You are more capable than you realize. We all are. Each of us must better understand our potential, become motivated to act, and enjoy the resulting rewards. If you haven't heard about your potential from your family, friends, teachers, coaches, acquaintances or yourself, read the following carefully. You and those around you can accomplish more than you ever imagined. You just need to get in there and do it. Right now, think about and marvel at the advances, generations before us and those now, have made. Many of those accomplishments seem nearly impossible, especially when you view yourself and your world through self-imposed limitations. You will be amazed by what you are capable of if you commit to accept challenges and follow through.

When I need a confidence boost, I look around to see examples of others who have succeeded. I remind myself that if others can accomplish so much, so can I. Then I jump in and take care of what is in front of me.

I am not suggesting spending all your time working on tasks and projects around the house. You need your family, recreation, work, and free time. Keep in mind, there are also projects that require a professional, especially when safety and major fixes are concerned.

What I am telling you is that you can accomplish most routine tasks successfully. When it comes to regular household and minor maintenance, stay ahead of it by doing one thing at a time, yourself.

My wife Cindy and I have gained experience over the years and accomplished some very satisfying projects. We started with small fixes and worked our way up to more complex projects. Together we dreamed up some big stuff and made complex projects happen from ideation to creation. We took on some creative home renovations that our friends would never attempt (think French courtyard in our family room and 50's diner in our basement). I am convinced that some of our friend's husbands didn't want to come to our home because they knew their wives would point out what Cindy and I had accomplished. Next would be a "Honey Do" list.

CHAPTER SIX: LIFE – MASTER CLASS

Stretch yourself – learn some new skills, learn to take care of tasks that you would otherwise neglect. Have some fun too!

The Value of a "Punch List"

I am a firm believer that if you write something down – be it a goal, task, or reminder – you are more likely to accomplish it. There are so many distractions in life, that it becomes difficult to filter and remember all the critical input. If I don't act with intent, I am much more likely to neglect a project. I may move on to some important task like surfing the net, just to fill my time – and let's be honest, that is probably time wasted. Keep yourself organized and you will be much more likely to accomplish the important tasks. I keep a Punch List, (think –To Do list) at all times. It is a simple, visual reminder.

Tailor your list to your specific needs. At a minimum include the task, supply list and priority (tackle your most important items first). If you never seem to have a pen and paper handy, use your smart phone Notes feature. It feels great to check-off tasks that are on the list!

Does Your Task Require A Professional?

Once you have made your Punch List, it is time to research and develop a plan of attack. There may be some items on your list that don't make sense for you to tackle – perhaps you don't have the tools or expertise, or something is too dangerous, especially absent specialized equipment and training.

When we have plumbing problems beyond a normal clog, we call a professional plumber. Most professionals have tools and knowledge that I don't. Plumbing problems are infrequent enough that I really can't afford to buy tools that I will probably never use again.

If the job requires a building permit, we call the appropriate professional.

Who to Hire

In our home state I was able to get a general building contractor license by studying 16-hours and taking a 45-minute multiple choice test. Where I live it is too easy to get a contractor's license and go into business. That fact keeps me on edge about which contractor to hire.

WIDE-EYED WISDOM

Ask your family and friends for contractor recommendations. Chances are your friends have had some of the same fix issues. Also, use online reviews from trusted sites. Positive recommendations from a trusted source are a must.

Urgency

There are some jobs that you must pay attention to right away, or risk major damage or unsafe living conditions.

Some examples:
- Smoke or carbon monoxide detector failure
- Leaky plumbing
- Faulty electrical
- Natural gas leak

In each of the above examples, failure to fix can lead to further damage and/or safety issues. Don't risk it. Take care of these fixes (with a pro!) immediately.

Once family safety is taken care of, your next responsibility is to mitigate damage, especially if you are insured. For example, if you have a water leak at a fixture, turn off the water to that faucet until you can get it fixed.

Time to DIY – My Approach

Usually, if I can visualize the task and the potential fix, I can do it without much coaching. That is not to say everyone approaches "do it yourself" the same way. We all have our own approach. By now I have quite a few "fix-its" under my belt. There are all sorts of resources available for do it yourself items. Here are a few resources for you to consult:
- *Local home improvement store* – Ask questions and check out their workshop offerings.
- *YouTube tutorials* – Be prepared for more than one method to accomplish your task. These are excellent, especially for visual learners. Plus, you can watch the tutorials over and over (if necessary).
- *Follow instructions* – This sounds like a no-brainer, but make sure to read *all* the instructions. Slow down…especially the first few times.
- *Check owner manuals* – Common questions are usually addressed.
- *Internet searches* – You can find just about anything you could ever want.

CHAPTER SIX: LIFE – MASTER CLASS

- *Family and friends* – Ask for help, trade work with a friend, work together and learn from one another.
- *Professionals* – You may need to hire a professional from time to time. Observe and ask questions as they work. Next time, you just might be able to handle the issue yourself.

Growing up in a large family with little money there wasn't much choice but to DIY. My dad and several brothers were in the building trades – we spent some great time working together and learning from each other. My family taught me things that gave me an advantage over others, those who have never been exposed to home maintenance projects. My wife and I moved away from our hometown and that learning turned out to be invaluable.

I was probably the one in our family that was a little slower on learning mechanical skills. My mind was wired a bit different than my dad and brothers. I was more interested in sports. While they were driving nails, I was driving golf balls. I took quite a bit of ribbing over that but would do it all over again if I had the chance.

You can make DIY a game. Keep score by comparing the cost to do it yourself versus the contractor estimate. Use some of your DIY savings for something fun and use the rest to reduce debt, invest, save for large purchases or education accounts for your kids. Here is that discipline word again…self-discipline is required so that you don't blow your savings on depreciating stuff or tap into the money for something other than an emergency.

Metamorphosis of the DIY'er
Phase One – DENIAL

Oh man – the maintenance projects are piling up. But looking around the house you don't even "see" the projects anymore. Constantly running toilet? You don't hear it. Holes in the drywall? Covered with a picture. Chipped paint…sticky front door lock…squeaking floor…missing weatherstripping… Yep, all still there. In a moment mixed with clarity and exasperation you decide to get things done, but by now the deferred maintenance feels insurmountable – so you contact the pros. As the estimates trickle back in, it doesn't take long to realize that you simply can't afford the fixes, so you put it off – all of it. The days turn into weeks, maybe months. But then something happens – you notice that the constantly running toilet has a pool of water around the base, damaged baseboard, and moldy drywall – now you *have* to do something. So, you find the first plumber you can muster and pay an emergency weekend fee plus the normal rates to fix the issue. Hey, at least the toilet works again. Your bank account however is none too happy.

Phase Two – ACCEPTANCE

After the toilet kerfuffle, your "maintenance blind" glasses have disappeared. Each and every unfinished task becomes glaringly obvious – and obnoxious…it's almost like they are taunting you. Enough is enough! You know you can't afford a pro to tackle this mess, so you take matters in your own hands.

Phase Three – ACTION

Your tool supply consists of a hammer and hand-me-down screwdriver set. In the back of the drawer is a rusty tape measure. Hmmhhh…that won't get you too far. As you head to the home improvement store you make a mental list of the projects waiting for you at home. But as you head into the store, you stop and stare, overwhelmed by the seemingly endless aisles and thousands upon thousands of items. Somewhere in this treasure trove are the materials you need to fix your problems…if only you knew *what* they were…and *where* they were…the hunt is on. With your cart loaded with your fix-it finds, you head to the checkout stand and then back home. A few YouTube videos point you in the right direction. Oops – you forgot some critical items and need to head back to the store.

Phase Four – PAIN

Back from the hardware store, you dig-in to your project. Ouch! You skin your knuckles and crack a pipe. Back to the store… Making progress now until you cut your finger…again… Sigh. You are tired, dirty, and frustrated. But by now you have figured out how to read the instructions, and mistakes one and two yielded success at try three.

Phase Five – MOTIVATION

Your early struggles and taste of success have lit an odd spark – you can't

CHAPTER SIX: LIFE – MASTER CLASS

quite put your finger on it, but you feel just a bit more capable to tackle the next task on your list. This time, you did a bit of research before heading to the store. With some measure of confidence, you ask questions of the associate as you gather supplies. At home you problem solve and work through the challenges. Look at that – another success.

Phase Six – CONFIDENCE

By now you have a host of fixes and experiences under your belt. You have figured out your favorite sources for information and even organized your newly purchased tools. The original list of fix-its has disappeared and you spy opportunities for improvements – that tired looking bathroom has long needed a refresh and you tackle installing a new floor and updated vanity. Look at that. You *can* get it done! And you do. Your friends now give you a call when they need some help, and you dive right in. It is easier to figure out how to get to the finish line and do it with excellence.

Phase Seven – CREATIVITY

The possibilities of what you can build/make/fix/repurpose become endless. Now in your free time you tackle some of these "fun" projects and enjoy adding to your home and gifting to others. Some may even say you are an artist.

Phase Eight – REWARD

Years later your home carries a sense of pride as you enjoy the fruits of your labor. Your confidence carries into other areas of your life as well, as you have learned that just about any challenge can be overcome when you put in the hard work of learning, trying, failing, and trying again until you succeed. In addition to the knowledge gained, the money you have saved over the years has allowed you to build equity in your home. You have been able to put your money to work where *you* want it, rather than someone else's pocket. Your grandchildren say, "Nana and Pop can fix anything". The skinned knuckles, cuts and sore back are totally worth it.

As I mentioned earlier, when I was a kid, our family didn't have the money to spend on hiring fix-it people. We could scarcely afford to buy the supplies to complete a small home fix-it task. My mom used to say, "Do you think money grows on trees?". (My siblings and I would give her a bad time, because we knew the fiber that went into paper money probably came from a tree – sorry Mom, we were obnoxious.)

Most of us do not have the money to hire someone to deal with every maintenance or fix it task. Look around and spot all the pent-up maintenance – it is everywhere. Make your list. If you are on a limited budget (most of us are), get started learning how to do things for yourself. You can save thousands of dollars by learning how to take care of simple fixes. Again, be reluctant to give your hard-earned money to someone else. You will be a major step closer to achieving your life plan!

I've listed several common fix-it areas. These are the items that all of us can learn to handle – yes, you too! We must keep our properties well maintained and, in the process avoid going broke paying repair bills. These fixes you can figure out yourself. For more complex jobs, hire a professional. **See Resources: Exhibit 7, p. 247** for a basic do it yourself tool kit.

101 Fix-Its You Can Do Yourself – *So easy even a monkey could do it*

Housekeeping
- Clean floors, kitchen, bathrooms
- Clean carpets
- Clean a dishwasher
- Clean a refrigerator
- Clean an oven
- Clean a clothes washer
- Clean minor mold buildup
- Learn to Cook

Plumbing
- Fix a leaky faucet
- Fix or replace a water shutoff valve
- Install a toilet
- Fix or rebuild a toilet
- Unclog a toilet
- Unclog a drain
- Install a sink
- Replace faucet fixtures
- Adjust water heater temperature

Appliances
- Install a dishwasher
- Install a clothes dryer
- Install clothes washing machine
- Install a refrigerator
- Replace an ice maker
- Install an oven
- Install a garbage disposal
- Install a smoke detector
- Install a carbon monoxide detector

Millwork
- Install a door
- Install baseboard and/or door trim
- Install doorknob and deadbolt
- Install door weather stripping

Walls/Paint
- Paint and stain
- Fill or patch drywall holes
- Texture drywall spots
- Apply caulking

CHAPTER SIX: LIFE – MASTER CLASS

Electrical
- Turn a circuit breaker on or off
- Replace a light switch
- Replace an electrical wall plug
- Add a dimmer switch
- Replace a three-way switch
- Test and reset GFCI electrical plugs
- Replace a clothes dryer electrical cord
- Install light fixtures
- Replace electric stove burners

Vehicle Maintenance
- Change a flat tire
- Check tire pressure include the spare tire (BEWARE, don't forget to check the spare tire. Think: flat tire – dark, cold, raining and a flat spare. Ugh!)
- Wash, wax and detail a car
- Put fuel in your car
- Check car motor oil levels and fill
- Change car oil
- Check car brake fluid, fill if necessary
- Check windshield cleaner fluid and then fill
- Change windshield wiper blades
- Install snow chains or cables
- Change car air filter/cabin filter
- Change car lights (headlights, tail, backup, and brake light bulbs)
- Change a car spark plug

Hard Surfaces
- Install tile floor or backsplash
- Install wood floor
- Fix a broken tile
- Fix cracked grout
- Seal countertops

Toys
- Fix a flat tire on a bike
- Assemble a bike, basketball hoop, kids' toys
- Build a child's playhouse
- Build a treehouse
- Repair broken toys

Exterior
- Pressure wash walks, deck, driveway
- Seal walks, deck, driveway
- Fix a sprinkler system
- Landscape
- Prepare and plant a lawn
- Mow a lawn
- Edge a lawn
- Weed the yard
- Plant a garden, trees, shrubs, flowers
- Diagnose and treat a damaged lawn
- Fertilize plants, shrubs, trees, and lawn
- Repair an exterior deck
- Clear clogged roof gutters
- Change a spark plug on outdoor equipment
- Change oil in a lawnmower

General Maintenance
- Replace HVAC filters
- Clean HVAC vents and filters
- Weatherize a home
- Repair exterior siding
- Replace cabinet hardware
- Repair cabinet and furniture scratches
- Fix stained surface on furniture and cabinets
- Refinish a cabinet
- Install new drawer slides
- Fix squeaky door and cabinet hinges
- Align and/or adjust cabinets
- Fix and reinforce loose drawers
- Level a table, chair, or cabinet
- Repair a stripped screw hole
- Fix a broken window
- Replace home window springs
- Fix a squeaky floor
- Replace window screens
- Remove old carpet
- Lubricate garage door tracks

WIDE-EYED WISDOM

Prepare for a Disaster

I had a chance to work with the folks at the Red Cross over a two-year period. Our task was to make sure that in the event of a major disaster, our company and our associates were well prepared.

You never know when a fire, earthquake, tornado, snowstorm, or other disaster may strike (think Covid pandemic). With some disasters, there may be advance warning, but you still can't predict the impact. In the event of a disaster you should be prepared to survive on your own for at least a few days. If there is a major local, regional, or national event, all the normal emergency personnel we come to rely on, will be overwhelmed and unable to help you.

Learn CPR and basic first aid, keeping both skillsets current. Develop and practice your personal emergency plan, which includes how you will communicate, home evacuation routes, first aid, family survival kits, and basic family survival tactics. I have built survival kits that I keep at home, work and in our cars. You never know where you will be when disaster strikes. You may be at work, on the road, or at home, so be prepared to take care of yourself and your family wherever you might be.

There are plenty of websites that will help you with building a survival kit. For the purposes of this book I used the American Red Cross. The Red Cross is an amazing organization that is ready to spring into action during an emergency. Take time to visit their website and learn everything you can about dealing with emergencies.

Also, take time as a family to build emergency kits. If you have children get them involved. They will benefit by being a part of the family project and you will pass along some valuable life skills.

Finally, keep in mind that you may need to "grab and go". When you need to be on the move there may not be time to gather the necessary survival items. Build survival kits in mobile and modular fashion. Kits should be readily accessible and easy to move when needed. The cost of the kits and supplies may not be in your current budget. If not, build your kits a few supplies at a time. Keep a checklist and start with the most important items first.

We all seem to struggle to figure out a great gift for a loved one – a survival kit is a great idea. What better way to say you care?

CHAPTER SIX: LIFE – MASTER CLASS

Home Emergencies: Be Prepared

There are three utility shutoffs that you should always know about before you spend the first night in your home. You will need this wisdom to respond to a major home emergency. Make sure you can act swiftly and confidently to avoid injury and limit damage. Be prepared…

1. **Gas Shutoff:** There is a shutoff valve on every natural gas meter. You can usually find the natural gas meter on one side of your home. Building supply stores have small metal wrenches available that can be strapped to the gas meter. The cost of the wrench is only a few dollars. If you have a gas leak or a house fire, ready access to the natural gas shutoff is a necessity. You can avoid major damage, injury, or loss of life if you know how to quickly turn off natural gas.

2. **Electric Shutoff:** Every electric breaker box has a main shutoff switch. The switch is usually larger than the breakers and is labeled as the main supply line. This switch will shut off all electrical power to the home. Knowing where your breaker box is located and how to operate the main power switch is essential. Even if there isn't an emergency, for certain home fixes, you will need to direct a professional electrician to the breaker box. (Spend some time learning about the breaker switches in the box. Each switch controls power, on and off, to plugs and switches in the home. When installing a light fixture, plug or switch, you must know how to shut off the electricity.)

3. **Water Shutoff:** One of the most common and expensive insurance claims is due to water damage. I am not talking about floods caused by natural disasters. Faucets, pipes, dishwashers, washing machines and plumbing of all kinds can and do fail. There is a main water shutoff valve for your home. The most recent time I used the main water shutoff was for a bathroom faucet with a faulty connection fitting. Luckily, we were home when the fitting burst. I shut the water off quickly but after just one minute of running water, we had over $20,000 in damage to tile, wood floor, wall board and paint. A few gallons of water running into places where it is not meant to be can

cause major damage — just ask someone who has been gone over a weekend and came back to find their personal possessions floating throughout the house.

There are a few places where the water can be shutoff.

    A. **Water Meter**. Make sure you locate the meter and the shutoff valve (usually near the street). Have a tool nearby so you don't need to search during an emergency.

    B. **Water Shutoff at the House**. Most homes are built to include a shutoff in or around the house. Ask questions and find out where the shutoff is located. It could be in your crawl space. You don't want to go searching when the water must be turned off immediately.

    C. **Faucets and Toilets**. There should be shutoff valves located at every faucet and toilet in the house. There may or may not be a readily accessible shutoff valve for a bathtub or shower so the main shutoff may need to be used.

    D. **Winterizing Outdoor Pipes**. There is usually a shutoff available for all outdoor irrigation. In most cases there will be inground boxes with handles to turn on and turn off water flow. Make sure you know where these are located and how to operate them. Once you turn off the water for winter you should empty the system so that in the event of a freeze, pipes do not break.

CHAPTER SEVEN
FINANCE – MASTER CLASS

In this chapter there are five major areas we will cover.

1. ***Wealth Factor*** – Take an inventory of your financial progress and judge if you are on track to achieve your life plan.

2. ***Common Investments*** – You will learn about investing basics and common investments.

3. ***The Stock Market*** – Gain knowledge about the Stock Market.

4. ***Rule of 72*** – The power of investment earnings.

5. ***"Nuclear" Spending Test*** – This exercise will test your ability to implement drastic expense cutting measures.

WIDE-EYED WISDOM

The Real Deal

Both of my parents grew up during the Great Depression. Dad was born in 1919 and Mom in 1920. They were elementary age children when the depression placed its nasty grip on our country. Now mere chapters in our history books, I don't think any of us can imagine what it was really like to live in the late 1920's and into the 1930's. I suppose World War II was the catalyst to propel the U.S., leaving the depression behind and set the country on the path to become the next world power.

In my opinion the entry into World War II and then the bombing of Pearl Harbor ignited an American "terrible resolve" that fueled decades of growth in the United States. WWII provided a compelling goal the country rallied around. I also believe the war caused an overwhelming number of citizens to become resolute in the drive to grow our country into a world power and never again experience a world war. None of us want war, especially on our home soil. As Admiral Yamamoto predicted, Americans became personally committed to a terrible resolve to achieve what others had only dreamed of. Those that lived through WWII invested heavily in future generations. They possessed the will, motivation, desire, self-discipline, and selflessness to tackle the most difficult of obstacles.

> "I fear all we have done is to awaken a sleeping giant and fill him with a terrible resolve."[62]
>
> *Admiral Isoroku Yamamoto*
> *Japanese Commander in Chief, WWII*

The recent decades have been kind to most of us. In fact, the decades have been so kind to the citizens of this country that as we have lost the WWII generation one by one, perhaps we have also lost that terrible resolve Yamamoto spoke of many years ago. Today, I fear the terrible resolve known to so many in the U.S., has now disappeared.

I for one can never recall being hungry or without my basic needs. As you read earlier, I grew up in a large family that was by no means monetarily wealthy. We had what we needed to live, and some of what we wanted. My parents did not possess the earnings potential to live beyond their means and mom made sure she and our father never went overboard on spending.

CHAPTER SEVEN: FINANCE – MASTER CLASS

The children in our family benefited from the "life lessons" that were passed along by both parents – lessons that were the direct result of decades of difficulty, lean times, hard work and the unwavering drive to succeed.

My mom was a simple woman who raised her large family with love, while also possessing more drive and discipline than most could imagine. (Try raising eight children.) She would often tell us "to save for a rainy day". As a child I didn't understand why she focused so much on that lesson, but as I grew and matured, I realized that she grew up during a time of great uncertainty starting with the Great Depression and then lived through several periods of war. In other words, the rainy day for those generations was more like a great flood caused by the steady stream of cataclysmic world events.

The lessons mom taught me, and Cindy's mom taught her, regarding education, work ethic, discipline, and the value of money, stayed with us. Those lessons helped us make wise decisions as we finished college, entered career jobs, started a family, and lived our lives.

My wife and I learned that saving was not enough to accomplish what we dreamed of. Yes, we had heard about keeping six months of living expenses in ready cash reserves, just in case of job loss. (None of us should be living paycheck to paycheck, not knowing how we are going to deal with an emergency – like the worldwide coronavirus pandemic in 2019-2020.)

Beyond "emergency" cash savings, we realized that our money was not earning much by sitting in a bank drawing miniscule amounts of interest. We needed something more.

Yes, I had to earn more money and yes, we had to budget and control our spending. But we also knew we needed to invest money for our future. As teenagers, hearing rumors that Social Security programs would go broke, we embarked on a path to save and invest money so that no matter what, we would be taken care of later in life.

Personal Wealth

You have read and perhaps become more interested and knowledgeable about how to create and live on a budget. Budgeting skills will help you achieve your long-term financial goals, which are an important part of how to fund your life plan. You learned about how to create a path toward your life plan. You also read about important steps in your education and career. Knowledge in these areas is indispensable. Proficiency in budgeting, investing, education and career are required to achieve your life plan.

So how do we bring all of this together? What other tools might help you realize your life plan? There are two concepts that I want to introduce here – "Financial Freedom Goal" and "Wealth Factor".

Financial Freedom Goal, *a definition*
Look – I didn't grow up in a rich family. There was no trust fund or grand inheritance waiting for me. I have had to pave my own path and make disciplined decisions to take care of my wife, my family, and I. Many, many years ago, Cindy and I set a goal – to be able to live entirely off our investment income in retirement. We had heard that the future of Social Security was shaky. We also knew that Social Security income just would not pay for the sort of lifestyle we envisioned for our future. This led to identifying a goal – our Financial Freedom Goal – which is the target we have used to signal if we are prepared for retirement. (In other words, we would no longer be reliant on a paycheck to meet our desired future needs/lifestyle.)

> ***Financial Freedom Goal:*** *The amount of accumulated investments/savings to satisfy all future income requirements.*

Wealth Factor
The unit of measure we use when evaluating progress toward our Financial Freedom Goal is our Wealth Factor. I like the term Wealth Factor – it's the plain English version of the accounting term Net Worth. Plus, Wealth Factor just *feels* more positive and personal to me. What is Wealth Factor?

> ***Wealth Factor:*** *Today's cash value of all you own minus what you owe.*

In football terms, think of the Financial Freedom Goal as the end zone, and the Wealth Factor as the yardage gained, step by step, toward the game-winning touchdown.

CHAPTER SEVEN: FINANCE – MASTER CLASS

Let's Get Fired Up

If right now all you hear is, *"blah, blah, blah…"* get back in the game and pay attention! Why should you care? Well, the degree to which your assets outweigh your liabilities (and generate income) is what you are working for! *This* wisdom is why you invest in yourself and your career and why you save, invest, and make thoughtful, and purposeful financial decisions. After all, a life of financial freedom allows you to pursue your life plan goals. If you aren't focused on building your Wealth Factor, chances are you are more focused on spending in the moment and strapped month-to-month with limited flexibility. You don't want to live your life at the beckon call of the debt collector, or woefully unprepared for your future. I don't know about you, but I choose to be wise and secure my own future by building my Wealth Factor.

Take some time to consider what a life of total financial freedom looks like to you – this is the point where you have enough money saved (plus investment and other income streams) to cover all of your expenses and the fun things you want to do (or own), without having to work for a paycheck. For most, a retirement date makes sense as our timeline (though there are many people who have achieved financial freedom much earlier).

Be realistic – life is expensive! You will need to have money, lots of it. Remember our favorite saying – **you are responsible for yourself, your life, and your future…and your financial freedom.**

Estimate Your Financial Freedom Goal

	The Process	Example
STEP 1	**Create a Financial Freedom BUDGET** *What is the average monthly cost (adjusted for inflation) of your future Financial Freedom life? Include the fun stuff – like travel and hobbies.*	**Monthly Budget:** $9,000
STEP 2	**Estimate Social Security INCOME at Retirement Age** *You may need to use an average – be careful if you are young, this program could be defunct or changed significantly, if retirement is well into the future.*	**Social Security Income:** $1,500

WIDE-EYED WISDOM

STEP 3 **Estimate Defined Benefit/Pension INCOME**

Depending on the career you choose, there may or may not be a defined benefit or pension income. Check with your employer to find out.

Defined Benefit Income: $1,500

STEP 4 **Subtract your INCOME streams from your EXPENSES**

Subtract your Social Security and Defined Benefit/Pension income from your Financial Freedom Budget estimate. The remainder is what you will need to earn during retirement or draw from savings/investments each month.

Monthly Budget	$9,000
- S.S. Income	- 1,500
- D.B. Income	- 1,500
Monthly Income Need	$6,000

STEP 5 **Calculate Annual Income Need**

Multiply your monthly shortfall by 12. This will tell you the annual amount of additional income you need to sustain your life of financial freedom.

Annual Need:
$6,000 × 12 =
$72,000

STEP 6 **Choose a Retirement Income Tactic**

A. Do you want to live off your investment earnings?
B. Do you want to live off withdrawals from your investment principal?
C. Or a combination of investment earnings plus withdrawals from your principal?

STEP 7 **Calculate how much in Investments or Savings you must accumulate to generate the required income.**

We will make some conservative assumptions for the purposes of these examples. Talk with a financial advisor to drill into your specific situation.

Strategy A:
Investment Income

The goal is to generate enough income without cannibalizing the investment.

Strategy B:
Savings

The Savings requirement will be largely dependent on the age you desire to reach Financial Freedom.

CHAPTER SEVEN: FINANCE – MASTER CLASS

Annual Need	$72,000	
Earnings	3%	4%
Minimum Invest.	$72,000 /0.03=	$72,000 /0.04=
Portfolio	$2.4M	$1.8M

You will need $1.8M - $2.4M in investments to generate enough annual income to cover your Annual Need without touching the investment principal. Your family, charity or other organization will inherit the investment principal one day.

Sticking with our annual need of $72,000 – here is the amount of Savings necessary, to cover your expenses with a life expectancy of 85 years (not adjusted for inflation).

Financial Freedom Age	Years of Financial Freedom	Savings Required
40	45	$3.24M
50	35	$2.52M
60	25	$1.80M
70	15	$1.08M

(*As you make future estimates and calculations, keep annual inflation in mind. Living expenses today will carry a higher price tag in the future. If the finish line is 30-years from now, then inflation compounded over 30-years will be necessary. Keep in mind these figures are estimates. Consult a financial advisor for your specific situation.)

Now you have the tools to estimate the end-game – your target Financial Life Plan Goal. The reality is that the examples above are by no means the only options – there are just too many factors and combinations of strategies to cover. You could decide to live off investment earnings and principal withdrawals (which would reduce the amount of investments and earnings), or you could decide to work as long as you possibly can and then live off both investment income and savings, etc. A financial advisor can run through a multitude of scenarios with you. You decide which fits your life plan best.

The point is for you to realize that you must actively plan for and work towards your Wealth Factor to live the life you have designed and desire for yourself. Don't let anyone else dictate your plan or tell you that you can't achieve it! Worse yet, don't stick your head under a rock and tell yourself that you will figure it out someday. (Someday is now.) These figures may look daunting, but instead of being overwhelmed, take a moment to celebrate this new knowledge, put it into action, and know that you are building your future.

How to Get There

Now that you know your future goal, how are you going to get there? There are a multitude of online planning calculators, just search for "Retirement Calculator" and you will be able to plug in specifics like your current age, salary, desired retirement age (think: desired Financial Freedom age). We will run through an example just so you can see how it plays out.

Monthly Savings Requirement to Achieve Target Wealth Factor

Current Age:	23		
Desired Retirement Age:	66	➡	$750/month
Investment Return:	6%		Savings Rate
Savings Goal:	$1.8M		

Based on the example above, a 23-year old must sock away about $750 per month to reach their Financial Freedom Goal by the age of 66. I know that sounds like a lot of money. Saving $750 per month *is* a lot of money and *will* require hard work and sacrifice. But before you throw in the towel, consider the following:

- The $750 monthly investment is a straight-line approach.
- Your big earnings years are still ahead of you, so don't despair. There are many options, such as increased investments as income rises.
- The example used a 6% after tax earnings rate, which could be conservative (that means the higher your earnings rate, the faster your investments grow).
- Many companies offer matching deposits on 401(k) plans. Depending on the organization match, you might only need to invest $500 a month, if your organization matches half your contribution (some companies match at higher or lower rates).
- There are companies that include stock as part of your compensation – many millionaires are minted regularly due to stock awards.

CHAPTER SEVEN: FINANCE – MASTER CLASS

Key Takeaway – *Start today. Don't wait!*

If you have a 401(k) available, sign-up and deposit at least enough to achieve the maximum matching dollar amount. When you are considering career direction and opportunities, the compensation and benefits package is a critical component. It will have a substantial impact on your future. On the other hand, wasteful spending will be the kryptonite to your financial future – become a steward of your finances and mindfully make decisions to support your own goals. <u>These are your decisions to make.</u>

Tracking Your Wealth Factor

Let's assume you have figured out the total amount of money you must accumulate in savings and investments, at retirement, to reach your life plan financial goals. There will be two amounts on your mind now.
1. Your Total Wealth Factor Goal – the amount you must accumulate to achieve Financial Freedom
2. The Monthly Investment Contribution to achieve your Wealth Factor

Good, let's move on. I'll show you how my wife and I track our progress. I like to monitor two factors of our future financial vitality, both which center on the principle of assets minus liabilities. Let me explain each.

Wealth Factor = ASSETS – DEBT – SELLING FEES

Vitality #1: INVESTMENT Wealth Factor
All the Investments You Own

The first wealth factor includes all the <u>investments</u> you own. This calculation does not include your personal residence, vacation home, or personal property. The reason we track this factor is because we don't want to sell our home or personal property to fund our Financial Freedom Goal. We don't consider those items "investment" assets. We require a bank of investments that are strictly meant to work for us and generate earnings.

Let's talk about how to calculate the current INVESTMENT Wealth Factor so we can track progress toward your required total dollar investment amount. Use today's current market value of all your investments and subtract any liabilities (debt).

How to Calculate Your INVESTMENT Wealth Factor

Include:
+
- Real Estate *(investment property, land, rental home)*
- Cash
- Savings
- Investments
- Valuable Collectibles *(rare/vintage cars, coins, etc…)*
- Any other item that can be quickly converted to cash *(you intend to cash out)*

DO NOT Include:
- Primary Residence
- Vacation Home *(unless you plan to sell to fund your retirement)*
- Hobby items *(ordinary collections with minimal values)*
- Cars
- Boats and Other Recreational Vehicles
- Personal property
- Furniture
- Anticipated inheritance

−
- Debt
Short Term (credit card debt)
Long Term (mortgage, car loan, student loan, etc.)

We don't include the items on the right side of the table because they are daily lifestyle items – consumables. You probably won't become a nomad and sell every item you own. Each of these *could* be converted to cash if you had to, but the market value is a fraction of what you might hope/estimate. Plus, you probably won't sell the home you live in, unless you decide to downsize.

It sounds like many people believe they will either win the lottery or inherit money from family members to build their wealth factor. All their financial "efforts" seem to point toward accumulating on the right side of the table, with absolutely zero impact on their own wealth or a secure future. Don't fall into this trap. This is a dangerous and foolhardy gamble. Don't believe that

CHAPTER SEVEN: FINANCE – MASTER CLASS

someone else is going to take care of you. Hate to break it to you, but you are not going to win the lottery – the lottery has astronomical odds against you. And a potential or promised inheritance can easily fail to materialize. After all, uncontrollable external forces are steering that ship.

Once you have the total value of your investments, subtract your liabilities to calculate your Investment Wealth Factor.

Vitality #2: TOTAL Wealth Factor
All the Investments You Own Plus Personal Real Estate

Once you have your INVESTMENT Wealth Factor nailed down, it is easy to calculate your TOTAL Wealth Factor. Simply add today's market value, minus selling fees of the personal real estate you own, to calculate your TOTAL Wealth Factor. Why is this factor important? Well, you may in fact decide that in retirement you don't really want a large home or vacation home. You may want to sell and downsize. This calculation gives you another viewing angle as you monitor the progress of your assets. Leave all the other items, consumables for living, out of your Total Wealth Factor calculation.

Tracking Progress

Our Wealth Factor is the direct measure of whether Cindy and I have reached our Financial Freedom Goal. We track it on a quarterly basis. Each quarterly investment statement is entered into a spreadsheet, as well as an update on any outstanding debt. The quarterly reviews allow us to make regular minor course corrections to monthly investment deposits, investment choices and spending. Much like flying an airplane, frequent minor course corrections are required to assure a safe trip from takeoff to landing. When forced to make drastic course corrections, you might be crashing the plane – oops, I mean your life plan.

Back to one of my favorite abilities, self-discipline. If you commit to a realistic target goal, plan how you are going to get there, have the discipline to follow through with regular contributions, and faithfully track your progress, I have no doubt that not only will you be in charge of your future and meet your goal, you just might exceed it. **See Resources: Exhibit 8, p. 248 for a sample Wealth Factor tracking sheet.**

WIDE-EYED WISDOM

As you will see in the coming sections, there are plenty of smart ways, aside from just saving cash, to grow your money to reach your goals today and in the future.

Common Investments

Different from savings, sound investments are a way to grow your money at a much faster rate. Each of us must figure out ways to set aside money (Savings) and put that money to work to grow and earn income on a regular basis. We want our money to work when we are not working (Investments).

Investment, defined:
To invest is to allocate money (or sometimes another resource, such as time) in the expectation of **some benefit in the future**. *In finance, the expected future benefit from investment is a return. The return may consist of capital gain and/or investment income, including dividends, interest, rental income etc.*[63]

Types of Investments
Pop quiz time! Yikes - does that just send chills through your body? Let's see how familiar you are with common and not so common investments. Write down your answers in the space provided. Answers are provided in the following pages.

1. What is an *annuity*?
   _____
   _____
   _____

2. What is *common stock*?
   _____
   _____
   _____

CHAPTER SEVEN: FINANCE – MASTER CLASS

3. What is *preferred stock*?

4. What is the difference between *common* and *preferred stock*?

5. What is a *401(k)*?

6. What is an *IRA*?

7. What are *529 plans*?

8. What is a *mutual fund*?

9. What is a *bond*?

WIDE-EYED WISDOM

10. If a company is bankrupt, who is *paid first* from the proceeds – *common stock, bond holder* or *preferred stock*?

11. What is a *CD*?

12. What is a *commodity*?

13. What is a *warrant*?

14. What is a *stock option*?

15. What is the *average annual* (pre-tax) *return* from the *stock market* over the past 90-years?

* * * * * * *

CHAPTER SEVEN: FINANCE – MASTER CLASS

The Answers:

1. **What is an *annuity*?**

    A financial product that pays out a fixed stream of payments to an individual. These financial products are primarily used as an income stream for retirees.[64]

2. **What is *common stock*?**

    Common stock is a security that represents ownership in a corporation. Holders of common stock exercise control by electing a board of directors and voting on corporate policy. Common stockholders are at the bottom of the priority ladder in terms of ownership structure; in the event of liquidation, common shareholders have rights to a company's assets only after bondholders, preferred shareholders and other debtholders are paid in full.[65]

3. **What is *preferred stock*?**

    Capital stock which provides a specific dividend that is paid before any dividends are paid to common stock holders and which takes precedence over common stock in the event of a liquidation. Like common stock, preferred stocks represent partial ownership in a company, although preferred stock shareholders do not enjoy any of the voting rights of common stockholders. Also unlike common stock, a preferred stock pays a fixed dividend that does not fluctuate, although the company does not have to pay this dividend if it lacks the financial ability to do so.[66]

4. **What is a *401(k)*?**

    401(k) Plan is a defined contribution plan where an employee can make contributions from his or her paycheck either before or after-tax, depending on the options offered in the plan. The contributions go into a 401(k) account, with the employee often choosing the investments based on options provided under the plan. In some plans, the employer also makes contributions such as matching the employee's contributions up to a certain percentage.[67]

WIDE-EYED WISDOM

5. **What is an *IRA*?**

    Individual Retirement Account. A tax-deferred retirement account for an individual that permits individuals to set aside money each year, with earnings tax-deferred until withdrawals begin at age 59 1/2 or later (or earlier, with a 10% penalty). The exact amount depends on the year and your age. IRAs can be established at a bank, mutual fund, or brokerage. Only those who do not participate in a pension plan at work or who do participate and meet certain income guidelines can make deductible contributions to an IRA. All others can make contributions to an IRA on a non-deductible basis.[68]

6. **What are *529 plans*?**

    A 529 plan is a tax-advantaged savings plan designed to encourage saving for future education costs. 529 plans, legally known as "qualified tuition plans," are sponsored by states, state agencies, or educational institutions and are authorized by Section 529 of the Internal Revenue Code.

    There are two types of 529 plans: prepaid tuition plans and education savings plans. All fifty states and the District of Columbia sponsor at least one type of 529 plan. In addition, a group of private colleges and universities sponsor a prepaid tuition plan.[69]

7. **What is a *mutual fund*?**

    A mutual fund is a type of financial vehicle made up of a pool of money collected from many investors to invest in securities such as stocks, bonds, money market instruments, and other assets. Mutual funds are operated by professional money managers, who allocate the fund's assets and attempt to produce capital gains or income for the fund's investors.

    Mutual funds give small or individual investors access to professionally managed portfolios of equities, bonds, and other securities. Each shareholder, therefore, participates proportionally in the gains or losses of the fund.[70]

CHAPTER SEVEN: FINANCE – MASTER CLASS

8. What is a *bond*?
   A bond is a fixed income instrument that represents a loan made by an investor to a borrower (typically corporate or governmental). A bond could be thought of as an I.O.U. between the lender and borrower that includes the details of the loan and its payments. Bonds are used by companies, municipalities, states, and sovereign governments to finance projects and operations. Owners of bonds are debtholders, or creditors, of the issuer. Bond details include the end date when the principal of the loan is due to be paid to the bond owner and usually includes the terms for variable or fixed interest payments made by the borrower.[71]

9. If a company is bankrupt, who is *paid first* from the proceeds – *common stock*, *bond holder* or *preferred stock*?
   Bond Holder

10. What is a *CD*?
    A certificate of deposit (CD) is a time deposit, a financial product commonly sold in the United States and elsewhere by banks, thrift institutions, and credit unions. CDs are like savings accounts in that they are insured "money in the bank" and thus virtually risk free.[72]

11. What is a *commodity*?
    A physical substance, such as food, grains, and metals, which is interchangeable with another product of the same type, and which investors buy or sell, usually through futures contracts.[73]

12. What is a warrant?
    Nope, we aren't arresting anyone. In finance, a warrant is a security that entitles the holder to buy shares of stock of the issuing company at a fixed price called exercise price, until a fixed expiration date.[74]

WIDE-EYED WISDOM

13. **What is a stock option?**
    A stock option gives an investor the right, but not the obligation, to buy or sell a stock at an agreed upon price and date. There are two types of options: **puts**, which is a bet that a stock will fall, or **calls**, which is a bet that a stock will rise.[75]

14. **What is the *average annual return* from the *stock market* over the past 90 years (pre-tax)?**
    The average annual return (pre-tax) from the S&P 500 for the past 90-years is about 10%.[76]

Investing Thoughts

If you made it through the quiz, I imagine that your eyes have glazed over a bit and you might have reached for your cell phone a time or two. Don't check out now. These lessons on Investments are too important to miss. The difference between having the knowledge to achieve your financial (and life plan) goals and wishing you did, is actually putting the time in now – yes, now – to learn the strategies to make your hard-earned money work for you to support your future. No one else is going to do this for you. Remember – **you are responsible for yourself, your life, your future**. And that includes your financial future. Pay attention and be ready to research and enact strategies in your own life – the sooner the better.

On that note, the first thing I learned about investing was to **start immediately**. You *can* afford to do something now. Saving and Investing should be a priority no matter your age. Of course, the earlier you start the better. Whether you have $50 or $50,000 now is the time to put the money to work for you. Don't wait or convince yourself that you can't afford to put money aside. It may be difficult at first, but once you see your investments grow you will experience a new feeling of satisfaction and freedom. The satisfaction of watching your investments grow will motivate you to become savvier and more committed to reach (and maybe even surpass) your Financial Freedom goal.

Figure out ways to make consistent investments, each month if possible. Find investment dollars by controlling monthly expenses (remember that

CHAPTER SEVEN: FINANCE – MASTER CLASS

Budget!), making more money (hello side-hustle) or by using unexpected tax refunds or cash windfalls. Holding expenses constant and making more money is a fast way to grow your investments.

Cindy and I arranged regular payroll deductions each month that went straight into a 401(k) plan. Once we adjusted to the idea of the automatic payroll deduction, we did not miss the money coming out of our paycheck. Over the long-haul our investments grew beyond what we had ever imagined.

If nothing else, make sure that you have taken advantage of your company/organization sponsored 401(k) plan. There is usually an employer match, ensuring an immediate return on your 401(k) investment. There is also a significant federal and in some cases state income tax benefit. Your 401(k) deduction is a reduction to your gross income. You won't be taxed on the income until you make withdrawals. Withdrawals from a 401(k) account can be made without penalty, (still taxed) after you reach the age of 59 ½. Keep in mind that if you withdraw money from a 401(k) account prior to the age of 59 ½, you will pay a 10% penalty plus Federal and State income taxes.

Right now, some of you are thinking, "But Keith, I barely have enough to make it month to month. And my income earning potential is limited. There's just no way I can invest." Sorry, but bull. That is an excuse. I have read many stories about people with modest incomes and lifestyles that left millions to families, friends, and charities. And no, they did not win the lottery.

Some examples from, "These People Donated Millions After They Died – But No One Knew They Were Rich"[77]:
- Former secretary left more than $8 million to education and scholarship funds.
- Retired grocer left $13 million to a Catholic school.
- Janitor left $5 million to a hospital.
- Special education teacher left $8.4 million, split between educational causes and the Humane Society.

What did these folks have in common? Each practiced modest spending. Each made smart investment decisions and left their money to grow. In some cases, they had no children to bequeath their estate to, so they left their money to benefit the "kids" they never had.

WIDE-EYED WISDOM

I'm not saying that you need to be as frugal as these folks must have been. What I am saying is that with good decision making and self-discipline, you will find the right balance of income, spending and investing. Identify the path to achieve your life plan goals, get on it and stay on it.

There is no magic in investing. If you think there is a way to "get rich quick" be careful. Remember the old saying, "if it sounds too good to be true it probably is". It takes discipline, research, knowledge, timing, and consistent deposits to make headway.

Investments are in some ways like your personality. Be comfortable with what you invest in – know and understand how your money is invested – and be comfortable with the risk and potential returns. Your investments should never cause you to be anxious or lose sleep.

A good rule of thumb is to ask…*How strongly do I believe in this source as a place to invest my hard-earned cash?* When your homework is finished, if the investment makes you uncomfortable, you might want to look for other places to invest. There are always other investment opportunities that may be a better fit for you.

The Stock Market

Is the stock market right for you? Picking individual stocks requires market knowledge, copious research, and the development of an investment strategy. If this sounds interesting to you, dig in and learn. Beginners may want to get their feet wet with <u>Index Funds</u> rather than investing in individual companies.

Common Stock

Most savvy investors will tell you to buy stock for the long-term. Don't look at stock as a regular trading game. Experts suggest you buy solid well-run companies that have great long-term prospects. Picking the right companies will usually result in growth of the stock share value and pay regular dividends.

You may find opportunities to buy stock at a low price with the intent of selling when the share price reaches a certain level. (I'm not telling you to do that. Timing the market may be a fool's game.) If you go this route, buying and selling regularly, understand the risk. Also, if you have sold your stock and it goes higher still, don't kick yourself. Be satisfied with your planned gain.

CHAPTER SEVEN: FINANCE – MASTER CLASS

Buying and selling common stock is not necessarily for first-time or casual investors. Most people elect to buy mutual funds. Mutual funds are managed daily by a team of professionals that understand investment strategies, financial markets, risk management and how to build a solid portfolio.

Investing Cycles

There are cycles to the stock market. **Look at the chart below.**[78] Note the peaks and valleys. Your greatest gains will likely be made with consistent investing over the long haul – the annual stock market return over the past 100-years has been about 10%.[79]

The Dow Jones Industrial Average stock market index since 1990:
- Average growth of 9.2% pre-tax over the past 30-years.
- Notice the correction periods in the years 1990, 2000 and 2008.
- This is a high-level example of historical earnings of the Dow Jones.
- You may choose to invest in something totally different.
- Invest in what you understand, makes sense, and will not cause you to lose sleep at night.
- Seek professional advice on where to invest your hard-earned money.

WIDE-EYED WISDOM

> "Be fearful when others are greedy and greedy when others are fearful."[80]
>
> Warren Buffett

What I have experienced (and what I think Mr. Buffett is saying) is to buy when an investment has hit a down cycle. The investment must make sense. Think: well-run company with good long-term upside. When individuals get nervous about investments, they sell. History tells us that people will sell at ridiculously low prices. When individual investors are jumping ship and selling at low prices, Buffet believes that may be the time to aggressively buy more stock in companies he believes in. Buffet won't buy on a whim or try to time the market.

Trying to time a market is difficult at best. If you take a long-term approach by buying stocks that are strong long-lasting organizations, you will be better prepared to hold onto your investments through the highs and lows.

There are investment advisors available that understand market fundamentals well enough to give you an idea of when to hold certain investments and when it is time to sell others. Choose wisely when you are in the market for a financial advisor. An excellent financial advisor will take the time to understand your goals and will help get you there.

If you are into buying common stock, maintain enough flexibility to take advantage of a major market pullback or down cycle. Be ready to increase investments in the best organizations when the opportunity is available.

Power of Compounding Interest: Rule of 72

I learned a lesson about the power of investment earnings for the first time when I was a junior in college. I could have used financial knowledge at a much earlier age – I was fully capable of understanding the concepts and so are you. Thank goodness I learned this lesson early enough to make a difference.

If you have never heard about the Rule of 72, do yourself a favor and pay attention – then enroll in a personal finance class at the first opportunity.

CHAPTER SEVEN: FINANCE – MASTER CLASS

Rule of 72 in Action – *a Hypothetical Example*
This situation may become very real to many of you.

Imagine yourself at the age of 21. You are one of three siblings. The oldest is 24 and the youngest is 17.

Fresh out of college you are working an entry level career job with good upward mobility. You don't make much money and can barely afford to pay rent, utilities, food, clothes, and occasional entertainment. Lucky for you, work is close enough to your apartment that you can take mass transit or bike.

You have always dreamed of owning your own car. You would love to travel. But your parents paid for your education, not wheels. You can still remember the speech, "When you can pay for a car, insurance, maintenance and gas on your own, then you have our permission". Clearly mom and dad were not about to pay for your car, after funding your college education. (Many of the rest of us had to pay for both schooling and car so you are in a great spot whether you admit it or not.)

The summer after graduation a family member of yours passes-away. (If that hasn't happened in your family yet, it will. Life and death are part of the journey.)

Of course, you are bereaved at the loss of a loved one. You are also the fortunate benefactor of their generosity. You and your two siblings will inherit the house your family member lived in.

The house is modest with a market value of about $220,000 and no mortgage or liens. The three of you agree to sell the house and split the proceeds. After closing costs and real estate fees there is $195,000 remaining. Each of you will receive $65,000.

*Mom has encouraged each of you to invest for your future. She insists that building a firm financial foundation will be important later in life. After the news spreads, your friends (and now several "new" friends have popped up) are talking to you about ways to spend the money. Adding fuel to the fire, you just heard a prominent billionaire daytime TV show host ask her audience what you would **buy first** if you won the lottery. If a self-made billionaire said it, then spending must be the answer.*

You have all kinds of possibilities in front of you – $65,000 is a lot of money. You and your siblings make three different choices about what to do with your inheritance.

Choice 1: *The oldest decides to travel the world. Money is spent on airfare, food, lodging, and incidentals. A great time was had and there are many stories to tell. You spend a whole hour looking at wonderful pictures of exotic destinations your big sister visited, not to mention all the social media posts you have enviously seen as she documented her journey.*

WIDE-EYED WISDOM

Now, with the money dried up and no job your sibling crashes at your place until she can find a new job that pays enough to support the necessities. You don't know how long this situation will last. Feeding another person has put a crimp in your already tight finances. But one thing is certain, if you continue to pay for her housing and food, your ability to survive will collapse and both of you will be asking your parents for support.

Choice 2: *What should you do with your $65,000? You are still paying for some of your older sibling's expenses, but you don't want to miss out on all the fun, so you decide to buy your first shiny new set of wheels. You live in an area with cold winters. Snow and ice are hazardous, especially if you don't have the right transportation. All-wheel drive will be your best bet. You would like to take up snowboarding and would like space for friends and equipment, so an SUV is the logical choice.*

The cost of a new fully loaded SUV is $45,000. If you take good care of the SUV it will last 8 to 10 years. Insurance is about $1,500 per year. Gas is another $1,500. For the first few years the car is under warranty so there will be little maintenance. Since you are new to the job market and are unsure if you can get a favorable auto loan you decide to pay cash for the SUV. The total first year cost of your new vehicle is $48,000.

Now that you have the SUV you decide to take your buddies on a vacation to snowboard at a cost of $2,000. After the spending spree that lasted a whole week, you are left with $15,000. Not knowing what to do with the money, but remembering your mom telling you to save, you leave the remaining $15,000 in a savings account earning 1%. (You will earn a little more than $150 per year on your $15,000.) Doesn't sound like much but after all, mom did say to save your money. You have also heard people talk about having funds available just in case there is an emergency like your oldest sibling moving in with you or losing your job.

Choice 3: *The youngest in your family is 17 and about to enter college. Mom and dad made the same college deal with the youngest, so if a "B" average is maintained, four years of college are paid. Best of all, the youngest has heard from you how great it has been without student loan payments after graduation.*

Mom, still the guardian for your underage brother, convinces him to invest the $65,000 at least until school is finished. The money will be available after graduation to either buy a car or pay for a master's program. Following mom's advice, your younger brother decides to invest the money and let it earn for him while he is in school – he won't need a car anyway. Mom and your little brother find an investment that will earn 6% after taxes.

CHAPTER SEVEN: FINANCE – MASTER CLASS

Decisions made! The inheritance has all been spent or invested.

If this was your real life, what would you do with this remarkable gift? How much would you have remaining a month or two after receiving your windfall?

People are predictable. Most would go the route of buying the car and spending until the money was gone. Yes, it would be fun for a while. But would the assortment of clothes, gadgets, entertainment, and travel leave any lasting positive impact on your life? Once the tags and packages are all disposed of and you have tired of your new purchases, then what?

> "Here is a new car, a new iPhone. We buy. We discard. We buy again. In recent years, we've been doing it faster."[81]
>
> Russell Hochschild

I am not saying you shouldn't spend *some* of the money. What I am saying is that with eyes wide-open, think, learn, and understand the options and consequences before you make your decision.

You might be thinking, "But this will never happen to me". Perhaps these specific details won't apply to you, but you *will* be faced with similar decisions whether the money is earned, gifted or borrowed.

Back to my college finance class. One of the first lessons was the **Rule of 72**. Albert Einstein determined that you could use a factor of 72 divided by your percentage earnings rate after taxes and calculate how long it will take for your investment to double in value.[82]

Rule of 72

If you invest a sum of money and leave it alone, no additions and no withdrawals, you can estimate the time it will take for the money to double in value.

The Formula: $\dfrac{72}{\text{Earnings Rate after Taxes}} = $ Number of Years to **Double** Your Investment

Let's look at our hypothetical example above to see how your younger brother's investment is faring.

When the youngest in the family picked up that first college finance lesson there was renewed enthusiasm in support of his $65,000 investment decision. Here is what he found when he plugged in his investment of $65,000 with a 6% annual after tax return.

WIDE-EYED WISDOM

$$\frac{72}{6\%} = \textbf{12-Years to Double His Investment}$$

Satisfied with his choice, your younger brother leaves the investment to grow and focuses on his studies. Three years later, he checks on the current value of his initial investment. What a pleasant surprise — that money has grown to $77,400. With the knowledge he has gained in finance class, he estimates the value of his account will be about $82,000 at graduation.

After graduation, your younger brother considers what to do with his inheritance. After all, it has grown — perhaps it is time to take some money out to buy his first car. But instead, your brother reasons that he has accepted a job with a promising career trajectory — he will be able to meet his basic financial requirements without tapping into those funds. He decides to leave the money alone and let it grow indefinitely. After all, the inheritance was a surprise gift — he never expected to receive that kind of money. Using his new financial skills, your brother calculates how much he will have accumulated in his investment if he leaves the money alone. Wow, your little brother will be a millionaire. Wait, he just finished school and he hasn't started his job yet!

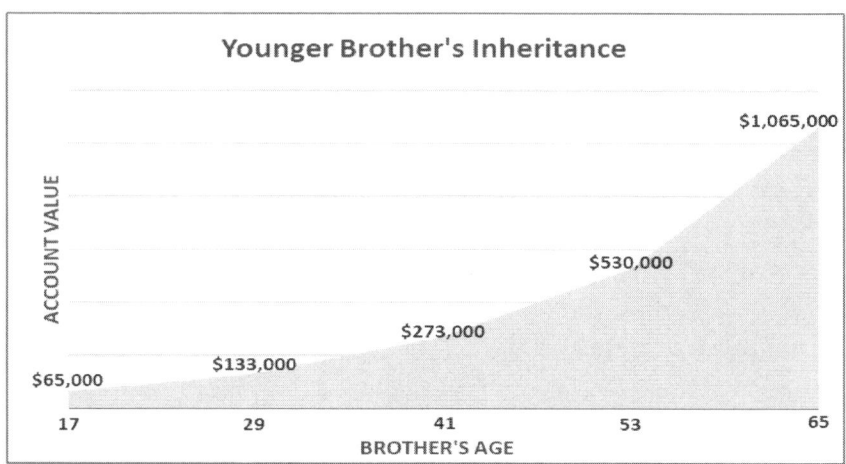

This example illustrates what can happen when you implement (Money + Basic Investment Knowledge + Discipline + Wisdom) x Earnings x Time. After reading this example you should have the skill to estimate the potential value of a sound investment, when allowed to grow over time.

Most important is to understand the potential long-term value of an investment before you decide to opt for buying some item that will give you short-term gratification and eventually be worth nothing.

CHAPTER SEVEN: FINANCE – MASTER CLASS

How dumb can you be?

Most of us have heard stories about lottery winners who have blown through their windfall of millions buying stuff. True story…I saw a show about a lottery winner (who had won *tens of millions of dollars*) bragging about all that he had bought. He opened a closet and proudly displayed his sound system that was "worth" $60,000. (Sorry sir, you *paid* $60,000 for that system.) Once installed, that depreciating asset was worth a fraction of what he spent. Later broke, the (poor – became rich – became poor) man either sold that system for pennies on the dollar or lost it entirely when his house was repossessed.

Yes, you read that right. This man who won *tens of millions of dollars* was flat broke in a few years. Can you believe it?!? If only he had invested those millions. He could have had about $2 million a year to spend (pre-tax income) without ever touching the principal. If only he had found and followed some great professional investment advice. A fool and his money…

In Conclusion: Next time you have a decision to spend on a can't live without item (that is soon to be worth nothing) or invest…keep the Rule of 72 front of mind and estimate potential investment gains. Is buying the item you just can't live without still worth it?

Let's Go Nuclear! – A Spend/Expense-Cutting Exercise

Now that you have learned about investments and the amazing power of compounded earnings, I bet you are ready to start making some smart, future-looking decisions with your money. I will also bet that for most, "finding" the money to get started may be a challenge. Well that is just what we are going to do – we are going to shake out your budget, evaluate your spending and find opportunities to save right now.

Before we get started, realize that these concepts and suggestions might seem radical. And this exercise will likely introduce some pain points. But what I want you to focus on, is that you are in charge, and you get to make the choices where you spend (or invest!) your money. Sacrifices today equal big returns, and progress toward your future goals!

If you worked through the Budget exercise earlier, this will be easier to accomplish. Our goal is to identify how much money you have available to save/invest by first identifying which expenses are necessary to survive and then eliminate all other expenses.

STEP 1: List All Monthly Expenses
Here is what I want you to do. Pull out your bank and credit card statements and list all monthly expenses. Get as granular as you can, which will help with the next step. (If you created a real Budget in Chapter 3, you already did this.)

STEP 2: Challenge
This is hard! Challenge your current thinking. Does each spend make the "absolute must" category? Do you have a house that outsizes your budget? Is your car a gas hog? Do you really need a daily latte? You already spend hours a day in front of a computer, do you need multiple streaming subscriptions?

STEP 3: Go Nuclear
Be realistic about what you truly must spend to survive. What spending could you eliminate or reduce?

STEP 4: Identify Saving/Investment $$$'s
How many dollars will the nuclear exercise free up for you to save or invest?

$$\text{Monthly Income} - \text{Current Spend} = \$$$
$$\text{vs.}$$
$$\text{Monthly Income} - \text{Nuclear Spend} = \$$$

CHAPTER SEVEN: FINANCE – MASTER CLASS

Nuclear Spending Challenge

CATEGORY	COMPONENT	CURRENT SPEND	CHALLENGE YOURSELF	NUCLEAR SPEND
TAXES	Income:	$		$
	Property:			
	Other:			
LIVING EXPENSES	Housing (Rent):		Roommate?	
	Food (Groceries):		Reduce by 10%	
	Utilities - Electricity:		Reduce by 10%	
	Utilities - Garbage:			
	Cell Phone:		Shop for a cheaper plan	
	Transportation (Fuel):		Carpool/bus/bike	
	Insurance:		Get Competing Quotes	
	Medical:			
	Other:			
DEBT PAYMENTS	Car Loan:		Trade-in and pay cash	
	Mortgage:		Ditch the McMansion	
	Student Loan:			
	Credit Card:			
	Other:			
CHARITABLE GIVING	Donations:		Be generous – you are more fortunate than you know	
DISCRETIONARY	Clothing:		Seriously, no more shoes	
	Eating Out:		It's called a brown bag - pack a lunch	
	Coffee:		You don't need the status cup, make coffee at home	
	Memberships (Gym):		Walk or run the block	
	Cable and Internet:		Sorry – you *could* do without, if you had to	
	Subscriptions:		Really, three services?	
	Entertainment:		Skip the movies and go for a hike or pick up a book	
	Other Retail:		Just stay away – it's a trap	
	Travel:		Think…staycation…	
	Other:		Leave the plastic at home	
	TOTAL:	**$**		**$**

WIDE-EYED WISDOM

STEP 5: Stop Making Excuses

Look – I am not steering your ship, you are. You are the one that makes the decisions. What is your life plan? Do you want to be in charge, or do you want spending to control you? You have the choice and the control. The ball is in your court. If you want to make wise financial decisions, do not let excuses stop you. You <u>can</u> do it!

So why did I ask you to do this exercise? Now you have learned to:
- Understand a need versus a want versus going overboard.
- Learn your <u>true</u> cost to live.
- In case of an emergency you identified expenses to cut.
- Understand you have more control over your finances than you think.
- Identify your saving and investing potential.
- Develop some "what-if" scenarios around spending habits.
- Determine if you can meet your life plan at your current income, or whether you must find another career or other income source(s).

Last Will and Testament

A last will and testament is a legal document instructing your wishes in the event of your death. You give instructions as to how you want your estate to be distributed, who becomes guardian for your children, who handles the final disposition of your estate, among other personal wishes.

Why is this important? If you pass-away with no will, the state will take control of your estate. Someone you don't know will determine how property, other assets and how your children will be cared for. How does it feel to know a stranger will decide what they want to do with your estate and your children? No not so good huh?

One last point before you create a will. Take special care with who you appoint as a beneficiary or beneficiaries for your bank accounts, retirement assets like a 401k, insurance policies, etc. Assign beneficiaries and avoid legal entanglements that will cost your heirs time and money.

CHAPTER EIGHT
CAREER – MASTER CLASS

This chapter is for those that may be in or wish to be in a leadership position during their career. Hopefully, that is you!

You will learn indispensable leadership/executive leadership skills:
- My **essential eleven** leadership skills. These are the lessons I focused on during my leadership development studies. Master these subjects, raise your professional ceiling, or perhaps blow it through the roof.

- **Patience**: Patience at work and what might be more important.

- Career **Involvement or Commitment**: A story about how to examine whether you are *involved* or *committed* to your career and life plan.

- Serious **Problems at Work**: Real life situations that make their way into many organizations. How to prepare and respond when faced with serious people issues.

- **Stretch Yourself**: Still wondering if you are capable? Read on for armed forces wisdom.

- **Business Ownership Financial Returns**: This lesson is a relatively short and simple acid test to judge business returns.

WIDE-EYED WISDOM

Essential Eleven

I bet you can think of at least a few TV or movie characters who rose to the rank of "leader" and ruled by manipulation, force, or coercive power. Usually these characters meet a dismal end – and you probably cheer. Power plus mean and nasty isn't likely to be effective for long. People make a conscious choice about whether to follow, or not. In the real world, generally a coercive leader is resisted by the team – perhaps not overtly, but the resistance is present. Team members may be unhappy, leave the organization, waste time complaining, and are highly unlikely to deliver optimal performance. Each of these behaviors will suck the life out of what is supposed to be a high-performance team.

Think of your own life – what sort of leaders do you respect and want to follow? Without hesitation I am most likely to follow a leader that I respect as an expert. **Expert power** is mighty, indeed. When *expert power* is combined with *effective leadership skills and with personal attributes; confidence, authenticity, trust, vision, compassion, drive, and curiosity,* results can be extraordinary.

Great leaders surround themselves with the right people who possess more skill and expertise in their specialty, than that of the leader. This is how I want you to approach leadership – developing, positioning, challenging, motivating, directing, and caring for your team members. When you provide these things, your team will execute beautifully.

I have often been asked what subjects and skills I recommend for somebody desiring to move up the corporate leadership ladder – I believe there are an essential eleven. It is not a requirement for you to be the very best at each of these subjects, but you should be well versed in all of them. The more you know about each subject and the proper application in your organization, the higher the likelihood that you will separate yourself from the pack of peers and raise your value.

Essential Eleven Leadership Skills

1. Lead

First let me say that nobody ever really arrives as a leader – there is always more to learn. The world and its inhabitants are far too complex for a leader to have all the answers.

CHAPTER EIGHT: CAREER – MASTER CLASS

We have a severe shortage of quality leaders. As a result, there are lots of people that have been put in leadership positions with little clue about how to lead effectively. Make sure you are one of the people that is truly qualified.

Learn what it means to **lead** – people don't want to be *managed*. Assets like equipment and property are managed. (For you HR professionals out there…consider using the term leader instead of "manager". The term "your manager" is dated by decades.)

You can't be a jerk and be an effective leader. The days of temper tantrums and pounding the table are over. Instead, seek to understand each individual and how they want to be treated. An effective leader must be approachable, predictable, and safe. Your team members should feel like you will always listen intently and remain calm as you work through issues.

There are countless books and courses on leadership. Figure out which are best for you and commit to be a lifelong student of leadership. The leadership risks are great and rewards exponentially greater. Here are some of the major items that will rest on your shoulders as a leader:

- **Personally**
    - Set the right example
    - Faithful steward of organization assets
    - Develop, model, and maintain trust and integrity
- **For Your Team**
    - Serve your team, customers, and organization – always protect their welfare
    - Effective and Timely Communication
    - Provide vision
    - Development of your team
- **For Your Organization**
    - Take care of customers
    - Strategy
    - Planning
    - Budgeting
    - Recognize talent, skills, and abilities
    - Hiring and discipline
    - Responsibility and accountability for results

2. Expert Knowledge

It amazes me how little information organizational associates know about the business they are in – this is the fault of leadership. To be an effective leader, take ownership of educating yourself and your team about the industry, how your organization fits, why each person is important and how to improve their own performance to be successful.

Hold yourself and your team accountable to understand priorities, strategy, and how to improve their personal performance to positively impact organizational results. Once your team knows "what", "how" and "why", they will make things happen, without you looking over their shoulder.

When you become an expert in your business the following happens:
- You understand how to impact results.
- You can connect the dots – actions to results.
- You exude confidence.
- You relate well with stakeholders.
- You see things others are unable to see.
- You can teach others.
- You anticipate problems and know exactly what caused them.
- You become a trusted information source.
- You have a firm grasp of the tactics and strategies that drive your organization's performance.
- You become more valuable to your organization.
- Your team is highly likely to follow you.

3. Finance

Time and time again I have witnessed an interesting phenomenon during financial statement reviews. Imagine a boardroom with a long table down the middle with every leather-covered chair filled, shoulder to shoulder. The latest financial statements are hot off the presses and distributed to the group of executives. One side of the table is totally confused – their eyes glaze over as they stare intently, without understanding, at the figures in front of them. The other side of the table also intently views the financial statements, but instead of staring dazed and confused, they eagerly analyze the facts and figures in

CHAPTER EIGHT: CAREER – MASTER CLASS

front of them while tying this objective measure of performance to the strategic objectives led by their teams. Which side of the table do you want to sit on?

Financial statements are a statistical synopsis of what has happened in the business, much like the batting average for a hitter in baseball. Financial systems are simply a group of buckets that collect similar purpose transactions. As the transactions are totaled, expenses are subtracted from revenues and there is either a profit or loss. Of course, that is a simple view, but that is really all you need to know to begin. That knowledge drives your understanding of how specific actions impact the financial statements. If you know that kind of detail, you know what buttons to push to enhance results.

Effective leaders and executives *must* understand financial statements. If you don't understand financial statements, you are at a significant disadvantage. Or, perhaps better said, if you *do* understand financial statements, you possess a significant advantage over your peers.

The Importance of Understanding Financial Statements:
- You are one of the few that can link organization actions to results.
- You understand the organization results, trends, and cycles.
- You understand what buttons to push to improve results.
- You can tell when something is wrong in the accounting.
- You know when something is going off the rails in the organization.
- You are not fooled by those that attempt to explain away the organization's performance.
- You can teach your team and others.

4. Strategy

Learn and practice the difference between strategy and tactics. Strategy is a buzzword thrown around liberally in many corporate cultures and is often misused. "Strategy" is not every action or reaction. Strategy is pro-active and usually something that has not been done before.

Tactics are reactive to some force or situation inside or outside the organization. Tactics are repeated over and over. In most discussions, the word tactic should replace the use of the word strategy.

Thinking strategically requires vision. Not everyone is a visionary or capable of strategic thought. Training yourself to think strategically is difficult but attainable. Do yourself a favor and pick up some books on strategy and strategic thinking.

Not all leaders are required to be strategic or visionary. Some roles in organizations require different skillsets. Don't kick yourself if strategic thinking is not your strength, but the leader that develops and hones strategic skills becomes a few steps closer to a senior officer position in their organization.

5. *Teambuilder*
For an organization to win regularly, effective teams (not just groups) are a must. There is a big difference between a group and a team.

Teams come together as they rally around the most important objectives. A team will see the goal as captivating and compelling enough to work closely together to achieve the desired end-result. Teams will go through fire for each other and to satisfy their objective. Highly productive teams are indispensable.

Groups meander. Groups may achieve their goal but are not really captivated by their desire to accomplish. Groups tend to slow down or take a step back from adverse situations, and lacking the cohesiveness, drive, and vision, will generally underperform.

High quality leaders know how to identify and communicate captivating goals. Leaders also know how to recognize talent and skills necessary to build great teams. Leaders are not intimidated by adding IQ and Knowledge (surpassing their own) to the room. With a clear target, the right knowledge, understanding and support, teams achieve despite significant risk and adversity.

Team members have different experiences, backgrounds, views, and ways they want to be treated. To get the most out of them, leaders must study and practice how to treat the different individual team members.

6. *Effective Meeting Leadership*
One way to become upwardly mobile and add to your leadership skillset is to learn how to lead an effective meeting. If you master this art, your colleagues become comfortable working on your projects and enjoy the satisfaction and success that comes with you as their leader. Colleagues will trust that they are in good hands – as being associated with and learning from you will help their own careers and bank accounts.

CHAPTER EIGHT: CAREER – MASTER CLASS

As you become known for success, the officers will call on you to lead important organizational initiatives. The same goes for managing projects. As you prove yourself, your profile will grow. Instead of having to shout or hold up your hand to be noticed, others will come looking for you. Your newest and biggest problem will become managing the demand for your skills (which, by the way, is a good problem to have).

Here is how you can improve your meeting leadership skills:
- Read materials on how to run an effective meeting.
- Watch how others lead meetings, note both the successes and failures.
- Make sure your meeting is necessary (if you can solve the issue with a phone call or visit, do it).
- *Establish meeting rules (allow the team to develop these rules).
- Limit the number of participants (do not invite the cast of thousands).
- Explain why each participant is important to a successful outcome.
- Don't allow participants to digress, tell stories or take you off track.
- Follow-up – send crisp notes and reminders of what is due and when
- As you progress, send crisp updates to participants and stakeholders.
- Celebrate milestones and wins.

Refer to Resources: Exhibit 9, p. 249 for a Meeting Rules sample.

7. Project Management

During their watch, leaders have ultimate accountability for the success or failure of projects. That said, it is imperative to put the right Project Manager talent in place. Unfortunately, many leaders neglect to follow-through on their oversight role, which can result in a project failure. If you are in the position to sponsor a project, don't blindly trust that your project leader has everything covered – stay involved, ask questions, clear roadblocks, and encourage the team. Poor planning or a misunderstanding of the size, scope, and difficulty of the project ultimately reflects on you as the sponsor.

Understanding the dynamics of project management – both the staffing and the process – will place you miles ahead of others in your organization. The right planning, staffing and leadership will increase project success rates in your organization, sometimes dramatically. It is far better to celebrate wins than explain why a project is late or why the initiative was a failure.

I like simplicity in project management:
- Create a simple "Envision Statement" – describe what success looks like in terms everyone understands.
- Use a spreadsheet or project software to outline the key tasks, who, what, when and why. *See Resources: Exhibit 10, p. 250*
- Identify Team Leads
    - Team leads are responsible for sub-projects (and their teams) that make up the master project.
    - Team leads attend regular project meetings. Attendance should be single digits – if you require a report/resource from someone that is not on the leadership team, invite them only to attend the pertinent meeting(s).
- Use a shared site for notes, task updates and progress reports.

Effective Project Management skills will increase your chances of being tapped to become involved in critical organizational initiatives. Project leadership success will ultimately raise your value, significantly. Regular project success is the precursor for senior leaders to ask for you by name. Senior leaders know exactly who they want alongside to help them be successful.

8. Effective Communication

Have you ever had a misunderstanding with a friend or partner? This happens all the time! Despite what you thought was perfectly clear, the other person took away a totally different message. As you know from experience, learning to communicate clearly and effectively is incredibly challenging, especially in a world where digital communication reigns. After all, I bet a fair share of your current conversations contain a mix of abbreviations and colorful emojis. Hate to break it to you, but despite this age of digital everything, *#Workhard* is just not going to cut it as a rousing message to your team. If you are headed for a leadership role, you *must* learn to communicate professionally and effectively. Here are a few tips to get you moving in the right direction:

CHAPTER EIGHT: CAREER – MASTER CLASS

- Face-to-face communication is best.
- Be open and share information readily unless it is confidential.
- Make conversations comfortable so that people will ask questions.
- Speak so simply that everyone in the room understands.
- Use word pictures, visuals, and stories.
- Successful communication is what you say and *how* you say it.
- Anticipate questions and answer them, even if no one asks.
- Monitor the team or group to make sure they understand.
    - Watch for verbal and non-verbal clues.
    - Check later for understanding, one-on-one.
    - Do not assume, that can get you in trouble.
- Use e-mail sparingly. Messages are frequently taken out of context.
    - E-mails should be just a few lines - use short crisp sentences and get to the point.
    - Think before you write, make sure the message is so simple everyone understands.
    - Read, proof, then read again.

9. Emotional Intelligence

The days of leadership by "pounding the table" are over. There may be an occasion when tempers are lost for one reason or another. But the tactics of using temper tantrums, fits and demands were dead and buried years ago. I think those archaic tactics are at least partially responsible for labor unions, labor laws, HR professionals and lawyers. An intimidation style is not sustainable in modern organizations. (Except for attorneys that litigate.)

Recent generations are built differently in many ways. To be a highly effective leader, one must understand more about how and why individuals and teams "tick". What you think works for you may not work for others. The team will decide whether to follow your lead. It is up to you to adjust to your team, not the other way around.

Emotional Intelligence has been important for decades, but the study, knowledge and understanding of E.I. is relatively new, having burst on the scene in the early 2000's. If you understand the emotional makeup – how and why people conduct themselves the way they do – you possess a powerful advantage. Commit to learn about the emotional construct of the individuals and the team. Then learn how to adjust your methods to your team.

If you haven't already, pick up some of the great books, assessment materials, and attend seminars on Emotional Intelligence. Commit to gaining an E.I. education and use it to power your leadership skills.

10. Negotiations

We covered the basics of negotiations earlier. Make a commitment to learn and practice – you will have many opportunities to negotiate. Understanding your own proficiency as a negotiator will help you decide when and where to assign someone more skilled to handle an important negotiation.

11. Risk

Leadership positions are risky business – so be prepared to assume the risk. Risk can be mitigated by doing your homework, studying effective leaders, and gaining knowledge.

If every fact and scenario were readily known, the world would run smoothly with no need for leaders to make tough decisions, nor work to build highly effective teams. Since that is not the case, leaders must make decisions *before* perfect/complete knowledge has been disseminated. Prepare yourself to work in an ambiguous and constantly changing world.

Summary

To succeed as an effective leader, high aptitude, deep knowledge and understanding of each of the *Essential Eleven* principles is vital. The more skilled you become in these areas, the more confident and effective you will be. If you aren't yet in the lead position, commit yourself to learning each of these skills now. You will build depth of knowledge and understanding, which will increase your value. If you are in a leadership position, commit to continuous learning. Load your development goals with one or more of the *Essential Eleven*.

Your market value may depend on how well you master these skills. Remember, a leader never "arrives" and is never finished learning. Humble yourself to accept that you don't know everything and there will always be a new tool, new skill or need to sharpen your skills. Much like a world class

CHAPTER EIGHT: CAREER – MASTER CLASS

athlete, once you have gained the knowledge and understanding in one or more of the *Essential Eleven*, practice relentlessly.

Leadership Patience
To be or not to be (patient) – a story...

I recall a time when our children were young and my wife was struggling with how to handle the demands of our household with three small children (one born with disabilities) who seemed to be experts at creating (or participating in) one disaster after another. From the time she woke-up to the moment her head touched the pillow, there was one demand after another ranging from referee, to art teacher, maid, cook, nurse, personal shopper, tutor, and then back around again. It felt like every moment was a mere act of survival to make it through the chaos of the day.

We attended a small neighborhood church. It seemed like everyone knew one another. One Sunday at the conclusion of our morning church service, we made our way to the foyer to visit with our friends. Cindy chatted with one of the women in our congregation who was blessed with about fifty years more "life" experience.

Cindy expressed her frustration with the demands of raising three small children and maintaining a household while I was at work (some of those days required me to travel out of town overnight – and left Cindy with no respite or help). As the two women talked, Cindy said that she just needed to learn to have more "patience". The older woman listened intently without interrupting, then when my wife finished, she looked her in the eye and in the most caring way told Cindy not to seek patience. My wife was a bit puzzled and wondered what she meant. The following words have been etched in my memory since that Sunday. "Cindy, you need to pray for wisdom," she said. "You see, patience by itself will not get anything done and worse yet could be damaging to your children. Wisdom with impatience makes good things happen."

I have rolled those thoughts over and over in my mind many times.
- Wisdom + Impatience = Positive Results
- Impatience (by itself) = Foolhardy
- Patience (by itself) = Prevents progress

WIDE-EYED WISDOM

There are times when patience is necessary. Hopefully your sixth sense and understanding of the situation will help you to determine when patience is the best approach.

If you are impatient without wisdom you may be on a fool's path.

It you are too patient, particularly at work, you may not accomplish what the organization and your customers expect and require. As Jack Welch, former CEO of GE once said, you must continuously "feed the beast" called a company or organization.

Challenges at Work

Serious People Issues
Nothing prepared me for what I had to deal with regarding the serious personal issues of the people I was responsible for leading. There were no college classes or workplace seminars – I was totally unprepared.

When there are people problems at work there is a good chance that something in their personal life is the root cause. People bring very stressful real-life problems to work with them. They don't mean to, it's just impossible to drop all personal baggage at the door and perform without distraction.

When personal problems make their way into the workforce, you cannot run and hide, be courageous. You will not solve their problems, but you can build a safe, caring, and compassionate environment.

Let me give you a few examples of serious personal problems brought to work by former colleagues, that I have had to help deal with:
- Drug/Alcohol addiction
- Infidelity
- Divorce
- Serious illness
- Death
- Office romance
- Sexual harassment
- Spying on a colleague outside of the workplace
- Inaccurate and damaging media articles

CHAPTER EIGHT: CAREER – MASTER CLASS

Dealing with People Issues

If your organization has guidelines regarding personnel issues, always follow organizational procedures. At times, not everything will be spelled out and you will have to rely on your own professional judgment to guide you – here are a few tactics to keep you on track:

- Slow down.
- Take a deep breath.
- Listen and take notes.
- Be empathetic.
- Take the high road.
- Be cautious about what you say.
- Do not assign blame and don't take sides or make hasty judgments.
- Do not let your emotions control you.
- Address the issue with Human Resources in a timely manner.
- Always do what is right.

There is no magic in dealing with people issues. Serious personal problems are stressful. Do your best to follow procedures and act in a timely manner. Check your own stress and emotional level – you may require professional help or an after-work method to relieve stress.

Harassment

I've called this one out because of the pervasive problems in our culture that impact women, minorities and vulnerable people. Most organizations require all associates to go through various types of training regarding harassment. Take these classes seriously – pay attention and learn. When the time comes, do exactly as you have been taught. You never want to be asked to explain to a judge why you did not report an incident even though you were made aware of it or were a witness.

I have dealt with harassment problems at work more than once. Whether an incident involved a leader, customer, associate, or visitor, if there was an indication of harassment, I made the report. Once the report was filed, I followed-up to make sure that we had done everything necessary to get to the bottom of the issue.

WIDE-EYED WISDOM

Don't Play It Safe: Stretch and Build Your Confidence

Several years ago, I worked for a struggling company. We had serious problems and the new officer staff did not understand the urgency of the situation. I was the last remnant of the "old guard". I knew and understood the depth and breadth of the company's financial trouble. During a meeting of the officers, I spoke up about our situation. My candor landed me in the new CEO's "doghouse". Once in the doghouse I was reluctant to get back in the game. I told the truth in a very businesslike fashion and was now paying a steep price for my honesty.

> "A ship in harbor is safe, but that is not what ships are built for."[97]
>
> John A. Shedd

A few weeks later a colleague and good friend of mine came to see me. His message…we need you, would you please, "get in the game"? He told me that I had too much to offer and somehow must get back in the thick of things so that I could help the organization. The lesson I learned that day has stuck with me. If I was going to stay with the company, I had to get back in the game. I did my best to get back into the inner company workings. The result was a success for the organization and for me personally.

Early in my doghouse days I questioned my confidence. Being isolated was no fun and I wasn't accustomed to sitting out. There may come a time (perhaps even now) when you suffer from lack of confidence, question your capabilities, or are afraid to fail. If that is the case, take a personal snapshot of what you think about your own capabilities. In your mind's eye what are you capable of achieving? Have you limited yourself? If so, why? Do you require more proof that you have untapped capabilities? Read on about capabilities.

The U.S. military has figured out ways to teach young people how to operate some of the most sophisticated equipment under the most trying conditions. Some military recruits are totally prepared and know exactly what they want. Others are just young folk, perhaps seeking goals and direction. Some new recruits are unruly and devoid of discipline and direction. (We have all heard families say that military discipline would be good for their son or daughter.) U.S. military branches seem to thrive in areas where many of our families and culture fail miserably. Why is that?

CHAPTER EIGHT: CAREER – MASTER CLASS

Imagine the mix of both disciplined and undisciplined young folks coming together in boot camp. One group is very motivated and knows exactly what they want – the other group is sort of meandering with little direction. Somehow, some way, both groups survive together and are molded into an awesome team.

Sample Cost of Military Equipment

Equipment	Approximate Cost
Tomahawk Missile	$1,400,000[83]
M1A2 Abrahams Tank	$9,000,000[84]
F/A 18F Hornet super	$70,500,000[85]
Nuclear Submarine	$5,500,000,000[86]
Aircraft Carrier (newest)	$13,000,000,000[87]
Computer Systems	Many more billions

The U.S. military has figured out that with consistent discipline, training and high expectations, they can mold young people, many with nothing more than a high school diploma, and develop them into men and women capable of operating some of the most expensive and sophisticated tools known to mankind. All of this while protecting hundreds of millions of people from our enemies. Young people are extremely capable. They have changed the history of our world.

A select group of our young people bear a tremendous burden. Yet some business owners I know, don't believe a young person can be trusted to unload or load a truck effectively. Here is my challenge to them, if the U.S. military can train young high school graduates to operate and maintain the machinery and technology for our country, then who really owns the truck-loading problem?

> "Older men declare war. But it is youth that must fight and die."[88]
>
> *Herbert Hoover*

What does this mean for you? Hold high expectations for yourself because **you are capable**. Others should expect great things from you too. Hold onto your confidence and build upon it each time you succeed or fail.

WIDE-EYED WISDOM

For parents who make excuses for sons and daughters, please stop. Instead of expecting and empowering young people to reach their potential, we blame someone else, a teacher, principal, coach, or the system. You give your children too much and expect little in return. Teach them self-discipline, a great work ethic, perseverance, honesty, and responsibility. Then, expect great things.

> "Young people need models, not critics."[89]
>
> *John Wooden*

When you feel less than capable, think about our fine young military men and women, who accept tremendous responsibilities, risk their lives, and accomplish the unbelievable. If they can do it – so can you and the rest of us.

(Do yourself a favor and read "Keep It At 17 Inches". Coach John Scolinos presents his views of what has contributed to the downfall of many in the U.S.A.)

Involved or Committed?

I learned a great lesson many years ago from a Florida college professor who conducted seminars for my company. Imagine a portly man about 5'8", friendly with a jolly disposition (visions of Santa Claus, anyone?). I can still remember him stuffing his suit jacket pockets full of sandwiches and a couple bottles of ice-cold beer (that was his ritual during a week of traveling seminars, as he retreated to his hotel room to grade term papers sent by his graduate students). One by one, each grad student would send their term paper to the hotel in whatever city the professor happened to be that night.

The late Dr. Karl Kepner of the University of Florida at Gainesville was that professor. Karl counseled my former company and our customers on effective strategy and planning.

> "Commitment is what transforms a promise into reality."[90]
>
> *Abraham Lincoln*

Karl would always ask the audience (business owners) if they were "involved" or "committed" to do what it took to ensure the future of their business. Karl's question inevitably resulted in quite a few puzzled looks from the audience. Or, as some of us would like to say there were quite a few "bass mouths" out there. You know, the blank stare of a fish with a partially open mouth. Anyway, I digress…

CHAPTER EIGHT: CAREER – MASTER CLASS

Karl went on to tell us a story about his neighbor, by the name of Kazuo. Kazuo was an older gentleman, probably about 20 or so years Karl's senior. Neither Kazuo nor Karl knew one another very well. Occasionally they would say hello or comment about the weather, until one day over the back fence a more serious discussion took place.

First it was the usual pleasantries but as the conversation continued, the two neighbors began to get to know one another. Kazuo finally worked up the nerve to ask Karl a serious question. He asked what Karl did during the "big one". Karl was a bit puzzled by Kazuo's question, given their age difference. Karl answered back, "you mean World War II?" Kazuo nodded his head in approval. Karl replied that he was born just before the war broke out, so he really doesn't remember anything about it.

Karl now more curious than ever, returned the query to Kazuo, "What did you do during the big one?" Kazuo answered, "I was a Kamikaze pilot in the Air Force. I flew 94 missions." By now Karl was totally confused. In history class he learned that Kamikaze pilots were trained to carry out a single suicide mission by crashing an airplane heavily laden with explosives, into a strategic target, usually a ship.

Karl could not help himself, so he asked Kazuo, "I thought a Kamikaze pilot flew only one mission?"

Kazuo nodded his head in agreement. Then he said to Karl, "That goes to show you what can happen when you are involved in a program but not committed."

Take time to identify the opportunities and important things in your life. Are you involved or committed?

Life is full of people who remain involved for the moment, but when the going gets rough they bail. Look for yourself. Identify situations in your own life where folks stuck around until they had to commit – and then out they went! Perhaps today it is more prevalent for someone to just "pass the buck" – blame someone else.

True commitment on the other hand is far less plentiful. Commitment is for the long-haul. It isn't easy. Perseverance is necessary. But the results of true commitment carry a bountiful harvest for those that are willing to do what it takes (not necessarily in Kazuo's case – I totally get why he wasn't committed). Case in point. I've had a fair amount of success in my life and career, but it hasn't come without hard work and sacrifice. During a phone call several years ago, someone told me that for some reason it seemed whatever I touched "turned to gold". They told me their life was much more difficult than mine.

WIDE-EYED WISDOM

The subject turned to what we had been doing the past few days. My conversation mate told me all about going out Friday night to the casino. They stayed out late and had a great time. I told them that same night I was

> "When confronted with a challenge the committed heart will search for a solution. The undecided heart searches for an escape."[91]
>
> *Andy Andrews*

stuck at Los Angeles International Airport until about midnight and finally got home around 2:30 a.m. Saturday. From the other end of the line I heard, "Oh, I would never do that". And that mentality explains the difference between involved and committed. So much for my Midas touch.

Business Ownership: Profitability…An Acid Test

Are you a business owner or want to be one? Assuming you have taken great care of your two most valuable assets…customers and employees, I have included one additional factor for judging the success of a business.

Many years-ago a man by the name of Roger Storm taught me his version of a simple measurement of Return on Net Assets Employed. This is a great way to judge the financial success of a business.[92]

Return on Net Assets Employed (RONAE)

Your profit before taxes divided by the net amount of money (capital) you have invested in the business, expressed as a percentage.

The Formula:

$$\frac{\$ \text{ Profit Before Taxes}}{\$\$\$ \text{ Cash Invested}} = \text{Return on Net Assets Employed \%}$$

The best way to understand this concept is with an example…

Example 1: You invest $250,000 of <u>your own money</u> in a business. You borrow $500,000. The business pays all expenses, including the interest and principle payment on the debt. At the end of the year you make $100,000 before tax.

$$\frac{\$100,000}{\$250,000} = \text{RONAE of } 40\,\%$$

CHAPTER EIGHT: CAREER – MASTER CLASS

There aren't many places to invest where you can make that kind of return.

Example 2: You invest $250,000 of <u>your own money</u> in a business. You borrow $500,000. The business pays all expenses, including the interest and principle payment on the debt. At the end of the year you make $10,000 before tax.

$$\frac{\$10,000}{\$250,000} = \text{RONAE of } 4\%$$

If this were a mature business, you might question why you have risked so much of your own money and expended so much effort for such a small return. Or, you may be wondering if there are expenses to cut and/or sales and gross margin that must increase. You may be selling your product or service well below what the market will bear.

There are plenty of places that will earn as much or more than 4% without so much effort, stress, and risk. (You may have bought yourself a job.)

If this return was on a new business you again might study how the expenses, sales and gross margin are impacting your return. This is a great time to pull out your plan and financial projections to ascertain if you are on-track.

*You may be asking why I used $250,000, when there was a total of $750,000 invested in the business. Return on Net Assets Employed considers just the cash that you <u>personally invested</u> in the business. Do not include borrowed money to calculate your personal return.

CHAPTER NINE
GET IN THE GAME

Dear Life Game Participant:

We are in the home stretch of *Wide-Eyed Wisdom*. I hope you have picked up wisdom lessons from my lifelong learning that will be advantageous, no matter the stage in life you happen to be in today.

In this final chapter, I share a collection of my thoughts on how I have aspired to live *my* life. I have made missteps, and have not always been successful, but I have done my best to live according to my vision and values.

This letter is also meant to motivate you to "get in the game". The world requires you to play a vital role, the right role...the role that you were meant to play. Your family, friends and colleagues need you to set positive examples for those around you and for people you will never meet. I have accepted the challenge to get in the game and change the world for the better. Do the same and live a life full of meaning, purpose, and integrity.

You were blessed with life. Your life is not an accident. There is a purpose you are meant to fulfill. Your purpose may not be clear to you. You have been blessed with strengths and abilities. What I have found is that as I use my strengths and abilities, I discover and fulfill my life purpose. As I have matured, my purpose has shifted. I have become more capable. You too will become more capable. You will experience a feeling of tremendous satisfaction as you use your strengths and abilities.

WIDE-EYED WISDOM

What do you believe in? Make no mistake, the universe and the inhabitants are not part of some cosmic accident. Our world is complex. There is intelligent design at work. Sit back and think about how our world and universe came to be. The creation of what we know and what we are yet to discover is mind boggling. Think about scientists spotting far off worlds in other galaxies – light years away. The universe is beyond our comprehension. There is something inside all of us that looks to a higher authority and there is something a lot smarter than us at work. Deep down we know that we are not descendants of algae. We were created and put on this earth. Take time to question and understand more about your own faith. Seek answers and learn. Don't stop until you find your answers.

Please continue to grow and develop. Each of us has been born with intelligence. We must commit to fill our minds with knowledge and understanding. Knowledge truly is power. Knowledge plus understanding is even more powerful. The more knowledge and understanding we gain, the greater our confidence and influence. You are capable. You are more than capable.

> "Do or do not. There is no try."[93]
>
> *Yoda*

Many of us live as if we are afraid to fail. We become disabled and never reach our full potential. Some of us never scratch the surface of our potential. Instead of being afraid, get in the game and if you fail, make it count by learning from the experience. Then, get going again and do not stop.

Dream of big things and set your goals high. Stretch yourself to grow and develop. What if you don't achieve every goal? If you aim high, succeed on some goals, and fail on others, my bet is that the total outcome will be much better than if you had set your personal bar too low. Nobody does everything they set out to do anyway. By getting in the game and *doing*, you will be better prepared for the next step in your journey.

By now you may be thinking, "The guy that wrote this book has more confidence in me than I do". I have heard that before and that statement is true. I know numerous people that didn't possess the confidence they should have had in themselves. Each of us are usually our own worst enemy. Quite often we limit ourselves with a shortage of confidence and a fear of failure. I've

CHAPTER NINE: GET IN THE GAME

experienced powerful outcomes, first-hand, what people do when they believe in themselves and put their heart into something.

Live your personal life to the fullest. Money and accolades won't mean anything when measured against your relationships with family and friends. Cherish each day, even the bad ones. When you look back the troubled times won't seem so bad.

If you have a problem with a family member or friend, offload it. Forgive them and forgive yourself. Don't carry personal baggage around with you. You won't be healthy if you are lugging around the weight of unresolved personal issues. I know this from personal experience. Forgiveness does not necessarily mean you will forget the hurt. After all, you are human. That said, you and the other person must get beyond whatever caused the issue. That is, if you can even remember what caused the hurt feelings to start with.

When you are choosing to be with family and friends, be intentional – turn-off your mobile device. Those you are with are infinitely more important than that little device. When you are glued to a mobile device you send the message that what is on that screen is more important than the people you are with. There is nothing worse than watching a group, sometimes a whole family, scarcely talking to one another because they are captivated by their little screens. You can't live a healthy life absent positive human contact and relationships. Face to face communication is still best, and if you can't visit someone in person give them a call.

Do not bully people, ever. You will not look better at someone else's expense. And there is nothing glamorous about taking advantage of another person. The actions of bullies are saddening and disgusting. Don't hang around bullies. If one of your friends engages in bullying behavior do them a favor and tell them to stop. If bullies ever learn how to conduct themselves properly it will be because each of us call them out and demand better.

If you witness the abuse of another person report it right away. Abuse should be addressed swiftly. If you are a party to abuse get help now, today.

Words are very powerful. Language and the ability to use it was given freely to each of us and carries an awesome responsibility. Take that responsibility very seriously. Once made, it is impossible to take back a comment whether spoken or in writing. Pause, calm down and think before you react. Think about an instance when someone said something to you that was either a lie or was meant to crush your spirit. It has happened to all of us. Have you been able to forgive and forget?

When something upsets me, I have found it best to wait instead of reacting. I've failed more times than I can count. I strive to let time pass so that I can calm myself and organize my thoughts for a response if a response is necessary. If you do not take control of your tongue and your written thoughts, who will? Unfortunately, the world seems to feast on negative messages. For some reason, many people freely express their thoughts and opinions on social media. Stay out of the loose talk and the resulting feuds. Be one of the people that takes the "high road". Control what you say and how you say it.

Get to know your neighbors. In the "olden" days we knew our neighbors. We helped one another, celebrated together, and provided emotional support. Be one of those people that interacts and develops amazing friendships.

When you get into an argument, do your best to be objective. Objective facts always outweigh subjective opinions. Never ever make personal attacks. Things are said that can ruin relationships forever. There are few things in life that are worthy of an argument. It does not really matter who is right and who is wrong. Pick your battles wisely.

If you are at fault, look the other person in the eye and take responsibility. A mature person will own up to their mistakes and apologize. When you take responsibility, you gain tremendous respect from the people that count.

Never tell lies. You cheat yourself and disrespect the other person. Lies are hurtful and disrespectful. Tell the truth always, no matter how much it might hurt. I remember a time as a teenager lying to my mom. I was 16-years old. My lie broke her heart. I should have just told her the truth and she would have understood. I could not bear to lie to her ever again. The more I matured, the more I realized the importance of truth. If

> "No man has a good enough memory to be a successful liar."[94]
>
> *Abraham Lincoln*

people cannot rely on what you say as true, then what kind of person are you, really? What will become of you? Dishonest people eventually pay the price for their actions.

At the root of who you are and will become is your self-respect. If you don't respect yourself don't expect others to respect you. Conduct yourself with the utmost respect for your mind, body, and soul. Self-respect will help

CHAPTER NINE: GET IN THE GAME

you to live a life of "terrible resolve" by doing the right things for yourself, your family and all those you impact.

> "Respect your efforts, respect yourself. Self-respect leads to self-discipline. When you have both firmly under your belt, that's real power."[95]
>
> Clint Eastwood

Respect others. If you respect others you will be respected. You may not like everyone, but you *can* respect them. You can also treat each person with dignity, no matter the circumstance. Your family members need care and respect from you. Show them the care and respect they need and deserve. Your actions will live on through your family, make sure you set great examples.

Do your best to compliment those around you and mean it. Compliment the person not an object. As an example, most people have learned to say, "That dress looks great on you". Instead say, "You look beautiful in that dress". To further prove my point here is a headline on MSN the day after I wrote this paragraph, from a US Weekly Article: "Serena Williams swears this dress will look great on you". They should have written… "Serena Williams swears you will look great in this dress".

Celebrate your wins and get over losses quickly. Winning and losing is just part of the journey. Chances are you will experience helpings of both. Sports fans can be the worst. When it comes to their favorite teams, some sports fans wear their psyche on their shirt sleeves. Don't take rivalries so seriously that you involve yourself in self-promoting behavior – always respect others. The good things

> "Losing builds character, winning is the supreme test of character."
>
> Keith A. Miller

about winning can be taken away during a moment of indiscretion. When you win, be a gracious and humble winner. Most people, at least those that count, appreciate, and gravitate toward genuinely humble people.

Be slow to criticize and do not gossip. Too many conversations revolve around making one person look good at someone else's expense. Stay out of that stuff, resist the peer pressure and just be yourself. People that really count will respect you for it.

WIDE-EYED WISDOM

Encourage those around you at every opportunity. Make encouragement a staple of how you treat people. Take the time to look for positives. You never know how your positive words will impact another. When you encourage, you might just help another person "launch" successfully or even save their life.

If you have a partner, show your affection. It is painful to watch people that never so much as give their husband or wife a hug in public. Appropriate public displays of affection are wonderful. For one, your family should witness your affection for one another.

Love others around you unconditionally – they need your love and care. Give love generously in all situations. You will receive more love than you give. When you become a parent make sure that you love your children. Let them know how much you care about them. Be part of every facet of their lives. Love from your parents, family and friends makes a huge difference in how secure a person becomes. People that are more secure find it easier to love themselves and those around them. A few days ago, I told our grandson, five-year-old James, that I loved him and would do anything to help him. He looked at me with those big beautiful brown eyes and said, "I know Pop".

Don't be afraid to discipline your children. Children must have boundaries to be healthy and gain confidence. As children grow, give responsibility, and stretch them. Teach work ethic, honesty, self-discipline, and integrity. A minister from our church used to say, "Don't protect your children *from* storms. Protect them *in* storms." I don't know where this quote originated but I'll always remember it.

Now for all of you that will one day marry and have children…To mature and grow, boys require stable loving men and women in their lives. I mean "men" not "males". There is a big difference. Boys must have men to be a role model for how they are supposed to grow up and live their lives. Men need to show boys the right way to treat women. Boys need a man to be a role model for what a man is supposed to be, how to love and how to conduct themselves. To mature and grow, boys must have a loving mother in their lives. A mother's nurturing and caring nature is important for boys to feel loved, gain confidence, learn how to love, and care for children and learn how to love their wives.

Girls need a father that is a "gentle man". Girls want a loving father to show them how they should be treated and cared for. Girls need a father's example to understand how to treat and care for her sons and daughters. Only

CHAPTER NINE: GET IN THE GAME

a gentle man can provide that kind of example. Girls must have a mother that is a strong woman. Girls need a mom's example to understand how to be a wife and mother. Girls need mom's example to understand the importance of her labor of love while shaping her children for their education, career, marriage, and family. Girls require a strong female role model to understand how to mature and grow.

Getting married is serious business. You agree to a contract. If you don't intend to fulfill your part, then don't get married.

Divorce is too common in our culture. My wife was in fifth grade when her parents divorced. I was 13-years old when my parents split. As a young teen, I needed more assurance from my parents. If you decide to divorce, please communicate with, and comfort your children. I would have felt much better if my parents would have addressed these three, simple points:
1. Mom and dad splitting up is not the children's fault.
2. Both mom and dad love each child unconditionally.
3. The children are all safe.

There is only one you. It is okay to be different. If we were all the same, the world would be a boring place and most of us would not be necessary. Embrace who you are. Continue to grow and improve every day. You will become a better person as you mature and develop.

If you don't think you have been blessed with gifts, look at the people that were born with challenges and without a choice in the matter. Children are born every day with significant disabilities and somehow make it through this world. The genetic lottery, an accident or an irresponsible parent dealt them a bad hand. If they can succeed so can you. If those with disabilities can't succeed on their own, then they need our help. When a disabled or disadvantaged person needs your help, give it to them. And, for goodness sake, don't make fun or discriminate. I can't think of too many things worse than taking advantage of those that have been disabled or disadvantaged.

Listen intently and mind the spoken and unspoken examples you exhibit. Whether you like it or not you are setting examples. Those around you pick up on what you say and do. Children will be the first to emulate your actions.

Really mean what you say and then do it.

WIDE-EYED WISDOM

If you ever find yourself falling into the mentality that you are entitled to whatever you want and the world revolves around you, beware. You are not a god. You won't be a god. Those types of thoughts are selfish and lead to destruction. That kind of individualism is a major problem in our world.

We stand on the shoulders of past generations. It may be in vogue to blame others for the state of our communities and country. Before you blame, remember that generations before us made innumerable sacrifices and made great things happen. Past generations did a lot of things right. Celebrate what they did right. Their sacrifices are immeasurable, all just to make our lives better. It's our watch now so let's make the best of it for future generations.

President Eisenhower believed that one of the few things in life that you carry with you that no one can take away is your integrity. It doesn't matter who you are, the color of your skin, the job you hold or the money you have. Integrity is one of the few things you will always keep regardless of the time or place.

> "Live with purpose and integrity."[96]
>
> *Dwight D. Eisenhower*

Decades removed from that terrible resolve, when Americans banded together to reach a compelling goal many have adopted a "self-interest" life model. Everything won't be in your best interest, so get over it. You will be required to make sacrifices along the way. It isn't always someone else's fault. You make mistakes just like everyone else. You won't look perfect when you take responsibility for a mistake or a problem…you will however be authentic. Respect other people and move forward! As a society we are ripping our country apart by catering to self-interests. Today, if something doesn't suit one person or group, just object and the silent majority must adjust. Instead, let's all get together and live as humans and fellow countrymen first.

For those of you that may cry foul. There is nothing wrong with differences in cultures or celebrating different beliefs. All of us should be allowed and respected as we celebrate our individual cultures and beliefs.

America is a "melting pot". The melting pot has always been a great strength. As William Shakespeare once said, "Your greatest strength is also your greatest weakness". Our country has gone too far in one direction and has lost the collective and compelling reasons we are Americans.

You will find out soon enough that everyone has serious problems. If you think you are alone, think again. Look around you. No one is immune to

CHAPTER NINE: GET IN THE GAME

problems. When problems come your way, step up and handle them. Most of what you deal with will be small. Once you learn to handle the small stuff, you will be better prepared when the bigger problems find you. Make no mistake – big problems will find you. You will get through problems and move on. If you are having trouble moving on, please get help. There is nothing wrong with seeking great counsel. Counselors are experts and are available to help you. Don't pay attention to people that think you are weak or flawed for seeking counsel. People that hold those beliefs are ignorant. All of us can use great counsel at different times. It takes courage to ask for help.

There is no question in my mind that you have some doubts about the future. I know I do. Our country seems to have strayed from what made us a powerful and favored nation. Our foundation and way of life has eroded. Delving into these issues would take volumes to discuss. What I will say is that there is a staggering price paid by our family units. Our families have shouldered pain and suffering to a magnitude that few would have predicted. Let's aspire to break the catastrophic family cycles that have taken over the past several decades. One by one we must heal the family unit in America.

The extremes in our political ideology have taken over the discussion about what should be acceptable and appropriate in our country, yet I don't think these extremes represent the majority. Today if an individual or group is courageous enough to offer a difference of opinion, instead of respectful discussion or understanding, there is belittling and name calling. In the past we could disagree and remain friends. What has happened? Stay true to your values and be respectful of others. If we listen to each other, we might discover that we want to achieve similar goals but just may have different ideas about how to get there.

Current generations are in control right now and have some influence over our communities and our country. We certainly have direct control over our own actions. The positive or "silver lining" in all of this is that we have the influence and control to lead and make a difference. If we take care of our own families and set great examples, others will follow. If we work together for the good of the whole, not of the one, collectively we will solve many if not most of our problems.

So, get in the game. If you have been silent, don't stay that way. Get involved.

WIDE-EYED WISDOM

My brother asked me several years ago what I was after in my life and career. He wanted to know what was driving me to do what I do every day. I told him I wanted to change the world. My commitment is the same today as it was then. Now, many years later, I have gained more knowledge, understanding and wisdom and have become more powerful.

No book, speech or program can tell you step by step what to do in your life. You hold the key. You must take the knowledge and understanding you gain and be motivated enough to learn and grow on your own. You own your direction. The time is now, make it count.

Hopefully, there were building blocks in this book that will help you and your family. Perhaps there is information that will motivate you to learn more and turn that knowledge and understanding into power to change your life and the world for the better.

In closing, live your life with purpose. Go your own way and do not bend to peer pressure.

And, please remember the following, **no matter what is going on around you, always do the right thing**.

Sincerely,

Keith Miller

Keith A. Miller

ACKNOWLEDGEMENTS

Cindy, I don't know what you saw in me as a teenager. You are the love of my life and I'm honored to be your husband (we just celebrated our 40th wedding anniversary). I am grateful for your love. You had confidence in me when I didn't have faith and confidence in myself.

Matt, you had to bear the burden of Mom and I learning to be parents. I do not remember much about what life was like without you. You have the strengths of compassion and emotional intelligence. You were blessed with qualities that are difficult to teach and learn. Be confident in yourself. You are very capable.

Teresa, without you, this book would have never come to fruition. You provided the ideas, energy, skill, and brainpower that has transformed my ramblings into concrete messages. Much like a great athlete, your presence raises the performance of those around you.

Chad, you are perhaps the most courageous person I know. You have one foot in one world while the other foot is planted in another world. There are a lot of people around us that need to learn from your courageous example and follow your lead. Stay strong!

To my brothers and sisters, thank you for helping little brother grow up and mature. You all had a hand in helping me along the way. Fortunately, we had a good upbringing. You all have a special place in my heart.

To my former colleagues, thank you for allowing me to join your team. Wherever I went, your arms were wide-open, allowing me to be a part of each team. I miss all of you and I can't thank you enough for your friendship and professionalism.

RESOURCES

EXHIBIT 1:	Values Word List	240
EXHIBIT 2:	Budgeting Made Simple	241
EXHIBIT 3:	Habitual Spending	242
EXHIBIT 4:	Car Loan Payment – Good Credit	244
EXHIBIT 5:	Car Loan Payment – Poor Credit	245
EXHIBIT 6:	Home Loan Payment Schedule	246
EXHIBIT 7:	DIY Starter Kit – The "Dirty Thirty"	247
EXHIBIT 8:	Wealth Factor Example	248
EXHIBIT 9:	Meeting Rules	249
EXHIBIT 10:	Project Task Tracker	250

WIDE-EYED WISDOM

EXHIBIT 1: Values Word List *(Wordpress.com and The Happiness Planner)*

Acceptance	Contentment	Fortitude	Meaning	Significance
Accomplishment	Contribution	Freedom	Moderation	Simplicity
Accountability	Control	Friendship	Money	Sincerity
Accuracy	Conviction	Fun	Motivation	Skill
Achievement	Cooperation	Generosity	Openness	Smart
Adaptability	Courage	Genius	Opportunity	Solitude
Adventure	Courtesy	Giving	Optimism	Spirit
Affection	Creation	Goals	Order	Spirituality
Alertness	Creativity	Goodness	Organization	Spontaneous
Ambition	Credibility	Grace	Originality	Stability
Amusement	Curiosity	Gratitude	Passion	Status
Assertiveness	Decisiveness	Greatness	Patience	Stewardship
Attentive	Dedication	Growth	Peace	Strength
Authenticity	Dependability	Happiness	Performance	Structure
Awareness	Determination	Hard Work	Persistence	Success
Balance	Development	Harmony	Playfulness	Support
Beauty	Devotion	Health	Poise	Surprise
Belonging	Dignity	Helping Others	Potential	Sustainability
Boldness	Discipline	Honesty	Power	Talent
Bravery	Discovery	Honor	Preparation	Teamwork
Brilliance	Diversity	Hope	Productivity	Temperance
Calm	Drive	Humility	Professionalism	Thankful
Candor	Effectiveness	Imagination	Prosperity	Thorough
Capable	Efficiency	Improvement	Purpose	Thoughtful
Careful	Empathy	Independence	Quality	Timeliness
Career	Empower	Individuality	Realistic	Tolerance
Caring	Endurance	Ingenuity	Reason	Toughness
Certainty	Energy	Innovation	Recognition	Traditional
Challenge	Enjoyment	Inquisitive	Recreation	Tranquility
Charity	Enthusiasm	Insightful	Reflective	Transparency
Cheerful	Equality	Integrity	Reliability	Trustworthy
Cleanliness	Ethical	Intelligence	Resourcefulness	Truth
Clear	Excellence	Intensity	Respect	Understanding
Clever	Experience	Intuitive	Responsibility	Uniqueness
Comfort	Exploration	Joy	Restraint	Unity
Commitment	Expressive	Justice	Results-oriented	Valor
Common Sense	Fairness	Kindness	Reverence	Victory
Communication	Faith	Knowledge	Risk	Vigor
Community	Family	Lawful	Satisfaction	Vision
Compassion	Famous	Leadership	Security	Vitality
Competence	Fearless	Learning	Self-actualization	Wealth
Competition	Feelings	Liberty	Self-reliance	Welcoming
Concentration	Ferocious	Logic	Selfless	Winning
Confidence	Fidelity	Love	Sensitivity	Wisdom
Connection	Fitness	Loyalty	Serenity	Wonder
Consciousness	Focus	Mastery	Service	
Consistency	Foresight	Maturity	Sharing	

RESOURCES

EXHIBIT 2: Budgeting Made Simple

The next task in the budget building process is to identify spending categories and estimate the amounts spent in each of the categories. Use this as a place to start. You will have other categories unique to you and your family.

- House payment/rent
- Home maintenance
- Homeowners/renters insurance
- Furniture
- Medical/Dental/Vision
- Subscriptions (Games and other)
- Yard maintenance
- Utilities
- Property tax
- Food
- Eating out
- Vacations
- Pets (Cost of the pet, food, toys, veterinary bills)
- Clothing
- Car Payment, Insurance, Maintenance
- Gas
- Car maintenance
- RV/Boat Payment, Insurance, Maintenance
- Entertainment
- Extracurricular activities
- Emergency Fund
- Family Gifts
- Donations
- Major Purchase Fund (Cars, major appliances, RV, home interior remodel, siding, paint, roof, furniture)
- School tuition and Education Expenses
- College Fund
- Investments
- Miscellaneous Allowance
- Personal Incidentals (Haircuts, impulse purchases like drinks/coffee etc.)

WIDE-EYED WISDOM

EXHIBIT 3: Habitual Spending

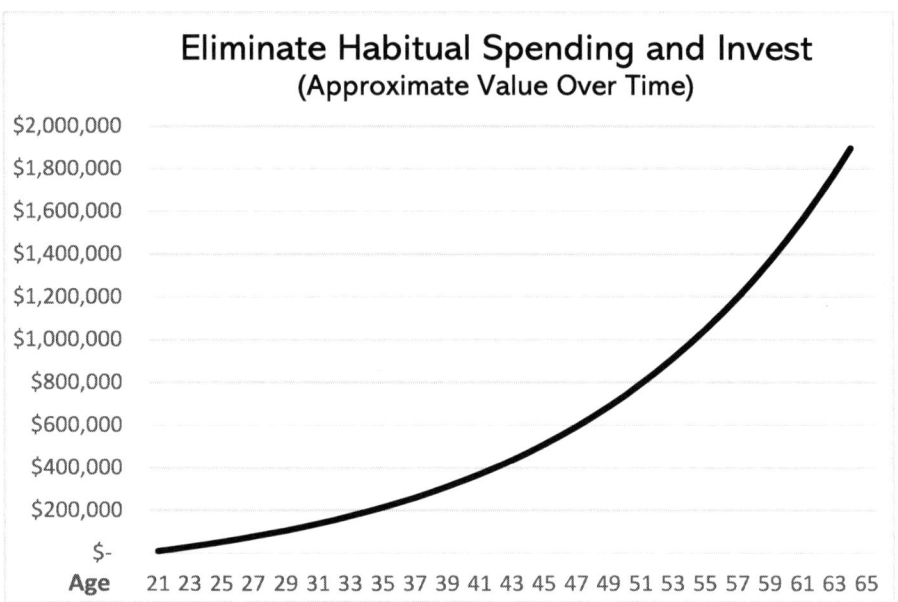

This graph represents what might have happened had our friend saved and invested the money that was being spent regularly on coffee, cigarettes, alcohol, and gambling.

- By saving $730 per month, then investing it with earnings of 6% after taxes, and continuing to allocate $730 per month throughout her working career.
- Our habitual spender, turned investor, will have accumulated about $1.9 million at the age of 65.
    - This of course assumes that she continues to invest $730 per month and does not withdraw money.
    - The estimate also assumes she has chosen investments that will yield 6% in after tax earnings.
- I'm not saying you should take all of your fun money and put it into investments.
- I am saying that you should examine your spending for saving and investment opportunities.

RESOURCES

- The money may be available right now, today, for you to build your personal wealth factor.
- Take the time to examine spending, allocating enough each month to savings and investments so that you fulfill your life plan.
- Do the math now, do not wait.
- The power of earnings compounding is tremendous.
- *Imagine the total, if $730 had been deposited in a 401(k) account with a modest employer matching deposit.

WIDE-EYED WISDOM

EXHIBIT 4: Car Loan Payment – Good Credit

Assumptions: New Car price $37,000 with 20% down ($7,400)
Borrow $29,600 @ 4.97% for 60-months
Total Cost of the Car: $40,891

Interest cost of $3,891 is less than half what is paid by someone with poor credit!

Payment	Interest Paid	Principle Paid	Payment	Payment	Interest Paid	Principle Paid	Payment
1	$ 123	$ 436	$ 558	31	$ 65	$ 493	$ 558
2	$ 121	$ 437	$ 558	32	$ 63	$ 495	$ 558
3	$ 119	$ 439	$ 558	33	$ 61	$ 497	$ 558
4	$ 117	$ 441	$ 558	34	$ 59	$ 499	$ 558
5	$ 115	$ 443	$ 558	35	$ 57	$ 501	$ 558
6	$ 114	$ 445	$ 558	36	$ 55	$ 503	$ 558
7	$ 112	$ 447	$ 558	37	$ 53	$ 505	$ 558
8	$ 110	$ 448	$ 558	38	$ 51	$ 508	$ 558
9	$ 108	$ 450	$ 558	39	$ 49	$ 510	$ 558
10	$ 106	$ 452	$ 558	40	$ 46	$ 512	$ 558
11	$ 104	$ 454	$ 558	41	$ 44	$ 514	$ 558
12	$ 102	$ 456	$ 558	42	$ 42	$ 516	$ 558
13	$ 100	$ 458	$ 558	43	$ 40	$ 518	$ 558
14	$ 99	$ 460	$ 558	44	$ 38	$ 520	$ 558
15	$ 97	$ 462	$ 558	45	$ 36	$ 522	$ 558
16	$ 95	$ 463	$ 558	46	$ 34	$ 525	$ 558
17	$ 93	$ 465	$ 558	47	$ 31	$ 527	$ 558
18	$ 91	$ 467	$ 558	48	$ 29	$ 529	$ 558
19	$ 89	$ 469	$ 558	49	$ 27	$ 531	$ 558
20	$ 87	$ 471	$ 558	50	$ 25	$ 533	$ 558
21	$ 85	$ 473	$ 558	51	$ 23	$ 536	$ 558
22	$ 83	$ 475	$ 558	52	$ 20	$ 538	$ 558
23	$ 81	$ 477	$ 558	53	$ 18	$ 540	$ 558
24	$ 79	$ 479	$ 558	54	$ 16	$ 542	$ 558
25	$ 77	$ 481	$ 558	55	$ 14	$ 545	$ 558
26	$ 75	$ 483	$ 558	56	$ 11	$ 547	$ 558
27	$ 73	$ 485	$ 558	57	$ 9	$ 549	$ 558
28	$ 71	$ 487	$ 558	58	$ 7	$ 551	$ 558
29	$ 69	$ 489	$ 558	59	$ 5	$ 554	$ 558
30	$ 67	$ 491	$ 558	60	$ 2	$ 556	$ 558
				Total	**$ 3,891**	**$ 29,600**	**$ 33,491**

*Source: Calculator.net

RESOURCES

EXHIBIT 5: Car Loan Payment – Poor Credit

Assumptions: New Car price $37,000 with 20% down ($7,400)
Borrow $29,600 @ 11.37% for 60-months
Total Cost of the Car: $46,343

Your interest cost of $9,343 is over $5,000 more than someone with good credit!

Payment	Interest Paid	Principle Paid	Payment	Payment	Interest Paid	Principle Paid	Payment
1	$ 280	$ 369	$ 649	31	$ 160	$ 489	$ 649
2	$ 277	$ 372	$ 649	32	$ 155	$ 494	$ 649
3	$ 273	$ 376	$ 649	33	$ 151	$ 498	$ 649
4	$ 270	$ 379	$ 649	34	$ 146	$ 503	$ 649
5	$ 266	$ 383	$ 649	35	$ 141	$ 508	$ 649
6	$ 263	$ 386	$ 649	36	$ 136	$ 513	$ 649
7	$ 259	$ 390	$ 649	37	$ 131	$ 518	$ 649
8	$ 255	$ 394	$ 649	38	$ 127	$ 522	$ 649
9	$ 252	$ 397	$ 649	39	$ 122	$ 527	$ 649
10	$ 248	$ 401	$ 649	40	$ 117	$ 532	$ 649
11	$ 244	$ 405	$ 649	41	$ 112	$ 537	$ 649
12	$ 240	$ 409	$ 649	42	$ 106	$ 543	$ 649
13	$ 236	$ 413	$ 649	43	$ 101	$ 548	$ 649
14	$ 232	$ 417	$ 649	44	$ 96	$ 553	$ 649
15	$ 228	$ 421	$ 649	45	$ 91	$ 558	$ 649
16	$ 224	$ 425	$ 649	46	$ 86	$ 563	$ 649
17	$ 220	$ 429	$ 649	47	$ 80	$ 569	$ 649
18	$ 216	$ 433	$ 649	48	$ 75	$ 574	$ 649
19	$ 212	$ 437	$ 649	49	$ 69	$ 580	$ 649
20	$ 208	$ 441	$ 649	50	$ 64	$ 585	$ 649
21	$ 204	$ 445	$ 649	51	$ 58	$ 591	$ 649
22	$ 200	$ 449	$ 649	52	$ 53	$ 596	$ 649
23	$ 195	$ 454	$ 649	53	$ 47	$ 602	$ 649
24	$ 191	$ 458	$ 649	54	$ 41	$ 608	$ 649
25	$ 187	$ 462	$ 649	55	$ 36	$ 613	$ 649
26	$ 182	$ 467	$ 649	56	$ 30	$ 619	$ 649
27	$ 178	$ 471	$ 649	57	$ 24	$ 625	$ 649
28	$ 174	$ 475	$ 649	58	$ 18	$ 631	$ 649
29	$ 169	$ 480	$ 649	59	$ 12	$ 637	$ 649
30	$ 165	$ 485	$ 649	60	$ 6	$ 643	$ 649
				Total	$ 9,343	$ 29,600	$ 38,943

*Source: Calculator.net

WIDE-EYED WISDOM

EXHIBIT 6: Home Loan Payment Schedule

Assumptions: Home price $250,000 with 20% down ($50,000)
Borrow $200,000 @ 3.0% fixed for 30-years
Monthly Payment: $843 (Rounded to Whole Number)
Total Home Cost: $353,480 (Total Interest Cost: $103,480)

Notice how the interest costs are <u>front-loaded</u>.

Payment Number	Year-End	Interest Paid: Month	Principle Paid: Month
1	First Payment	$ 500	$ 343
12	1	$ 490	$ 353
24	2	$ 480	$ 363
36	3	$ 469	$ 374
48	4	$ 457	$ 386
60	5	$ 445	$ 398
72	6	$ 433	$ 410
84	7	$ 421	$ 422
96	8	$ 408	$ 435
108	9	$ 395	$ 448
120	10	$ 381	$ 462
132	11	$ 367	$ 476
144	12	$ 353	$ 490
156	13	$ 338	$ 505
168	14	$ 322	$ 521
180	15	$ 306	$ 537
192	16	$ 290	$ 553
204	17	$ 273	$ 570
216	18	$ 256	$ 587
228	19	$ 238	$ 605
240	20	$ 220	$ 623
252	21	$ 201	$ 642
264	22	$ 181	$ 662
276	23	$ 161	$ 682
288	24	$ 140	$ 703
300	25	$ 119	$ 724
312	26	$ 97	$ 746
324	27	$ 74	$ 769
336	28	$ 51	$ 792
348	29	$ 27	$ 816
360	30	$ 2	$ 841

*Source: Calculator.net

RESOURCES

EXHIBIT 7: DIY Starter Kit – The "Dirty Thirty"

1. Screwdrivers (Basic Set)
2. Hammer
3. Measuring Tape
4. Stud Finder/Laser Level
5. Cordless Drill
6. Drill Bits
7. Wrench Set
   (Metric and Standard)
8. Socket Set
   (Metric and Standard)
9. Pliers Set
10. Pry Bar
11. Paint Brushes
12. Hand Saws: Power and Manual
13. Power Saws: Miter and Chop
14. Power Palm Sander
15. Sandpaper
16. Putty Knife
17. Utility knife
18. Hack Saw
19. Wire Stripper/Cutter
20. Electrical Circuit Tester
21. Work Gloves
22. Toolbox or Bucket
23. Shovel
24. Rakes: Two of them (Bow Rake and Steel Rake)
25. Action Hoe
26. Fertilizer Spreader
27. Lawn Mower
28. String Trimmer
29. Tire Pressure Gauge
30. Compact Air Compressor

You now have your Birthday and Christmas wish list. Your family and friends will be pleased that you can give them some real ideas for sensible gifts. Plus – the regular use of these gifts will keep on giving!

WIDE-EYED WISDOM

EXHIBIT 8: Wealth Factor Example

This is a sample that shows the progression of the following:
- Increases in Real Estate Values
- Debt Reduction
- Contributions to Investment Accounts
- Earnings on Investment Accounts

It is likely that your investment advisor or bank will have an online tool.

Asset	Period			
	Quarter 1: 2020	Quarter 2: 2020	Quarter 3: 2020	Quarter 4: 2020
Real Estate				
Home (Market Value)	$ 350,000	$ 351,000	$ 352,500	$ 354,750
Home Loan Balance	$ (300,000)	$ (298,000)	$ (295,850)	$ (293,200)
Broker Fees & Closing Costs	$ (22,750)	$ (22,815)	$ (22,913)	$ (23,059)
Net Real Estate Equity	**$ 27,250**	**$ 30,185**	**$ 33,737**	**$ 38,491**
Bank + Investments				
Checking: Ajax Bank	$ 2,500	$ 2,344	$ 1,985	$ 2,612
Savings: Ajax Bank	$ 1,100	$ 1,632	$ 1,248	$ 1,174
Common Stock: XYZ Co.	$ 3,200	$ 3,028	$ 3,009	$ 2,931
Mutual Fund: A Company	$ 12,653	$ 12,888	$ 13,012	$ 13,256
Mutual Fund: B Company	$ 16,549	$ 16,541	$ 16,989	$ 17,158
Mutual Fund: C Company	$ 12,019	$ 12,124	$ 12,298	$ 12,555
401k Account #1	$ 45,125	$ 47,899	$ 50,232	$ 53,689
401k Account #2	$ 31,832	$ 32,465	$ 34,215	$ 36,874
Tax Free Bond Account	$ 4,125	$ 4,185	$ 4,255	$ 4,315
Total Bank + Investments	**$ 129,103**	**$ 133,106**	**$ 137,243**	**$ 144,564**
Other Debt:				
Credit Card #1	$ (1,215)	$ -	$ -	$ -
Credit Card #2	$ (852)	$ -	$ -	$ -
Car Loan #1	$ (18,450)	$ (17,650)	$ (15,700)	$ (14,600)
Car Loan #2	$ (21,859)	$ (20,855)	$ (19,715)	$ (18,500)
Student Loan #1	$ (15,125)	$ (14,850)	$ (14,450)	$ (13,850)
Student Loan #2	$ (16,416)	$ (16,012)	$ (15,012)	$ (14,783)
Total Other Debt	**$ (73,917)**	**$ (69,367)**	**$ (64,877)**	**$ (61,733)**
Total Wealth Factor With/Home	**$ 82,436**	**$ 93,924**	**$ 106,103**	**$ 121,322**
Total Wealth Factor WO/Home	**$ 55,186**	**$ 63,739**	**$ 72,366**	**$ 82,831**

RESOURCES

EXHIBIT 9: Meeting Rules

1. Meetings should be held only if necessary. (Some examples: Clearly communicate information and gather feedback, solve a problem, or coordinate projects.)

2. Have a clear Purpose and stated Objective. Both items should be made clear in the meeting invitation.

3. Meetings must have a clear Agenda of discussion topics to be followed in the meeting. Agenda should clearly state purpose and objective(s), discussion topics, preparation materials, and time commitment.

4. Send an Invitation and Agenda <u>in advance</u> to all necessary participants.

5. Begin and End on time

6. Appoint the meeting Leader (Chair), responsible to facilitate and attendees must have clear roles for attending the meeting. The Leader will coordinate who will be responsible for note taking, as well as facilitate the session.

7. All Participants must:
    - Arrive on time
    - Be prepared
    - Encourage open and honest discussion
    - Listen and ask questions
    - Be concise and to the point in their remarks
    - Stay focused on the meeting task/subject matter
    - Avoid side discussions

8. The Leader will communicate next steps, responsibilities, and time frame for completion. (Who, What and When)

9. Notes and Decisions made must be Documented and sent to participants.

10. Fulfillment of the Meeting/Project Purpose or Objective must be achieved.

WIDE-EYED WISDOM

EXHIBIT 10: Project Task Tracker

*This is a simple Excel spreadsheet that everyone will understand.
- Update the tracker regularly.
- Track specific tasks.
- Make the Project Task Tracker visible to team members.
- Use simple English, so that all understand.
- Celebrate closed tasks.
- All task closure should equal your finished project.
- Add columns for other reasons, such as team member identification, task number, if desired.

Task #	Task Title	Description	Team Lead	Start Date	Due Date	Dependencies	Status	Resolution

*Source: Gene Puhrmann, Associated Grocers Inc.

WORKS CITED

[1]Steverman, Ben. "Half of Older Americans Have Nothing in Retirement Savings." Bloomberg, 27 March 2019, www.bloomberg.com.

[2]Shaw, George Bernard. "George Bernard Shaw." Good Reads, www.goodreads.com/author/quotes/5217.George_Bernard_Shaw.

[3]Twain, Mark. "Mark Twain." Brainy Quote, 13 June 2019, www.brainyquote.com/quotes/mark_twain_153869. n.d. webpage.

[4]Reagan, Michael and Bob Phillips. The All-American Quote Book. Eugene: Harvest House Publishers, 1995. p 194.

[5]Franklin, Benjamin. Letter to Jean-Baptiste Le Roy. 13 November 1789.

[6]Bennet, Roy T. The Light in the Heart. 2020.

[7]Task, Aaron. "Money 101: Q&A with Warren Buffett." Yahoo! Finance, 8 April 2013, finance.yahoo.com/news/money-101--q-a-with-warren-buffett-140409456.html.

[8]"Intelligence." Oxford Dictionary, 19 January 2015, www.oxfordlearnersdictionaries.com/definition/american_english/intelligence.

[9]Owens, Jesse. "Jesse Owens Quotes." BrainyQuote, www.brainyquote.com/quotes/jesse_owens_166163.

[10]Cosell, Howard. Cosell by Cosell. Chicago: Playboy Press, 1973.

[11]Berra, Yogi and David Kaplan. When You Come to a Fork in the Road, Take It!: Inspiration and Wisdom from One of Baseball's Greatest Heroes. Hachette Books, 2001.

[12]Friedman, Zack. "Student Loan Debt Statistics In 2020: A Record $1.6 Trillion." Forbes, 03 February 2020, www.forbes.com/sites/zackfriedman/2020/02/03/student-loan-debt-statistics.

[13]Edison, Thomas. "Thomas Edison Quotes." BrainyQuote, BrainyQuote.com/quotes/thomas_a_edison_104931.

[14]"Richard Branson." Wikipedia, 26 April 2020, en.wikipedia.org/wiki/Richard_Branson.

[15]Waring, David. "Small Business Failure Rates: Why All the Stats Have it Wrong." Fit Small Business, 26 July 2017, https://fitsmallbusiness.com/small-business-failure-rates.

[16]Hubley Luckwaldt, Jen. "The Best Jobs for Trade School Graduates." The Balance Careers, 20 November 2019, www.thebalancecareers.com/best-trade-school-graduate-jobs-4125189.

[17]"What is work ethic? definition and meaning." Wikipedia, 18 March 2018, en.wikipedia.org/wiki/Work_ethic.

[18]Lake, Rebecca. "What is the Average Age of Marriage in the U.S." The Balance, 14 April 2020, www.thebalance.com/what-is-the-average-age-of-marriage-in-the-u-s-4685727.

WIDE-EYED WISDOM

[19]Treacy, Michael and Fred Wiersema. The Discipline of Market Leaders. Reading: Wesley Publishing Co. Inc., 1996.

[20]Robbins, Tony. AZ Quotes, www.azquotes.com/quote/858076.

[21]"Definition: Financial Literacy." Wikipedia, 2 April 2020, en.wikipedia.org/wiki/Financial_literacy.

[22]Hammer, Dennis. "How to Follow the 50/30/20 Rule." Wealthsimple, 25 September 2019, wealthsimple.com/en-us/learn/50-30-20-rule.

[23]"Impulse." Bing, www.bing/com/search?q=impulse+definition&form.

[24]"Top 10 Lessons from Warren Buffett." Forbes, https://www.forbes.com/pictures/eede45imgh/if-you-buy-things-you-do/#3f3f24b3e10f.

[25]Rogers, Will. AZ Quotes, www.azquotes.com/quote/249442.

[26]Deaton, Jaime Page and Nate Parsons. "Average Auto Loan Rates in April 2020." U.S. News & World Report, 03 April 2020, cars.usnews.com/cars-trucks/average-auto-loan-interest-rates.

[27]Bundrick, Hal M., CFP. "How much house can I afford?" Nerdwallet, https://www.nerdwallet.com/mortgages/how-much-house-can-i-afford.

[28]DeCambre, Mark. "U.S. consumer debt is now above levels hit during the 2008 financial crisis." MarketWatch, 19 June 2019, www.marketwatch.com/story/us-consumer-debt-is-now-breaching-levels-last-reached-during-the-2008-financial-crisis.

[29]Irby, LaToya. "What are the 3 Major Credit Reporting Agencies?" The Balance, 25 February 2020, www.thebalance.com/who-are-the-three-major-credit-bureaus-960416.

[30]Laryea, Brittney. "FICO Score vs. Credit Score." Lending Tree, 17 June 2019, www.lendingtree.com/credit-repair/fico-vs-credit-score.

[31]Szmigiera, M. "Leading credit card companies in the United States in 2019, by number of cards in circulation." Statista, 16 December 2019, www.statista.com/statistics/605634/leading-credit-card-companies-usa-by-number-of-card-holders.

[32]Amadeo, Kimberly. "Average U.S. Credit Card Debt Statistics." The Balance. Dotdash, 11 March 2020, www.thebalance.com/average-credit-card-debt-u-s-statistics-3305919.

[33]"MSN Money." MSN Money, 28 04 2020, www.msn.com/en-us/money.

[34]Sirull, Ellen. "Cash vs. Credit Cards: Which Do Americans Use Most?" Experian, 15 March 2018, www.experian.com/blogs/ask-experian/cash-cs-credit-cards-which-do-americans-use-most.

[35]Bradney-George, Amy and Kliment Dukovski. "What you need to know about cash advance interest rates." Finder, 28 April 2020, www.finder.com/cash-advance-interest-rates-credit-cards.

[36]Mayer, Britney. "9 Best No Balance Transfer Fee Credit Cards (2020)." CardRates, 31 October 2019, www.cardrates.com/advice/no-balance-transfer-fee-credit-cards.

[37]Jefferson, Thomas. "Thomas Jefferson." AZQuotes, www.azquotes.com/quote/145683.

[38]"U.S. National Debt Clock April 2020." Dave Manuel, 28 April 2020, www.davemanuel.com/us-national-debt-clock.php.

[39]Duffin, Erin. "Federal debt of the United States - Forecast 2019-2030." Statista, 29 January 2020. www.statista.com/statistics/216998/forecast-of-the-federal-debt-of-the-united-states.

[40]"Household Debt and Credit Report." Federal Reserve Bank of New York, Q4 2019, newyorkfed.org/microeconomics/hhdc.html.

[41]"Wells Fargo account fraud scandal." Wikipedia, 28 December 2018, en.wikipedia.org/wiki/Wells_Fargo_account_fraud_scandal.

[42]"Definition: Mission Statement." Wikipedia, 2 February 2020, en.wikipedia.org/wiki/Mission_statement.

[43]"Definition: Vision statement." Wikipedia, 1 December 2019, en.wikipedia.org/wiki/Vision_statement.

[44]"Corporate Values." BusinessDictionary. 2020. www.businessdictionary.com/definition/corporate-values.html.

WORKS CITED

[45]Mencken, H.L. "H.L. Mencken." AZ Quotes, www.azquotes.com/quote/1456761.

[46]Page, Scott E. and Lu Hong. "Groups of diverse problem solvers can outperform groups of high-ability problem solvers." PNAS (2004): 01.

[47]Michael, Reagan and Bob Phillips. The All-American Quote Book. Eugene: Harvest House Publishers, 1995. 251.

[48]Wooden, John. "John Wooden." Good Reads, www.goodreads.com/quotes/595960-you-are-not-a-failure-until-you-start-blaming-thers.

[49]Richardson, Chae. "Quote About Courage and Fear." Juicy Quotes, juicyquotes.com/quote-about-courage-and-fear.

[50]Horsager, David. "You can't be a Great Leader Without Trust - Here's How You Build It." Forbes, 24 October 2012, https://www.forbes.com/sites/forbesleadershipforum/2012/10/24/you-cant-be-a-great-leader-without-trust-heres-how-you-build-it/#ded23fa4ef7a.

[51]"Robert Benchley Society." RobertBenchley.org.

[52]Wooden, John. "John Wooden." Good Reads, www.goodreads.com/quotes/45142-it-is-amazing-how-much-can-be-accomplished-if-no.

[53]"Definition: re-creation." Dictionary, dictionary.com/browse/recreation.

[54]Hope, Bob. "Bob Hope." Brainyquote, www.brainyquote.com/quotes/bob_hope_100536.

[55]Einstein, Albert. "Albert Einstein." GoodReads, www.goodreads.com/quotes/118182-you-never-fail-until-you-stop-trying.

[56]Reagan, Michael and Bob Phillips. All-American Quote Book. Eugene: Harvest House Publishers, 1995. 111.

[57]"48 Famous Failures Who Will Inspire You to Achieve." Wanderlust Worker, www.wanderlustworker.com/48-famous-failures-who-will-inspire-you-to-achieve.

[58]"Anonymouse Greek Proverb." GoodReads, www.goodreads.co/quotes/666987-society-grows-great-when-old-men-plants-trees-whose-shade.

[59]Spurgeon, Van D. "'Win-Win' Negotiations." Spurgeon Management Services.

[60]"TINSTAAFL." CyberDefinitions, www.cyberdefintions.com/definitions/TINSTAFL.html.

[61]Proverb. "If you want a thing done well, do it yourself." Wiktionary, en.wiktionary.org/wiki/if_you_want_a_thing_done_well,_do_it_yourself.

[62]Yamamoto, Admiral Isoroku. "Isoroku Yamamoto." Brainy Quote, www.brainyquote.com/quotes/isoroku_yamamoto_224334.

[63]"Investment Defined." Wikipedia, 16 April 2020, en.wikipedia.org/wiki/Investment.

[64]Kurt, Daniel. "What is an Annuity?" Investopedia, 10 December 2019, www.investopedia.com/ask/answers/12/what-is-an-annuity.asp.

[65]Chen, James. "Common Stock." Investopedia, 31 January 2020, www.investopedia.com/terms/c/commonstock.asp.

[66]"Preferred Stock." InvestorWords, www.investorwords.com/3778/preferred_stock.html.

[67]"401K Plan Overview." IRS, www.irs.gov/retirement-plans/plan-sponsor/401k-plan-overview.

[68]"IRA." InvestorWords, www.investorwords.com/2641/IRA.html.

[69]"An Introduction to 529 Plans." U.S. Securities and Exchange Commission, 29 May 2018, www.sec.gov/reportspubs/investor-publications/investorpubsintro529htm.html.

[70]Hayes, Adam. "Mutual Fund." Investopedia, 24 February 2020, www.investopedia.com/terms/m/mutualfund.asp.

[71]Hayes, Adam and Gordon Scott. "Bond." Investopedia, 22 February 2020, www.investopedia.com/terms/b/bond.asp.

[72]"Certificate of deposit." Wikipedia, 11 April 2020, en.wikipedia.org/wiki/Certificate_of_deposit.

[73]"Commodity." Investorwords, Web Finance, www.investorwords.com/975/commodity.html.

WIDE-EYED WISDOM

74 "Warrant (finance)." Wikipedia, 19 September 2019, en.wikipedia.org/wiki/Warrant_(finance).

75 Chen, James and Gordon Scott. "Stock Option Definition." Investopedia, 03 February 2020, www.investorpedia.com/terms/s/stockoption.asp.

76 Maverick, J.B. "What is the average annual return for the S&P 500?" Investopedia, 19 February 2020, www.investopedia.com/ask/answers/042415/2hat-average-annual-return-sp-500.asp.

77 LaBianca, Juliana. "'These People Donated Millions After They Died – But No One Knew They Were Rich." Reader's Digest, 21 May 2019, www.rd.com/true-stores/inspiring/secret-millionaires-donations-after-died.

78 "Dow Jones 100 Year Historical Chart." Macrotrends, 27 April 2020, www.macrotrends.net/1319/dow-jones-100-year-historical-chart.

79 Royal, James, PH.D. and Arielle O'Shea. "What is the Average Stock Market Return?" Nerd Wallet, 02 April 2020. www.nerwallet.com/blog/investing/average_stock_market_return.

80 Brownlee, Adam P. "Warren Buffett: Be Fearful When Others Are Greedy." Investopedia, 5 April 2019, https://www.investopedia.com/articles/investing/012116/warren-buffett-be-fearful-when-others-are-greedy.asp.

81 Hochschild, Arlie Russell. "Arlie Russell Hochschild Quotes." BrainyQuote, www.brainyquote.com/quotes/arlie_russell_hochschild_512756.

82 Yosukeyamada. "Einstein's Rule of 72." Success Financial Freedom, 29 August 2016, www.successfinancialfreedom.com/2016/08/29/einsteins-rule-of-72.

83 Macias, Amanda. "US tax-payers paid millions of dollars for the airstrikes on Syria. Here's a breakdown of key costs." CNBC, 17 April 2018, www.cnbc.com/2018/04/16/syria-airstrikes-cost-to-us-taxpayers.html.

84 Parker, Brandon. "How much does an M1A2 Abrams battle tank cost." Quora, 5 May 2016, www.quora.com/How-much-does-an-M1A2-Abrams-battle-tank-cost.

85 "Boeing F/A-18E/F Super Hornet." Wikipedia, 17 May 2020, https://en.wikipedia.org/wiki/Boeing_F/A-18E/F_Super_Hornet.

86 Eckstein, Megan. "CBO: Navy's Next Nuclear Attack Submarine Could Cost $5.5B a Hull." USNI News, 10 October 2019, news.usni.org/2019/10/10/cbo-navys-next-nuclear-attack-submarine-could-cost-5-5b-a-hull.

87 "Meet the Navy's New $13 Billion Aircraft Carrier." Cnet, 10 December 2019, www.cnet.com/pictures/meet-the-navys-new-13-billion-aircraft-carrier.

88 Hoover, Herbert. "Herbert Hoover." Goodreads, www.goodreads.com/quotes/22005-older-men-declare-war-but-it-is-youth-that-must.

89 Wooden, John. "John Wooden Quotes." BrainyQuote, www.brainyquote.com/quotes/john_wooden_447019.

90 Lincoln, Abraham. "Abraham Lincoln." GoodReads, www.goodreads.com/quotes/34059-commitment-is-what-transforms-a-promise-into-reality.

91 Andrews, Andy. The Traveler's Gift: Seven Decisions that Determine Personal Success. Thomas Nelson Inc, 2005.

92 Storm, Roger. Western Region Director of Merchandising - Fleming Foods, Inc. "Return on Net Assets Employed." 1983.

93 Star Wars Episode V, The Empire Strikes Back. Dir. George Lucas. Perf. Frank Oz - Yoda. 1980.

94 Lincoln, Abraham. "Abraham Lincoln Quotes." BrainyQuote, www.brainyquote.com/quotes/abraham_lincoln_105816.

95 Eastwood, Clint. "Clint Eastwood Quotes." BrainyQuotes, www.brainyquotes.com/quotes/clint_eastwood_392797.

96 Eisenhower, Dwight D. "Dwight D. Eisenhower Quotes." BrainyQuote, www.brainyquote.com/quotes/dwight_d_eisenhower_109026.

97 Shedd, John. "John Augustus Shedd." Wiki Quotes, Wikimedia, 13 May 2019, en.wikiquote.org/wiki/John_Augustus_Shedd.

ABOUT THE AUTHORS

Keith A. Miller is a life coach, author, consultant, and senior executive with over 40-years of experience in food wholesale distribution. His professional experience is broad and deep with expertise in Executive Coaching, Marketing, Procurement, Product Development, Business Turnaround, Mergers and Acquisitions, Enterprise Risk Management, Operations, Business Continuity, Strategy, Negotiations Instructor, Project Management, Change Management, Leadership and Team Building.

Keith lives in the Pacific Northwest with his wife Cindy, near their three children and three grandchildren. In his free time, you can find him watching a sporting event, visiting the spectacular Oregon coast, traveling, working on their property, crafting furniture and art projects, or playing with his grandkids.

Teresa Miller-Weston is a first-time author and proud Oregon State University grad. Having graduated summa cum laude and Management Student of the Year, her critical attention to detail has led to success in corporate communications strategy, marketing, data analysis, project management, event management, and design. Whether personally or professionally, she is driven to continuously improve, loves a challenge and the opportunity to learn and problem solve by imagining and creating unique solutions. Teresa resides on 20-acres of farmland in the beautiful Pacific Northwest with her husband and three young children.

For more resources and information regarding their coaching and consulting services, including the upcoming book, *Don't Whip the Horses*, visit: www.wide-eyedwisdom.com.